Malcolm Chalmers is now at the s[...] Bradford University. Previously h[...] the universities of Glasgow, Cambridge and East Anglia. He also worked for two and a half years as an economist with the government of Botswana. He is the author of *The Cost of Britain's Defence* and *Trident: Britain's Independent Arms Race*. He was born in Glasgow in 1956.

Militarism State and Society
General editor: Dan Smith

Malcolm Chalmers

Paying for Defence

Military Spending and British Decline

Pluto Press

London and Sydney

First published in 1985 by Pluto Press Limited,
The Works, 105a Torriano Avenue, London NW5 2RX
and Pluto Press Australia Limited, PO Box 199, Leichhardt,
New South Wales 2040, Australia

Photoset by AKM Associates (UK) Ltd,
Ajmal House, Hayes Road, Southall, Greater London
Printed in Great Britain by Guernsey Press, Guernsey, C.I

British Library Cataloguing in Publication Data
Chalmers, Malcolm
    Paying for defence: military spending and
    British decline.
    1. Great Britain — Armed Forces — Appropriations
    and expenditures
    I. Title
    355.6′22′0941   UA649

ISBN 0 7453 0023 5

Contents

Acknowledgements

The work for this book began while I was a student at the University of East Anglia in 1981. I am grateful to John Cameron, Ken Cole, Steve Smith, and Steve Rankin for their encouragement at this initial stage.

Most of the research necessary was undertaken while at the School of Peace Studies at Bradford University. I am particularly grateful to Howard Clarke, George Crossley, Janet Dando, Malcolm Dando, Andrew Kelly, James O'Connell, and Paul Rogers for help and advice. For efficient typing of successive drafts of the manuscript over a period of more than a year, I would like to extend my thanks to Helena Larkin and Deborah Robinson. I would also like to thank the School for permission to use sections from 'The Cost of Britain's Defence', (Peace Studies Paper Number 10, 1983) in Chapters 6 and 7.

Dan Smith and Ron Smith both provided detailed comments on an earlier draft of the book. The final product has been much improved as a result. Jane Hayball, Pete Finlayson and Mark Ormerod generously provided accommodation on frequent trips to London to gather material. Most of all, my gratitude goes to Christine Halsall for her support and encouragement.

Introduction

Since 1945, as a direct consequence of its continued aspiration to remain a Great Power, the UK has consistently spent more of its national income on the military than any other major European state. Even in the 1980s the longing for a world role continues to exercise a decisive influence on government policy. Indeed, there has recently been an increased emphasis on those military commitments – such as the 'independent' nuclear force – most clearly associated with this longing.

Paradoxically, however, the attempt to retain international political status has led to accelerating economic decline. Britain's heavy military burden has diverted scarce resources from investment and exports, and impeded economic growth. Together with other legacies of Britain's imperial past – such as the commitment to sterling's reserve currency role and the encouragement of overseas investment – high military spending has ensured that the UK has fallen further and further behind its main economic competitors.

The revival of the peace movement in the 1980s gives study of these issues a new relevance. By reopening discussion on the fundamental issues in defence and foreign policy, the peace movement has ensured widespread interest in proposals for alternative defence policies. This in turn is opening up new opportunities for a radical reformulation of Britain's international role, bringing it into line with both its legitimate security interests and its economic resources.

This book is also relevant to discussions of the alternatives available in economic policy. These discussions have often devoted too much attention to short term issues of economic management – reflation and deflation, import controls and devaluation, inflation, money supply and incomes policy. Comparatively little attention has been given to the deep-seated structural problems of poverty, inequality and growth, to which these short-term remedies are often of little relevance. Yet, if a viable alternative to present economic policies is to be constructed, it must tackle these problems. Otherwise its success is bound to be both short lived and reversible. It is clear that such an alternative will be considerably more difficult to construct unless it is willing to remove the burdens which high military spending, and other legacies of Britain's international role, continue to place on the economy. Realistic and politically acceptable policies for cutting defence spending are as necessary to an alternative *economic* policy as they are to an alternative *defence* policy.

To understand current policy, and in what ways it needs to be changed, it is necessary to go back several decades in order to appreciate how we arrived where we are today. That is why most of this book is contemporary history, tracing the evolving relationships between defence policy, military commitments, and domestic economic performance in the 40 years since the Second World War.

Before looking at the postwar period, however, Chapter 1 provides some historical background, looking at the relative decline of the British economy from the 1870s onwards. Until the 1930s peacetime military spending was relatively low despite extensive overseas commitments. These commitments, however, were already imposing a growing burden on the economy in other ways.

In the period since the Second World War, Britain's aspiration to a world role was reflected in the simultaneous adherence to five major commitments in defence policy: the retention of a military role outside Europe ('East of Suez'); the permanent stationing of substantial forces on the European continent; the construction and development of an independent nuclear force; the 'special relationship' with the United States; and the policy of self-reliance in the production of most major weapons systems. These commitments, taken together, explain why Britain's defence spending remained higher than that of most of its major allies. The discussion of these five commitments then helps us to understand their continuing attraction to British leaders.

The next four chapters (Chapters 2–5) trace the reluctant nature of the retreat from Great Power status since 1945. While governments have recognized, at least to some extent, the links between high military spending and poor economic performance, they have been unwilling to sacrifice the trappings of international status to provide resources for industrial growth.

The story begins with the failure of the post-war Labour government to reassess adequately Britain's position in the world. Its decision to retain a series of costly military commitments ensured that the relative economic success of this period proved to be temporary and illusory. In 1950, when a choice had to be made between economic growth and Britain's status as a Great Power, it chose the latter. Under intense American pressure, defence spending was increased by more than 50 per cent in two years with disastrous economic consequences.

For the next two decades both Conservative and Labour governments made repeated attempts to reduce the burden of military spending on the economy. Their continuing belief that Britain remained entitled to the position of 'number two' within the Western alliance, however, ensured that Britain's major military commitments would remain unquestioned. As a consequence Britain continued to devote a greater proportion of its national income to the military than most of its allies (and economic competitors).

Chapter 6 then summarizes the economic consequences of this persistently high level of military spending. It discusses in turn the relationship of military spending to investment, civilian technological resources, and the balance of payments. It comments on the importance of 'spin-off' from military research into civilian industry, and on the costs and benefits from arms exports. Finally, it links high military spending to other effects of Britain's foreign policy during this period and concludes that the failure sufficiently to adjust that policy to Britain's limited economic resources helps us to understand why decline has significantly accelerated since the Second World War.

Chapter 7 brings us up to date with a discussion of the substantial increase in defence spending in the 1980s. It examines the reasons for, and effects of, this increase. And it argues that, despite this increase, there is likely to be a squeeze on the defence budget in the late 1980s, forcing a further 'review'. The possible outcomes of such a review under a Conservative government are briefly examined.

Chapter 8 concludes the book by discussing the possibilities for reducing defence spending which would be available to a disarmament-orientated British government taking office in the later 1980s. It argues that such a policy could reduce the defence budget substantially by abandoning capabilities and commitments with little value in terms of national or NATO security. And it contends that, carefully implemented, a lower-cost defence policy could make a major contribution to national economic recovery.

Finally, a number of caveats are necessary in order to define the limitations of this book, and to prevent its arguments from being distorted by misuse. First, it concentrates on the determinants and effects of military spending in the specific case of Britain since 1945. It makes no claim to present a more widely applicable theory of the relationship between military spending and economic development. There may well be other cases in which military spending has had a positive impact on economic performance.

Secondly, no attempt has been made to examine the international links between military spending and underdevelopment. The discussion of Britain's defence commitments 'East of Suez' has been confined to their impact on the UK economy. Their effects on the course of Third World economic and political development have not been analysed.

Finally, it must be emphasized that this volume is not presenting a general explanation of Britain's economic decline. High military spending since the Second World War, it is recognized, is only a significant *contribution* to that decline. And, though some links are made with other costs incurred by overseas policies, in order to suggest how military spending might fit into such a general explanation, the detailed consequences of these other aspects are not examined. For those readers interested in pursuing these and other issues, the book concludes with a guide to further reading.

1. Paying for greatness

Britannia in retreat

Britain's industrial and commercial dominance of the world economy reached its height in the middle of the nineteenth century. At that time it produced two-thirds of the world's coal, five-sevenths of its steel, and over 40 per cent of its entire output of traded manufactured goods.[1] This dominance was based on an initial monopoly of industrialization, and reinforced by military power. The Napoleonic Wars at the beginning of the century had left the Royal Navy militarily unchallenged and had thus allowed British commerce to expand into markets protected from potential trading rivals. The Wars had also finished off Amsterdam as a rival financial centre to the City of London, and inaugurated a century during which sterling was the world's main international currency. Moreover, military and financial strength continued to reinforce each other. While 'gunboat diplomacy' ensured the protection of British commerce against local discontent, and global naval power ensured the security of British shipping against potential trading rivals, financial and economic dominance reduced the need for the exercise of military force.

The maintenance of the Pax Britannica (in contrast to the later Pax Americana) was a remarkably low-cost affair. Even in 1870, the naval budget was only £9.8 million. The relative weakness of the army (although it cost more at £13.4 million) mattered little as long as the balance of power on the European continent continued to prevent the emergence of a dominant power which could pose a direct military threat to the UK. Imperial military power, moreover, was mainly financed from colonial – rather than British – exchequers, and enforced by the use of colonially-raised troops. It was the Indian Army, for example, that provided the only professional officers on the British side in the Crimean War, and which enabled Britain to conduct campaigns in the Middle East and Africa during both world wars.[2]

The British economy in the mid-nineteenth century thus obtained considerable benefit from the world economic system as it then was, while incurring relatively little cost for its military protection. Having overcome the traumas of Chartist revolt in the 1830s and 1840s and the splits occasioned by the abolition of the Corn Laws in 1846, the ruling classes were united in their support of the ideas of free trade and laissez-faire capitalism and in their belief in British superiority, not only in industrial and military power, but also in culture, morality and wisdom. The latter beliefs were to considerably outlast the demise of the former.

From this position of predominance, it was inevitable that there should be some decline as industrialization spread to Europe and North America, helped by British exports of machinery, skilled personnel, and knowledge. Particularly crucial in this process was the creation of railway networks, which were essential for economic and political development in all the continental powers – the US, Russia and Imperial Germany.[3] The greater natural resources and larger populations of these countries would, over the next century, be the underlying cause of the decline in Britain's *relative* economic position, and thus ultimately in its financial and military pre-eminence.

These trends were, however, accelerated by a drastic decline in *absolute* British industrial performance. In the late nineteenth century, annual growth in industrial production declined to just over $1\frac{1}{2}$ per cent in the 1880s and 1890s compared with around 4 per cent in the 1820s and 1830s and 3 per cent in 1840–70.[4] Two structural features of the British economy appear to have played a key role in this decline. The first was the growth in overseas investment, encouraged by the development of other economies and by the existence of the international financial markets in the City of London. Around 1870, annual investments abroad began to exceed net investment at home; in the great boom of 1911–13, investment abroad was twice that at home.[5] More and more, Britain began to live off the accumulated wealth of its imperial past rather than its industrial strength.

The second feature was that the domestic investment that did occur was concentrated in sectors protected from international competition by Britain's monopoly of important international services and by its political control of many colonial and semi-colonial markets. As industry developed in Europe and America, cotton, iron and steel exports were diverted instead to Argentina, India and Australia. Two of the country's biggest industries – shipbuilding and coal – relied on the continued dominance of British shipping in world trade, and on its policy of domestic purchase. Increasingly British firms compensated for technical inferiority by reliance on protected colonial or semi-colonial markets and on the natural protection of the home market.[6]

As Britain's relative economic position declined, so too did its military predominance. The last decade of the nineteenth century saw the beginnings of an arms race with the new industrial powers. Imperial rivalry between France, Germany and Britain grew as the balance of economic power shifted. The costs of maintaining world naval supremacy increased as Britain attempted, simultaneously, to keep control of the North Sea against Germany, and to protect its far-flung interests in Asia and Africa. Increasing reliance had to be placed on 'understandings' on spheres of influence with Japan in the Far East, Russia in Asia, the United States in the Western Hemisphere and France in Africa.[7]

Table 1 UK Defence Spending 1870–1932

(£ million)	Naval budget	Army budget	Total defence budget	% Gross Domestic Product (GDP) market prices
1870	9.8	13.4	23.2	2.1
1880	10.2	15.0	25.2	1.9
1890–1	14.1	17.6	31.7	2.1
1900–1	29.5	91.7*	121.2	5.9
1910–11	40.3	27.4	67.4	2.9
1921–2	. . .	. . .	189	3.6
1932	. . .	. . .	102	2.3

* including Boer War.
Source: B.R. Mitchell, *Abstract of British Historical Statistics*, London: Cambridge University Press 1962; Paul Kennedy, *The Realities Behind Diplomacy*, London: Fontana 1981, pp. 35, 231.
Note: . . . not available.

Thus, even before the two world wars, British military power was overstretched. The Boer War of 1900–2, which cost the British taxpayers £222 million, demonstrated the drastic rise that modern warfare was bringing to the costs of maintaining military dominance.[8] Moreover, it also illustrated the limited gains that were to be made from such interventions, as most of the rebel Afrikaaners' goals were achieved anyway shortly afterwards. The lesson was, however, not learnt. It was to be repeated time and again in the long and expensive retreat from Empire that followed the war against Hitler.

The war of 1914–18 accelerated many of the economic tendencies of the previous decades. It saw the loss of more overseas markets to the United States and Japan, with shipbuilding particularly badly hit as it concentrated its efforts on domestic warship orders. It also meant increased orders for US industry, financed by massive British borrowing in New York, which transformed the United States into a major creditor nation, and led to the demise of London as the world's most important financial centre.

In the aftermath of victory, however, the ruling elite remained committed to the institutions and policies evolved in the nineteenth century. The frontiers of Empire were extended as a result of German defeat, and rebellions in India and Ireland were not seen as signals of more fundamental long-term changes or of impending imperial collapse. The Indian Army continued to be the main instrument of political control in much of the Empire: even in 1939 it was equal in size to the British Army, and financed largely by the Indian treasury.[9] The return to isolationism of the US and the temporary weakness of both Russia and Germany appeared to preclude immediate military challenges. Indeed so confident was the government that, as part of the policy of financial stringency, it adopted the 1919 Ten Year Rule, which instructed the armed services to plan their budgets on the assumption that the Empire would not be engaged in a major war during the next ten years. This rule, to be interpreted on a 'shifting' basis, was not abandoned until the early 1930s when Japan and Nazi Germany began to pose new threats to British interests. Defence spending fell as a result from £189 million in 1921–2 (3.6 per cent of GDP) to the relatively meagre sum of £102 million in 1932 (2.3 per cent of GDP).

In the 1920s, many of Britain's traditional industries suffered catastrophically. Output of cotton, steel, coal and shipbuilding all fell as competitiveness declined. The experience of these 'staple' industries, however, was in marked contrast to that of the City of London. By the middle of the 1920s, British overseas investments, financial and insurance services, were earning more than ever before. This disparity between the fortunes of manufacturing and the City was due in large part to the state's attempt to recreate the supposed 'golden age' before the war by sacrificing the needs of domestic industry to those of overseas financial policy. Montague Norman, Governor of the Bank of England from 1920 until 1944, and the unquestioned, though unelected, master of that policy, saw the Bank as above the concerns of purely national interests. Its role, he believed, was to provide stability for the world financial system by restoring the pre-1914 financial order that the gold standard had provided.[10] As a result of his policies, sterling was revalued to an artificially high rate (the parity with gold it enjoyed in 1913), and severe deflationary policies were implemented to keep it there. The result was a further deterioration in the British economy, and an attempt to enforce wage cuts that culminated in the General Strike of 1926. Only in 1931, when faced with severe world slump, and French opposition, was the gold standard eventually abandoned. By that time, however, much damage had been done.

The 1930s saw a clear break from these policies. The Great Depression of 1931 had destroyed the world financial order, and with it the prospects for overseas investment and sterling's reserve currency role. For a period, British industry and government were forced to direct their attentions inwards to the domestic economy. As a consequence this period saw the beginnings of a major shift in the British economy away from its previous dependence on its export industries and services towards new industries geared to the domestic market for consumption goods – housing, vehicles and consumer durables. It was a shift encouraged by tariffs to protect industry against foreign competition and by a low level of military spending. The 1930s were, partly as a result, a period of relative economic success, particularly when compared to other industrial nations.[11]

Yet, while the 1930s saw some economic modernization, foreign policy was unable to break with the imperial legacy. The resources available to Britain were clearly insufficient to defend the Empire against the simultaneous threats from Germany, Italy and Japan. It was feared, with some justification, that another world war would bring national bankruptcy and eventually the end of the Empire. Until 1938, therefore, the ruling class consensus favoured appeasement. Even after war with Germany had formally commenced in September 1939, some powerful voices urged a negotiated settlement which allowed Hitler free rein in Eastern Europe in return for the preservation of the Empire. For Churchill's rejection of such an option many millions today have cause to be grateful. There is no doubt, however, that it accelerated the end of Britain's world role, as we shall see in Chapter 2.

Falling behind

After the Second World War, from the late 1940s until the early 1970s, the world saw the longest and most dramatic economic boom in recorded history. Unprecedented rates of growth allowed rising real wages, improved welfare services and a high level of employment. Only in the last decade have the ghosts of the 1930s – slump, mass unemployment and financial crisis – once again returned to haunt the peoples and leaders of the capitalist nations.

Britain was not unaffected by this success. Real wages rose, the welfare state was established and mass unemployment became only a bitter memory. National income grew at a rate faster than at any time since the nineteenth century. Compared with its own historical experience, the period from the Second World War until the 1970s was a success for the British economy.

The picture, however, is dramatically different when we compare Britain's performance with that of other countries. As Table 2 shows, Britain's rate of growth was well below those of its main competitors. During the long boom in the world economy, its national income per head fell behind those of one after another of the industrialized nations. The unearned bonus of North Sea oil since the late 1970s did not improve the position.

It should be noted, moreover, that the gap in performance between Britain and its major competitors has never been as pronounced as in the period since the Second World War. As Table 2 shows, productivity growth in 1870–1913 was 1 per cent per annum less than Britain's most successful competitor at that time – the US – and only 0.8 per cent per annum less than in

Germany. This is a dramatic contrast with the 1950–76 period (which excludes immediate post-war reconstruction) when those competitors with lower military burdens had growth rates between 2.1 per cent and 4.7 per cent per annum faster than the UK. The 'economic miracle' in most of the industrialized world seemed to leave remarkably little impression in the UK. Though its absolute level of income per head rose at a rate somewhat faster than before, its level relative to other industrial nations fell at an unprecedented pace. The only other major country with a similar record was the US – which had even heavier military commitments than the UK.

Table 2 Phases of Productivity Growth (GDP per person-hour), 1870–1976 (Per cent per annum)

	1870–1913	1913–50	1950–76
France	1.8	1.7	4.9
Germany	1.9	1.2	5.8
Italy	1.2	1.8	5.3
Japan	1.8	1.4	7.5
Netherlands	1.2	1.5	4.1
United States	2.1	2.5	2.3
United Kingdom	1.1	1.5	2.8

Source: A. Maddison, 'The Long Run Dynamics of Productivity Growth' in W. Beckerman (ed.), *Slow Growth in Britain*, London: Oxford University Press 1979, p. 195.

Britain's decline in the three decades since 1950 has been a process in which a number of interacting factors – low investment, poor productivity growth, declining export shares – have all been involved. Each factor reinforced the others: together they constituted a set of vicious circles which, once started, it proved difficult to break. Output and productivity rose relatively slowly, and British shares of external and domestic markets fell as industry became less and less competitive. In turn this led to a worsening balance of trade (imports rising faster than exports), and to balance of payments crises. The response to these crises – domestic deflation – further weakened the incentives for investment and thus continued the process. The expectation of low growth, punctuated by government-imposed cutbacks, became built into investment decisions, and fixed the economy still more firmly on a path of relative decline.

The priority given to a continued Great Power role made a fundamental contribution to this process of decline. For the costs of this role to the domestic economy now far outweighed the benefits. The Empire had helped to form the basis of British industrial strength in the nineteenth century. In its decline, and in the attitudes and structures it left, it was to help destroy it.

Still a Great Power?

After the Second World War the commitment to a world role continued to dominate the policies of the British state. Its institutions and traditions, its financial and industrial structure, and the prejudices and priorities of its leaders, were all tied closely to the needs of Empire. As with so many states in history, however, attributes and behaviour patterns which had contributed to its success at an earlier stage of its life now prevented a remedy to its subsequent decline. Commitments and attitudes associated with Empire were continued long after they made economic sense. The result was the accelerating decline of the British economy.

It would be misleading to see the British state in the period since 1945 as acting simply in the interests of national capitalism as a whole. The failure of the British economy, and of both profitability and capital accumulation, must cast some doubt on that idea. More plausibly, perhaps, it can be argued that the state acted in the interests of a particular section of the British bourgeoisie – the pre-industrial 'Establishment' of southern mercantile and financial interests.[12] It has always been willing to subordinate the needs of the national economy to those of this section of capital and thus of international capitalism as a whole: as the Bank of England did in the 1920s. It is, indeed, precisely this lack of identification with the interests of national industry which is the peculiar characteristic of the external policies of the British state.

Such an explanation provides useful insights into the origins of the peculiar role of the British state during this period. It needs to be complemented, however, by an understanding of the factors that ensured its continuing strength. The autonomous power of state structures, aided by pervasive imperial ideologies, ensured that Britain sought to fulfil the role of a Great Power many years after it ceased to be 'rational' to do so. As Carlo Cipolla commented in his comparative study of imperial decline:

> Whenever we look at declining empires, we notice that their economies are generally faltering. The economic difficulties of declining empires show striking resemblances . . . All empires seem eventually to develop an intractable resistance to the change needed for the required growth of production . . . what appears *ex post* as an obsolete behaviour pattern was, at an earlier stage in the life of an empire, a successful way of doing things of which the members of the empire were justly proud . . . The more a mature empire is proud of its cultural heritage, the more emotionally difficult it is for its people to change to new modes of being and to new ways of doing things, under the pressure of external competition and growing difficulties.
>
> Change implies imaginative effort. Change hurts vested interests. It is not difficult to explain why change is generally opposed. It would be surprising if it were not. The tendency to resist change is strengthened by existing institutions.
>
> Owing to its past growth and development, an empire is inevitably characterized by a large number of sclerotic institutions. They hinder change for their very existence. Moreover, they give invaluable support to that part of the population which opposes change for one reason or another. Institutional rigidities reflect cultural rigidities. Conservative people and vested interests cluster around obsolete institutions, and each element supports the other powerfully. If the necessary change does not take place and economic difficulties are allowed to grow, then a cumulative process is bound to be set into motion that makes things progressively worse. Decline enters then in its final, dramatic stage.[13]

The continuing commitment of the British state to a Great Power role remains the fundamental reason for its inability to tackle the problems of domestic economic decline. This commitment is both an *institutional* and an *ideological* one. Institutionally, it is reflected in financial and industrial structures that are formidable barriers to policies for economic renewal. Ideologically, the perception of Britain as a world power continues to prevent such policies being given precedence over the requirements of political and military prestige.

Britain's institutions, however, cannot be understood simply as instruments of a Great Power ideology. Shaped by an imperial past, each has a momentum of its own. The complex of interests involved in weapons production, for example, derives much of its continuing influence from its role in the futile attempt to remain a world power. Yet the particular ways in which this general requirement is met are also decisively shaped by the conservatism of the institutions charged with fulfilling it. It will be a recurring theme of this book that the power of Britain's arms lobby has not only reinforced the commitment to a Great Power role, but also ensured that the means chosen to fulfil that commitment have often been both inefficient and militarily questionable.

The British establishment's skill in adapting to decline, paradoxically, has also been a factor in enabling it to avoid more drastic change. Pax Britannica had been based, since the nineteenth century, more on diplomatic skill and willingness to compromise and co-opt than on its continually overstretched armed forces. The British Empire has always been, in Basil Liddell Hart's words, 'an astonishing achievement – and the biggest bluff of all history'.[14] Unlike the two new superpowers, the British ruling class had never felt that its international power rested mainly on quantitative superiority in either industrial production or in military force.

The illusion that this imperial 'bluff' could continue was further strengthened by Britain's apparent success in the Second World War. In 1945 it had emerged financially bankrupt but militarily victorious. It was the British prime minister who, along with the American and Soviet leaders, attended the Yalta and Potsdam conferences. And it was Winston Churchill himself who, in Moscow in 1944, had agreed with Stalin a division of Europe into spheres of influence.[15] It appeared inconceivable then that Britain was simply a medium-rank offshore island in Europe.

Over the next three decades, as other nations recovered from war and as its own relative decline accelerated, Britain did adjust its commitments to some extent to new realities. Though this was often 'too little, too late', it did prevent the possibility of more radical upheaval. The managed and gradual withdrawal from the colonies in the 1950s and 1960s was held to be a success compared with the trauma of France in Vietnam and Algeria, and of Portugal in Angola and Mozambique. No governments were overthrown and the Establishment kept its grip firmly on the levers of state power. Even in 1983, the Governor of the Bank of England, the Chief of Defence Staff, the editor of the *Times*, the head of the Civil Service and the head of the Foreign Service were all ex-pupils of one major public school – Eton – whose traditions were firmly linked to Britain's imperial past.[16]

Success in managing decline meant that Britain did not experience the psychological and structural upheaval that would have been necessary for it to abandon its imperial aspirations and seek a new, more modest, role in the world. The armed forces successfully avoided military defeat in a way that reassured political leaders of Britain's continued power and influence. The most important post-war exception to this rule – the brief Suez adventure – demonstrated the fragility of that influence. But both the subsequent reassertion of the 'special relationship' with the US, and the skilful use of independent nuclear weapons as a symbol of national status, ensured that its impact was largely absorbed.

Britain's continuing aspirations to Great Power status were reflected in its simultaneous adherence to five major commitments in defence policy:
  – the imperial, extra-European, role
  – the European commitment
  – the independent nuclear force
  – the 'special relationship' with the United States
  – the commitment to self-sufficiency in arms production.

The attempt to maintain all these commitments, and the partial nature of the eventual retreat from the least tenable amongst them, explains why British military spending has been higher than that of most of its allies throughout the post-war period. And it also helps us to understand why it is considerably higher than Britain's peacetime military spending before the Second World War. For, compared with that period, the perceived military requirements for international status have been greatly increased. The European and nuclear commitments are both entirely new and expensive. The costs of maintaining the imperial role and an independent arms industry have both considerably increased. And the need for close co-operation with the US has both permitted the continuance of otherwise untenable commitments and attitudes, and has created pressure for Britain to make a 'special contribution' to Western security as a whole in order to maintain its 'special relationship'.

Holding on to Empire

By the first decades of the twentieth century, the Empire was already, on balance, probably more of a burden on Britain's economy as a whole than a bonus. This burden, however, largely took indirect forms – the emphasis on overseas investment, the anti-technical bias in the upper classes, the maintenance of sterling as a reserve currency. The direct, military costs of Empire remained relatively cheap until the Second World War. After that war, however, the balance of advantage shifted markedly. The rise of national liberation movements increased the need for military forces and provoked a series of costly counter-insurgency wars. Newly independent states and guerrilla fighters equipped themselves with modern weapons, supplied from both the West and the Soviet bloc, which further increased the capabilities required for British forces.

The key event in transforming the balance sheet of Empire, however, was the gaining of independence by India in 1947. British India had been not only the Empire's main economic asset, an employer of a substantial section of the home country's middle classes and a major protected market for its industries. It was also the source of most of its military manpower and the hub round which its string of military bases – Malta, Suez, Aden, Singapore – had been built and without which they made little sense. It was therefore remarkable how slow the impact of Indian independence was on Britain's commitment to the retention of its remaining possessions. Indeed humiliation at Suez in 1956 probably had a greater, or at least more immediate, effect on national opinion.

Until the mid 1960s, reluctant retreat from Empire was

accompanied by continued attempts to retain a residual imperial commitment. Only after 1965, as the country's economic plight worsened and the costs of the East of Suez role continued to climb, did a Labour Cabinet agree to withdraw from most remaining bases in the Gulf and Far East by 1972. Even then the longing for a British military role outside Europe did not die. A number of residual commitments were maintained in the Mediterranean, Hong Kong, Belize and the Falklands, the last of which has proved extremely costly. And the structure and attitudes of the armed services – particularly those of the Royal Navy – continue to reflect to this day a desire for an intervention role outside Europe.

Arguments for a return to a 'maritime strategy', in which priority is given to surface naval forces at the expense of the land/air commitment to Europe, reflect this continued yearning for a world role amongst important sections of the ruling elite. It is a policy popular amongst Conservative MPs, many of whom have close links with the influential Navy lobby, and it even enjoys support from a number of prominent Labour politicians. Indeed, partly in response to such pressure, the present government has already taken important steps to reverse what it believes was the overconcentration of forces in Europe that characterized the 1970s. The Empire may no longer exist as an administrative entity, but its spirit lives on in the minds of admirals, politicians, and, not least, a large section of the British people.

Committed to Europe

In the past, the security of Britain itself, and its sea links with the Empire, have been ensured by a policy of preventing the domination of the European continent by a single power. Britain has never been interested in controlling its European neighbours, only in preventing a threat to itself and its overseas possessions. As a result, throughout its imperial history Britain's leaders have looked with suspicion at, and feared entanglement in, European politics, and have pursued a policy of having no permanent allies or permanent forces in Europe.

This policy broke down temporarily, with disastrous human consequences, when Britain intervened in 1914 to prevent German domination of the Continent which, it was believed, would pose a direct threat to British naval power and national security.[17]

Immediately after that war, however, the army was quickly withdrawn and Britain reverted to its traditional policy. Only in the aftermath of the Second World War did Britain feel forced to agree to a permanent military alliance in Europe – the North Atlantic Treaty Organization (NATO). With the rise of Soviet military power it was believed that a British commitment was now needed to ensure West European resistance to a further expansion of Soviet influence. In direct contrast to past policies, therefore, Britain actively promoted an alliance between the major West European powers and committed a large proportion of its armed forces to that alliance. This questionable strategic rationale – the need to avoid the possibility of Soviet dominance of Europe – was powerfully reinforced by the ideological antipathy of both Conservatives and most Labour leaders to Soviet-style socialism. Anticommunism – the foundation of the Cold War – became both an explanation of and justification for Britain's military commitments in Europe and elsewhere.

However, the European commitment, as in the past, was somewhat ambiguous, continually competing with Britain's world role for military resources. In 1952, Britain refused to merge its armed forces into a European army – the European Defence Community (EDC) – largely because of its continued belief in its role as an independent world power. At first, it refused to join the European Economic Community (EEC) for the same reason. In the 1960s, its applications for membership were rejected on French insistence because of its continued close links with the Commonwealth and Empire, and with the United States. And by the time Britain did succeed in joining – in 1973 – the political momentum for unity had been dissipated, and the economic advantages of membership had diminished.

In Britain's first decade of EEC membership both main political parties have been eager to stress their commitment to maintaining national 'sovereignty' and protecting national interests. Mrs Thatcher appeared to be shifting foreign policy away from Europe and towards a strengthening of both the 'special relationship' and Britain's world role. And, although some Labour opponents distinguished between the capitalist-dominated EEC, which they oppose, and a united socialist Europe, which they would support, many of their colleagues continued to believe in quasi-imperial illusions about Britain's world role, of which an exaggerated importance given to Commonwealth economic links, *inter alia*, is a notable example.

The nuclear illusion

Reinforcing Britain's self-image as a great power has been its involvement with the most powerful weapons of all – the atomic and hydrogen bombs. In 1940, Britain had, briefly, led the world in atomic weapons research; and its scientists played an important role in the wartime Manhattan Project, which developed the weapons used on Hiroshima and Nagasaki.[18] Even today, the link between international influence and possession of nuclear weapons is symbolized in the membership of the UN Security Council. The permanent members of that body – the US, the USSR, France, China and the UK – are the five states with acknowledged nuclear arsenals. Britain's nuclear force undoubtedly has contributed to the illusion that it is a step above most other medium-sized powers in the international pecking order, even if it is not a superpower. And, within NATO, the nuclear force, and the close nuclear co-operation with the United States, has reinforced Britain's feeling that it is number two in the alliance.

Moreover, the nuclear force helped to encourage, especially in the 1950s, the idea that Britain could afford to fulfil its military commitments in Europe and in Asia simultaneously without ruining its domestic economy. In Europe, it was argued, tactical nuclear weapons and a policy of 'massive retaliation' could compensate for NATO's supposed conventional inferiority. Non-nuclear land and air forces could therefore be reduced to a 'tripwire' function, sufficient only to make it clear that a fullscale assault was underway before using nuclear weapons on a large scale. Even outside Europe, it was believed that nuclear weapons could be a cheap substitute for overstretched conventional forces in limited conflicts.

Both concepts proved to be illusions. In Europe, the growth in the Soviet nuclear arsenal, which had been virtually non-existent in the 1950s, led to an increasing reluctance in NATO to give up entirely the conventional option; and the political need for a symbol of Britain's commitment to Europe also meant that the cuts in its continental forces were not as great as had been hoped. In the Empire, nuclear weapons proved to be unusable in counter-insurgency warfare, or in limited confrontations such as that with Indonesia. If Britain wished to maintain both its European and imperial commitments, it discovered, it would have to pay dearly for them, or give one of them up.

In some respects, the nuclear force clearly complemented the imperial commitment. By encouraging continued illusions of national power, it reinforced support for a world role and delayed a reappraisal. Yet at the same time, it also proved to be a compensation for the retreat from that role when it did take place. At the crucial moment after the Suez fiasco, an increased emphasis on Britain's independent nuclear status helped to silence those arguing for a more radical reappraisal. The British place at the 'top table' of arms talks served to further quell doubts domestically.

The nuclear force thus encouraged pretensions of being a world power, and indirectly contributed to overcommitment in defence policy as a whole. Its direct costs were, moreover, also considerable: certainly greater than governments liked to admit publicly. At the peak of the V-bomber project, nuclear forces took between 10 and 20 per cent of the defence budget.[19] Though the proportion spent on strategic nuclear weapons fell in the 1960s, some of the £12,500 million spent in the 1970s and 1980s on the Tornado bomber – now assigned to a 'theatre nuclear' role – should also be attributed to nuclear spending. And, in the late 1980s, the Trident project will ensure that nuclear costs will rise again, on conservative assumptions, to as much as 15 per cent of total defence spending.

A special relationship

Since the Second World War, British leaders have placed a high priority on maintaining their 'special relationship' with the United States. The war itself forged extraordinarily close military and economic ties between the two governments. And, once it had ended, the survival of the Empire was clearly dependent on US approval, or at least tolerance. Moreover, the world's capitalist economies, and those of Western Europe in particular, needed an American lead in the 1940s to prevent a recurrence of the political traumas that followed the First World War. Binding together these two ideas – tolerance of colonialism and aid to rival capitalist nations – was the global contest with the Soviet Union. A narrow view of national economic advantage might have suggested that

Europe, Japan and the British Empire were potential rivals in a conflict for domination of world markets, and that the US had little interest in their economic reconstruction. Its assumption of the role as leader of the capitalist world from 1947 onwards – a Pax Americana not unlike Britain's nineteenth-century dominance – led to such considerations being subordinated to the requirements for prosperity and unity between advanced capitalist states in the confrontation with the Soviet bloc. The Cold War therefore proved the cement of American foreign policy, enabling short-run sectional economic interests to be overcome, and the US to commit itself to a leadership role in the capitalist world system.

If the Cold War enabled the US to reconcile the elements of its own foreign policy, it was the 'special relationship' with the Americans that was the keystone enabling Britain to retain the trappings of its world status despite the crippling effects of the war. Its imperial – and later 'out of area' – policing role in the Third World was supported by the US as a contribution to the confrontation with the Soviet Union and with national liberation movements. In Europe, the US supported Britain's efforts to act as a bridge between North America and Europe, as an ally in opposing communist expansion on the Continent, and in sharing the financial burden of defence in Central Europe and the North Atlantic. And Britain's independent nuclear force could not have been maintained without American help – at least not without sacrificing other military commitments.

The 'special relationship', for Britain, had an important additional advantage, as much psychological as material. It helped the transition from Pax Britannica to Pax Americana to be made relatively smoothly, and it provided the old, declining power a role as an experienced advisor to the less sophisticated, if more powerful, 'new boys' – a role as elder statesman writ large. This conception accorded with British perceptions of their own greater wisdom and maturity. The willingness to compromise and manoeuvre, essential to Britain's past world leadership, would, it was thought, act as a valuable constraint on American impetuousness, its simplistic worldview and its reliance on brute power. Britain could in this way, its leaders believed, influence the path of world events without directly controlling them.

The price paid for this intangible 'advantage' was, however, considerable. In return Britain was expected to support the US stewardship of the capitalist world in words and in deeds. British policymakers believed that, in order to influence American policy, they had to support it. To preserve the trappings of its past power, Britain had to subordinate them to US designs. Though important scope remained to influence policy at the margins, especially in the first post-war decade, major decisions taken by the US government were shaped by its conception of its own interests. Britain, by contrast, found itself bearing the burden of a world role, while its political and economic influence declined still further. In return for its high level of military spending, it found itself with only the illusion of international political power, rather than the reality. The latter belonged to the United States.

Britain's commitment to high defence spending was, from the United States' point of view, an important component of the 'special relationship'. If Britain wished to have greater influence in Washington than other medium powers, it was argued, it had to share the costs of America's military leadership. The most costly consequence of this belief occurred during the Korean war in 1950–2 when, in response to demands from the US, Britain agreed to a massive rearmament programme which halted the domestic economy in its tracks. More than any other event, this programme handicapped Britain in competition with the emerging economies of West Germany and Japan, which had no comparable military burden. It raised defence spending to a higher plateau, on which it remained for the next three decades. Yet the increase in expenditure was motivated mostly by Britain's concern to retain influence in Washington and thus avoid America becoming embroiled in a major Asian war. Fears of a new and immediate Soviet offensive – then sweeping the United States – appeared to have been very much a secondary factor in British considerations.

Finally, the 'special relationship', linked as it is with imperial and nuclear commitments, has played some part in preventing Britain's transformation into a European power. Other European countries, and France in particular, have often voiced suspicions that the UK would be a 'Trojan Horse' for the Americans within Europe, as it was at least as interested in maintaining its close Atlantic ties as it was in European co-operation. Indeed the 1962 Nassau agreement, under which the US agreed to sell Polaris ballistic missiles to the UK, was one of the factors which precipitated de Gaulle's veto on British EEC membership shortly after. It is significant that the most enthusiastically pro-European Prime Minister – Edward Heath – was also the one who placed least emphasis on the 'special relationship'. For, if the 'out-of-area' and American commitments were complementary, both have in practice often been alternatives to closer ties with Europe. Under the Conservatives in the 1980s, there are signs of a modest, but significant, shift back towards these old priorities.

Buying British

The final factor that explains Britain's high level of military spending is its continued commitment to maintaining the domestic arms industry. Self-sufficiency in weapons supplies has been seen as an important requirement for both political influence and operational independence. Occasional doubts have found difficulty making progress against this view in the face of a powerful industrial and military lobby anxious to protect the interests of uncompetitive, but profitable, arms manufacturers. Yet, in reality, the arguments of that lobby have become increasingly dubious. For not only has the cost of only 'buying British' in arms grown considerably, but the military value of such independence has also been reduced.

The costs of remaining independent in military production have escalated ever since the beginning of the Second World War. The 'advances' in military hardware during that conflict – radar, jet aircraft, nuclear explosives, rockets, etc. – proved to be only the beginning of an extended technological arms race. The post-war confrontation between the two superpowers created external pressures for continually refining weapons systems, while the acceleration in industrial technology as a whole provided new opportunities for military innovation. As both superpowers devoted massive scientific and industrial resources to improve their relative position in the Cold War, the costs to other powers of keeping up with them grew. Though the basic types of non-nuclear weapons – planes, tanks, ships – were the same as had been used in the 1939–45 conflict, new technologies were transforming their destructive capabilities. And, as a result, the cost of producing each unit of equipment rocketed. One of the more remarkable, but by no means exceptional, examples of this process is in military aircraft. The cost (after making allowance for inflation) of producing 385 Tornadoes for the RAF of the 1980s will be greater than the cost of 21,000 Spitfires made before and during the Second World War.[20]

For Britain to keep up technologically with this arms race has required a massive investment in military research and development (R & D). Growth in R & D was particularly marked in the 1950s, when it grew from £69 million in 1949–50 (9.3 per cent of total defence spending) to £204 million in 1956–57 (13.3 per cent of the total).[21] Yet it still proved impossible for a relatively small power, as Britain was and is, to develop and produce the entire range of modern weapons. The R & D cost for each new type of weapon is largely independent of the number to be produced. Those countries with a much larger order book can, therefore, spread these overheads more thinly than is possible for the UK, and thus lower the average cost of each unit. Unless British producers are able to export a considerable proportion of their output, or collaborate successfully internationally, they will start with a severe handicap in competition with larger US producers.

As a result of this logic, the 1960s and 1970s saw exceptions to the principle of self-sufficiency being made in some of the most difficult 'high tech' areas – notably ballistic missiles (i.e. Polaris) and military aircraft. In general, however, these concessions were reluctant and partial. In the 1980s Britain continues to devote a higher proportion of its defence budget to R & D than any other NATO member,[22] and still produces a wide, though now incomplete, range of different weapons. The unit costs of its producers, consequently, often compare unfavourably with foreign competitors; and the numbers produced of each type have tended to diminish with each successive generation. If cost escalation continues at past rates, further erosion of the principle of self-sufficiency is inevitable.

As the costs of self-sufficiency have risen, moreover, the need for it has diminished. There are several reasons for this, two of which, in particular, should be noted. The first is that the importance of weapons ready for use has increased compared to the capability for producing more weapons in future. In the two world wars, victory had been won by mass mobilization of men and mass production of weapons in a struggle lasting several years. The bulk of these resources were provided during the war itself by adaptation of civilian assets – people and machines – to military purposes. Yet, since 1945, the growing sophistication of weapons has been such that they require considerably longer to be produced, yet will be used up in a much shorter time. The next major war in Europe, even if confined to 'conventional' weapons, is likely to deplete the armouries of both sides so quickly that the war will be won or lost within weeks rather than months. It will therefore be fought with equipment, and to a large extent trained men, already at hand. In such a conflict, a capability for providing supplies of ammunition, spares, and fuel, and for rapid repairs and modifications, will be crucial. But the ability to develop and produce complete new weapon systems – planes, tanks, missiles – will be of marginal use at best. The war will be over long before they can be completed.

The second reason to doubt the value of complete self-sufficiency is that Britain is now a member of a permanent military alliance, NATO, other members of which are able and willing to supply arms in peacetime. Since it will be forces already acquired in peace which will count in war, there is therefore less need than in the past for independent production if the weapons required can be bought from allies at a significantly lower cost. Indeed there are positive advantages, in both operational and financial terms, in having greater standardization of equipment between Alliance members.

The government has, and will, wish to provide for the possibility that, in the unforeseeable future, there will be a rift between itself and its NATO allies. Nevertheless, while such a contingency cannot be ruled out, it would appear reasonable to suggest that such provisions should be given a lower priority than if there is an imminent threat of having to 'go it alone'. And were that to occur, and the perceived threat to British security drastically alter – for example, from the Soviet Union to another source – then no area of defence policy would be untouched.

In recent years, the strength of these arguments has been reflected in an increasing tendency to collaborate with other NATO countries in the production of major weapon systems. The most notable current example is the project, jointly with West Germany and Italy, to produce the Tornado aircraft, which will be the RAF's mainstay in the 1990s and beyond. By retaining a capability for producing only parts of that plane, each nation is demonstrating that it does not consider self-sufficiency necessary, in this case at least, for national security.

Britain's arms lobby

So far, however, the British government has remained reluctant to increase reliance on arms imports, even when these would be much cheaper. In the late 1970s, only 10 per cent of equipment spending was on imports, 15 per cent was on collaborative projects, and 75 per cent was local.[23] The explanation for this reluctance is not primarily military. It lies partly in the identification of domestic arms production with national independence and status. The use of uniquely British equipment is still a symbol of Great Power aspirations and thus of continuity with the past. The two superpowers are virtually 100 per cent self-sufficient in military equipment. Medium-rank countries such as Britain and France are reluctant to part with the principle of self-reliance as it would all too clearly represent a further retreat from the level of the two giants, and thus a fresh reminder of their decline from past glory.

Perhaps a more important underlying factor in explaining Britain's adherence to domestic procurement, however, has been the political clout which arms manufacturers possess. The existence of continuous lobbying for further defence projects from the companies, and often the trade unions, involved has reinforced the prestige arguments in favour of domestic manufacture. It has meant that there is a cohesive, politically visible, constituency continually pressing for the high levels of defence spending necessary to fund these projects. Those politicians sceptical of the need for high arms spending have to face a strong military and industrial lobby opposed to them. And their more hawkish colleagues recognize that the domestic 'military-industrial complex' adds political weight to their case. Were equipment to be bought overseas at a lower cost, they fear, with some justification, that savings incurred would be used for civilian programmes rather than for increased military power.

The implication of this argument is that, to some extent, the production of ever more sophisticated and expensive armaments is a self-perpetuating process, often largely unrelated to military needs. Equipment manufacturers, like the armed forces, will tend to argue for the projects that are most suitable for their own industrial and bureaucratic interests. Factories on defence work with a limited timescale, as most major equipment projects are, will lobby continually for 'follow-on' projects in order to prolong their existence. Their arguments will be strengthened by the perceived need to preserve teams of workers with 'up-to-date' knowledge in areas where a 'general capability' is thought to be necessary. One of the prime functions of the Chevaline nuclear project in the 1970s, for example, appears to have been to keep the Aldermaston design team together as a way of retaining the option of a Polaris successor system in the 1980s and 1990s.[24]

To the extent that manufacturers are successful in arguing for 'follow-on' projects, their industrial requirements will be determining the future structure of the armed forces, rather than vice versa. This produces a conservative bias in the whole procurement process which protects existing producers and organizations, and prevents the full exploitation of new developments in technology.

Such a conservative bias tends to be a feature of most large organizations. In civilian industry, however, outdated and inefficient products are subject to continual testing in use and comparison with alternative products and methods for achieving the same results, and to competition from alternative producers. Firms which do not adapt to new technologies or the needs of consumers are likely to go out of business. In military production, on the other hand, these incentives for productive innovation and efficiency are considerably blunted. Given the absence of a major European war, the contingency for which most weapon systems are now designed, the testing of military products in use is of necessity much more imperfect than for civilian ones. As a consequence, it is often easier to continue to produce weapons which assume the next war will, in many respects, be much like the last one. Moreover, the effective monopoly which domestic manufacturers often have within the British market ensures that the second spur to innovation, competition with other producers, is also severely constrained.

The commitment to independent arms production has, therefore, tended to reduce the cost-effectiveness of British defence spending, while also increasing the pressure for it to remain high. If governments had been more willing to question that commitment, Britain would perhaps have been able to adjust its defence policy more quickly to the resources available and to a realistic role for itself in the world. In the event, the pressure of the arms lobby has acted as a powerful brake on Britain's slow and faltering retreat from policies based on outmoded ideas of national grandeur.

2. Opportunity lost: the 1940s

The consequences of the Second World War are still with us today. Indeed the history of the period since 1945 can be seen largely as that of the institutions and structures formed in the cataclysm of those years. The war saw the emergence of both the United States and the Soviet Union as superpowers and the beginnings of the Cold War. It strengthened the forces of nationalism amongst the subject peoples of the old European empires, and clearly signalled for the first time that the days of colonialism were numbered. It made clear that capitalism in Europe could only survive by making major concessions to the demands of the working class, determined to avoid repeating the experience of mass unemployment after the first European war of the century. Finally, with the destruction of Hiroshima and Nagasaki with atomic bombs in August 1945, it signalled a transformation in the nature of warfare which was to dominate international relations in the decades to come. The conflicts and disputes which had plagued humanity for centuries – and showed no sign of disappearing – would now have to be resolved without total war. The alternative was global holocaust.

For Britain, the war effort brought it close to bankruptcy. Overseas assets were sold, often at knockdown prices, and foreign debt increased sharply. Shortly before the approval by Congress of American war supplies on credit ('Lend-Lease') in March 1941, all new import orders had been frozen.[1] Without US aid, Britain would have been obliged to seek some form of settlement with Hitler to prevent a choice between economic collapse and capitulation.

Moreover, once they entered the war, the United States and the Soviet Union rapidly overtook Britain in the size of their military effort. In Asia, the United States soon emerged as the dominant Allied power. The development of nuclear weapons – in which

Britain had been the pioneer in 1940–1 – was made possible only by the US's massive economic resources, and the success of the European war rested on the sheer size and brute force of the emerging superpowers. Britain's participation in victory, therefore, was tempered by a radical reduction in its financial and military power. With other medium-size nations – Germany, Japan, France – temporarily in chaos, Britain could still claim a status as No. 3. Yet even that would only last until other economies recovered from war.

These underlying and far-reaching changes in the balance of world power were not clear to the leaders of Britain in the 1940s. The pressure from United States President Roosevelt to grant colonies independence was strenuously resisted by Churchill who insisted that 'he had not become the King's First Minister in order to preside over the liquidation of the British Empire'.[2] Indeed, while the British people fought, and died, to protect their homeland and to liberate others from the evils of the Nazis and their allies, the primary objective of their leaders appears to have been the preservation of the British Empire.

This was most clear in the continuing dispute over British participation in the war in Asia. Against objections from the US military chiefs, Churchill had demanded a large share in that war, once Hitler was defeated, in order to regain Britain's lost colonies of the Far East.[3] His pledge 'to devote our whole resources to the defeat of Japan after Germany had been brought to her knees' was given with no regard to either its economic consequences or its military necessity. It was, quite simply, an attempt to thwart American ambitions for a decolonized Pacific under its own dominion. As things transpired, the Hiroshima and Nagasaki bombs ended the war one year ahead of schedule. As a consequence the Americans were able to exclude both Britain and the Soviet Union from the occupation regime, and structure post-war Japan to meet their own requirements.[4]

A new consensus

The war united the leaders of Britain's major political parties round a new set of beliefs. On the one hand it was recognized that major social reforms and state economic intervention were necessary. Indeed it was the Conservative-led Coalition government that introduced many of the reforms that, collectively, made up the Welfare State. On the other hand, it was generally held that Britain had a right, even a duty, to continue to play a major role in the affairs of the world as a Great Power. The Labour government under Clement Attlee did not dissent from this belief.

That this consensus – reform at home, imperialism abroad – was economically untenable did not appear obvious to many at the time. For the years immediately after the war were to be marked with considerable economic success and with a fulfilment of the objectives of the consensus on domestic policy. As we shall see, the simultaneous achievement of economic growth and imperial grandeur was only to be temporary.

The Labour Party victory in the General Election of July 1945 was the clearest indication of the hopes of millions of working men and women for a better society. The war against Hitler not only ended unemployment and demonstrated the advantages of government direction of the economy. It also made a psychological impression on the class barriers that bedevilled British society, creating an increased sense of confidence amongst working people, and a willingness to accept change amongst the middle classes.[5] The belief that a return to the divisions and degradation of the 1930s was unacceptable had already led the wartime coalition government to make major reforms. The most important of these were encapsulated in the Beveridge Report (1943), with its proposals on comprehensive social security for the unemployed, elderly and sick; the proposal for a National Health Service (1944) which called for health care free of charge to all; the White Paper on Full Employment (1944), which committed the government to maintain a high level of activity and employment in the economy; and the 1944 Education Act. Given the radical nature of public opinion in 1945, the Attlee government proved depressingly conservative. It did little more than implement the policies agreed by the wartime coalition. Its nationalization of basic industries – coal, electricity, gas, railways – was uncontroversial, and the public support for much wider public ownership went unheeded. As Anthony Howard remarked, 'the overwhelming Labour victory of 1945 brought about the greatest restoration of traditional social values since 1660.'[6]

Yet the economic record of the government was impressive. Most commentators had thought that the post-war period would see a short-lived boom followed by a severe recession, as had occurred in 1919. Instead the retention of wartime controls enabled the government to keep inflation at very low levels, and simultaneously to maintain a remarkably high level of employment. Government planning also enabled the rapid conversion of much of industry to peacetime use. Discussion today about the problems of conversion from military to civilian production could draw much from the experience of 1945-7. Over two years, the labour force engaged in the war effort fell from 9 million to $1\frac{3}{4}$ million, yet, with the exception of the fuel crisis of early 1947, the number unemployed never rose above 2 per cent of the labour force.[7] This achievement surpassed even the expectations of Beveridge, who had suggested 3 per cent as the practicable minimum level of unemployment that could be attained in peacetime Britain, a figure then thought to be hopelessly optimistic.

The industrial capacity shifted from military use went mainly into increasing exports and investment. The Lend-Lease agreement of 1941 had allowed Britain to concentrate its personnel on all-out military mobilization, while the US produced most of the weapons and supplies. But it also left the UK at a severe disadvantage in overseas markets, as indeed the US had intended. As Attlee commented after Lend-Lease had been cut off at the end of the war:

> It has been made possible for us . . . to mobilise our domestic manpower for war on an intensity unsurpassed elsewhere – without having to produce exports to pay for our imports of food and raw materials or to provide the cash we were spending abroad. The very fact that this was the right division of effort between ourselves and our allies leaves us, however, far worse off, when the sources of assistance dry up, than it leaves those who have been affording us the assistance.[8]

The magnitude of this problem can be appreciated by noting that the volume of exports in 1945 was less than half that in 1938 and the foreign deficit was one tenth of total national product.[9] The losses of earnings from overseas investments, adverse terms of trade, and decline in invisible earnings (especially shipping), meant that a 75 per cent rise in exports *over pre-war levels* was needed to balance the nation's trade.[10]

Yet, to many people's surprise, that target was met in 1950, a year ahead of schedule. And the performance of investment and industrial production was also satisfactory. Both could be expected to increase quickly to pre-war levels as capacity was converted from wartime use in 1945 and 1946; and they did. More impressively, they continued to grow thereafter. Investment, 12 per cent of national income in the pre-war years, now stood at 15 per cent. Industrial production grew at an average of 7 per cent per annum in the years 1948–50 (see Table 3).

Table 3   The British Economy 1946–50 (1938=100)

	1946	1947	1948	1949	1950
Volume of exports	99	109	138	153	177
Volume of imports	68	78	81	89	89
Industrial production	102	108	117	125	133

Source: J.C.R. Dow, *The Management of the British Economy 1945–60*, London: Cambridge University Press 1964, Tables 2.1, 2.2.

Unfortunately for the British economy this unbroken growth was not to last. In 1950 it was interrupted by the rearmament programme that followed the outbreak of the Korean war. The body blow to the economy which that event dealt was one from which it never fully recovered, as we shall see in Chapter 3.

The Korean war period was also to see the end to two temporary conditions that had contributed to the economic progress of the late 1940s, and had to some extent disguised the continuing over-extension of the British state. The first was the absence of industrial competitors, with the exception of the US, in overseas markets. The economies of Western Germany and Japan were not to commence their 'economic miracles' until 1947 and 1951 respectively. Not until the early 1950s were these countries to begin to capture large shares of markets previously dominated by Britain. Meanwhile, UK exports were pulled up by the need for reconstruction and re-equipment of a war-devastated world, and further aided by the chronic, worldwide, dollar shortage.

The second temporary condition was the reduction in military industrial capacity made possible by the 'Ten Year Rule' adopted in 1946. This instructed the services to plan their requirements on the official assumption that there would be no major war for a decade. As a consequence of this, the large stocks of equipment left from the war would satisfy immediate military requirements, and military production could thus be run down. Although it was recognized that defence spending would not fall to pre-war levels, the 1947 White Paper on Defence stated that:

> It is both inevitable and right that the rehabilitation of the civil economy should increasingly absorb the country's efforts and resources, to the diminution of activities in the defence field.[11]

The result of the Ten Year Rule was, however, to encourage the illusion that Britain still had the resources to be a Great Power without damaging its domestic economy. The experience of the 1950s was to show that illusion for what it was, as the long-run cost of Britain's defence commitments became more apparent.

External policy: much as before?

These two temporary circumstances, then, contributed to the good economic performance in these years. In doing so, they also helped to ensure that the basic foundations of Britain's external policy would not be altered, even by a Labour government. Dissenting voices included, at moments in 1946 and 1947, both Attlee and his Chancellor, Hugh Dalton.[12] But the dominating figure of Ernest Bevin, Foreign Secretary and previously leader of the Transport and General Workers' Union, fought and defeated their proposals with the help of the military and diplomatic establishment. Bevin summarized his view of Britain's future role in 1947:

> His Majesty's Government do not accept the view . . . that we have ceased to be a Great Power, or the contention that we have ceased to play that role. We regard ourselves as one of the Powers most vital to the peace of the world and we still have our historic part to play. The very fact that we have fought so hard for liberty, and paid such a price, warrants our retaining this position; and indeed it places a duty upon us to continue to retain it. I am not aware of any

suggestion, seriously advanced, that by a sudden stroke of fate, as it were, we have overnight ceased to be a Great Power.[13]

Few challenged the assumption that Britain was a Great Power, if not on a par with the US and USSR, then at least well ahead of any of the others. This perception was greatly strengthened by the result of the war and by the process by which the 'Big Three' decided the fate of the post-war world at the Yalta and Potsdam conferences in 1945.[14] Few had the radicalism, or the foresight, to suggest that Britain should abandon its global pretensions and adjust to the middle ranking to which its economic strength entitled it.

The end of the war left the government with a string of overseas commitments from which it was unwilling to extricate itself. At the same time the war had also heightened aspirations for an end to colonial rule throughout Africa and Asia. To contain these aspirations and restore the pre-war position required large numbers of troops. By the beginning of 1947, there were 300,000 British service personnel stationed outside Europe: as many as the total armed forces in the mid 1930s.[15] Political unrest in Palestine and India necessitated substantial garrisons. The historic outposts of the Empire in Gibraltar, Malta, Suez, Aden, Hong Kong and Singapore demanded more. In the Middle East, fear of Soviet intentions towards Iran necessitated a strengthening of bases in that region. And in the Far East, Malaya was soon to be faced with a major revolt against colonial rule. Moreover, in Europe, Britain had a further 200,000 troops as late as 1947. Many were needed as armies of occupation in Germany, Austria and Italy, and aid to the authoritarian Greek government against left-wing rebels tied down additional forces.

Only a small proportion of the half a million British troops overseas at this time would have been needed to provide the basis of temporary occupation regimes and an orderly transition to independence. The vast majority were, instead, needed as a result of a determination by the government both to restore imperial rule and influence to its pre-war position and to prevent expansion of Soviet influence beyond its gains in Eastern Europe. The latter involved not only countering direct military threat, but also suppressing left-leaning and nationalist movements that threatened

Western economic interests in general.

Uncertainty as to the position of the US strengthened the need for substantial military forces to back up this dual determination. The US not only continued to oppose the existence of European colonialism – as Roosevelt had made clear to Churchill in 1941. It also seemed less than ready to associate Third World nationalist movements with communist expansionism. Indeed the US government openly pressed for the granting of self-government to British colonies such as Palestine and India.

This uncertainty was compounded by the rapid withdrawal of US troops from Europe (to a level of 115,000 by early 1948)[16] and by the ending of most military co-operation between the UK and the US. In September 1945 President Truman had agreed to the early abolition of several Anglo-American 'Combined Boards' responsible for combining staffs, co-ordinating operations and pooling resources; and this was implemented in 1946 against British objections.[17] Of particular importance were the moves by the US to prevent Britain developing an independent nuclear weapon capability. Britain had made a substantial contribution to the Manhattan Project and had desisted from further independent work in order to give top priority to the early development of an American bomb. Now the US appeared to be seeking a national monopoly of the new weapons.

These steps suggested to the British that the Americans might be returning to their isolationist position of the inter-war period. As a consequence, British demobilization proceeded at a relatively slow pace, with the plans to return service manpower and defence spending to the pre-war level being shelved. A stepping up of the A-bomb project also took place, as the government's view that it needed such a weapon for Great Power status was reinforced by the freezing of nuclear collaboration by Washington.[18]

Propping up the Empire

The uncertainty in Britain's 'special relationship' with the US was dramatically emphasized by President Truman's decision to end Lend-Lease aid to Britain only one week after Japan's surrender. Even goods already on their way across the Atlantic were included in the order. The decision embarrassed the new Labour government and created a sombre mood in ruling circles. The move was widely felt to reflect the American government's hostility to British colonialism and its reluctance to subsidize a future economic competitor.

This interpretation appeared to be vindicated by the severe conditions which the US insisted on including in the $3.75 billion Loan Agreement signed in December 1945. The two most important were that sterling should be made convertible within one year of the agreement coming into operation; and that Britain should not seek to discriminate against US goods in Empire markets. The effect of these conditions would be to subordinate Britain to an American-dominated international economic system.[19]

The Loan was opposed by both the imperialist wing of the Conservative Party, fearing further weakening of the Empire, and by the left of the Labour Party, who questioned the alliance with capitalist America. In the end, however, only Bevan and Shinwell opposed it in Cabinet.[20] The House of Commons debated it in an atmosphere of gloom and disillusion. 'We are sitting here today as the representatives of a victorious people, discussing the economic consequences of victory,' said one MP. 'If a visitor were to come . . . from Mars . . . he might well be pardoned for thinking that he was listening to the representatives of a vanquished people discussing the economic penalties of defeat.'[21]

Despite the relatively harsh terms for Britain, the Loan also ran into severe political trouble in the US from Congressmen opposed to propping up British 'socialism' and imperialism. At one stage there was a possibility that it would not be approved. As a result of this uncertainty, serious consideration was given by Britain's government to alternative schemes. The retention of Great Power status, even at the expense of domestic economic development, was a central, if implicit, starting point for most of this thinking. The most striking example of this tendency was a scheme, advocated by some of the country's most senior officials, that would have ended Britain's role as an industrial nation.

In 1946, Lord Alanbrooke and Sir Henry Tizard advocated the transfer of as much British skilled labour and industry as possible to the white Dominions as a response to Britain's approaching nuclear vulnerability.

> The essential idea of the latest thinking on imperial defence
> is that essential war industries, skilled white manpower,
> research organisations, and raw material stocks, should be
> dispersed throughout the Commonwealth . . . the
> suggestion was quite seriously made by the British Chiefs of
> Staff. It was presented as part of an outline plan of imperial
> defence, for study by the Dominion Prime Ministers [at the
> Commonwealth Conference of April/May 1946], with the
> approval of a Labour Cabinet well aware of the manpower
> problems looming ahead . . .[22]

> [The question must be asked] whether the British Isles, with
> their present concentration of population and industry, can
> be held and defended as a base against the forms of warfare
> that might be directed against them . . . the question was
> being asked before the end of the last war when it was
> thought that the Germans might get the atomic bomb first.
> [It is argued] that Britain would be neither so tempting, nor
> so vulnerable as a target, if there were distributed in the
> Dominions and Colonies six or seven alternative centres of
> British industrial strength and striking power.[23]

That such a policy was even seriously considered shows the extent
to which the policy-makers of the time saw their role in international, imperial, rather than purely national, terms. Such
radical, imperial solutions were, however, abandoned, along with
the option of rapid withdrawal from Empire, when the US
eventually approved the Loan Agreement. That approval enabled
the British state to remain committed to an imperial role, albeit
one increasingly subordinate to US interests. Both the social
upheaval involved in the radical imperial solution of mass
emigration, and the shock to its ruling class of abandoning the
British Empire so soon after 'winning' the war, were successfully
avoided.

Churchill's speech in Fulton, Missouri, in March 1946 played an
important part in overcoming the obstacles to the Loan. Speaking
of the 'Iron Curtain' that had descended across Europe, he argued
for the 'fraternal association of the English-speaking peoples' and
for a permanent military alliance between the US and the British
Empire. His speech helped the shift in the US to a more openly
anti-Soviet position and thus ensured the Loan's final approval by

219 votes to 155 in July 1946. A common line of thought was expressed by one Republican congressman. 'The economic arguments in favour of the loan,' Christian Herter wrote, 'are on the whole much less convincing . . . than the feeling that the loan may serve us in good stead in holding up a hand of a nation whom we may need badly as a friend because of impending Russian troubles.'[24]

A point seldom emphasized, however, is the importance of military considerations in the UK need for the Loan. It has been assumed that the American conditions had to be accepted as no real alternative existed; and that the continuance of necessary imports required the Loan to be granted. In fact the Loan was financially necessary only because of Britain's high level of overseas government spending. In February 1946, during discussions on what would happen if Congress rejected the Loan, Keynes had emphasized this point in a private memo:

> the main reaction of the loss of the American loan must be on our military and political expenditure . . . The American loan is for £937 million . . . estimated political and military expenditure [in the three years 1946–1948] is £1000 million. Thus, it comes out in the wash that the American loan is primarily required to meet the political and military expenditure overseas . . . The main consequences of the failure of the loan must, therefore, be a large-scale withdrawal on our part from international responsibility. (Perhaps there might be no harm . . . in letting the State Department appreciate a little more vividly . . . that this would be inevitably the most striking consequence.)[25]

The purpose of the Loan, therefore, was not to ensure the survival of the British economy or the preservation of full employment. It was to provide the resources necessary for Britain's military commitment to 'containment' of the Soviet Union and other anti-Western forces. Far from weakening the Empire, it was essential for its continued existence – albeit an existence largely subordinate to United States global interests. It enabled the US government to maintain the stability of the global system it wished to create, despite continuing domestic opposition to American military involvement overseas. For, if an anti-Communist consensus did not exist amongst the American people in early 1946, their government already saw the Soviet Union as the primary threat, far more important than the secondary problems of British imperialism and economic competition.

The Loan enabled the British state to avoid making drastic adjustments in foreign policy. Britain could continue to be a world power, one of the Big Three, with a significant say in the affairs of the whole planet. Perhaps more importantly it could *appear* to be one, and thus avoid the demoralization of its ruling classes that a more drastic curtailment of overseas commitments would have brought. In retrospect, it is clear that the political restructuring resulting from Congressional rejection of the Loan would have accelerated Britain's adjustment to its diminished economic power. Withdrawal from East of Suez could have been completed two decades before it was eventually forced upon the government by later economic crises. Resources could have been used for domestic economic development rather than the doomed attempt to maintain a world role for which only the United States had the industrial muscle. One of those closely involved in overseas financial policy at the time, Sir Richard Clarke, was to write:

> Thirty years later, when one sees the relative success of Germany, Japan, France, which were forced to make great social and economic changes, one cannot be absolutely sure that our right long-term course was to display remarkable ingenuity to retain the status quo.[26]

The success in maintaining a global role also foreclosed the possibility of Britain entering a European federation. Throughout the next decade, Britain was to argue that its Commonwealth and Empire commitments, along with its 'special relationship' with the US, prevented it from full participation in any supra-national Western European institution. It thus lost the opportunity to influence those institutions to take account of British national interests. When a turn to Europe was made, and the UK entered the European Community in 1973, it had to accept conditions of membership drawn up while it had been outside. Some of these – such as the Common Agricultural Policy – have proven to be persistent economic and political problems ever since: ones that perhaps could have been avoided had Britain's position in 1945 as temporarily the strongest West European power been used in a different direction.

From Pax Britannica to Pax Americana

The Loan, however, could not prevent increasing balance of payments problems by 1947. The gold and dollar deficit of £50 million a month in early 1946 increased to £135 million in the last quarter of that year, £200 million by February 1947, and over £500 million in July.[27] The fuel crisis in February contributed to the problem, causing export losses estimated at £800 million and a temporary level of unemployment over two million. The introduction of convertibility (a condition of the 1946 Loan) further increased the outflow of dollars. By the time it was retracted – in August 1947 – £3.6 billion of the £5 billion credits from the United States and Canada had been exhausted. The Loan, intended to last three years, in fact lasted only 18 months.[28]

As a result of these crises, there was pressure by the Treasury for more cuts in overseas military spending. In November 1946 Chancellor of the Exchequer Hugh Dalton wrote to Prime Minister Attlee: 'I am very doubtful indeed about this policy of propping up, even with American aid, weak states in the Eastern Mediterranean against Russia . . . Nor, even if we had the money, am I satisfied that we ought to spend it this way.'[29] Dalton, on this occasion, won this argument and, on February 21, the British sent a message to the American government announcing that UK aid to Greece would terminate at the end of March.

By this time the anti-communist consensus was more firmly established in Washington. State Department Under-Secretary Dean Acheson was able to convince Congressional leaders that: 'Like apples in a barrel infected by the corruption of one rotten one, the corruption of Greece would infect Iran and all to the East . . . Africa . . . Italy and France . . . and open three continents to Soviet penetration.'[30] The result was the 'Truman Doctrine', publicly announced on March 12, which marked a major turning point in American foreign policy. It signalled an acceptance of a hawkish line towards the Soviet Union and a determination that America should take the lead in 'containment' of communism worldwide. The Pax Americana was born.

The most serious threat to the policy of containment was in continental Europe itself. Its economies were, by 1947, in severe crisis. Industrial and food production were dislocated and the US supplied seven times as much to Europe as it received.[31] Only

American aid, it was felt, could prevent further economic deterioration. Moreover, the war had discredited most right-wing politicians through their collaboration with Nazism; while communist and socialist activists had played a leading role in the resistance movements in occupied countries. The establishment of socialist regimes in some of the Western European nations was a real possibility. The main 'threat' to US policy in Europe was, therefore, home-grown socialism, not Soviet military intervention. The Soviet economy was shattered after the struggle against Hitler and incapable of conducting a major offensive war. Given this assessment, rearmament in Western Europe was unnecessary and costly. The main requirement was economic, not military. For prolonged economic crisis would further discredit pro-capitalist political forces and strengthen those for radical change.

The US, therefore, agreed in July 1947 to a massive infusion of 'Marshall Aid' into the West European economies, conditional on the expulsion of communists from governments in France and Italy – a move reciprocated by Stalin with the removal of non-communists from government in Hungary and later in Czechoslovakia.[32] The creation of the two ideological blocs in Europe was accelerated.

The British Labour Party bears no little responsibility for this polarization in Europe. It opposed European politicians arguing for a 'Third Way' between American free enterprise capitalism and Soviet totalitarian socialism. It encouraged splits in the Labour movements between communist and social democratic factions. As a result of Labour's commitment to the Empire, a 'special relationship' with the USA was essential. This, in turn, effectively precluded support for an independent socialist Europe, free from both superpowers. Britain threw all its weight behind an incorporation of Western Europe into an American-led international system.

Failure to reappraise

These American moves, providing economic and military leadership in the reconstruction of world capitalism, had indicated to the British government that the possibility of US isolationism was fading. Henceforth it was clear that the US was ready to act to prevent the spread of socialism and anti-Western forces in any 'theatre'. Moreover, as the Pacific war had demonstrated, only the US had the military resources to protect the smaller nations of Asia from external attack. Indeed this fact was recognized by Australia and New Zealand, Britain's old Commonwealth allies. They concluded new defence arrangements (later formalized in the ANZUS Treary) with the US, from which Britain was deliberately, and humiliatingly, excluded.[33]

The justification for retaining Britain's military role in Asia was brought further into question with the independence of India and Pakistan in August 1947. At a stroke, the heart of the British Empire was removed. For the chain of bases held by Britain, from Gibraltar and Suez through to Singapore, had been constructed round the pivot of India. The defence of Australasia – now also out of British hands – had been an additional, if secondary, factor. Indeed Curzon had clearly stated, four decades before, the implications were India to be 'lost':

> Your ports and coaling stations, your fortresses and dockyards, your Crown Colonies and protectorates will go too . . . they will be unnecessary as the toll-gates and barbicans of an empire that has vanished.[34]

Indian independence not only removed the main justification for British imperial policy. It also removed one of its main props – the Indian Army. That force had been central to imperial defence East of Suez, and was one of the secrets of the low cost of Pax Britannica. Former Chief of the Imperial General Staff, Lord Alanbrooke, described Indian independence as 'a crippling blow to British military power'.[35] It was therefore remarkable how slowly the effects of this change were felt in defence policy. Doubly remarkable, in fact, given that American willingness to replace the UK as 'guarantor' of Western interests as a whole had now clearly been demonstrated.

In fact an important debate did take place within the government on the utility of military bases in the Middle East, particularly that at Suez. Prime Minister Attlee argued that the indefensibility of the Mediterranean route in wartime, together with the impending independence of India, meant that the line of communication through the Suez Canal made little sense. He pressed these views on the Cabinet Defence Committee, arguing that Mombasa in Kenya could be used as a base for the protection of the African colonies. His view was, however, defeated, with the Chiefs of Staff, in January 1947, telling him that they would resign were Britain to withdraw from the Middle East.[36]

The Truman Doctrine and Indian independence weakened the dual justification for the high level of British military spending: the need to 'hold the fort' against socialism while America dithered, and the desire to maintain the Empire intact. Neither now applied. Partly as a result defence spending did fall and demobilization of soldiers continued as commitments in Greece, Palestine, India and Burma were relinquished. But the failure to reappraise the entire British role East of Suez was to lead to a series of costly local wars whose relevance to the needs of the British people was difficult to discern.

Table 4 Defence Spending 1945–50

	1945–6	1946–7	1947–8	1948–9	1949–50	1950–1
£ million (cash)	4,410	1,653	854	753	741	777
As % GDP	. . .	16.1	7.7	6.3	5.9	5.8
£ million (1984–5 prices)	55,482	20,653	10,329	8,649	8,350	8,558
Change		–62.8%	–50%	–16.3%	–3.5%	+2.5%

Source: see Appendix. GDP data for 1945–6 not available.

Nevertheless, in the late 1940s considerable progress was made in reducing both defence spending and the military's demands on scarce resources. Partly as a result of this, and partly because of the rapid economic recovery in Europe that the Marshall Plan initiated, British industrial growth continued to be impressive. Unemployment was kept to an unprecedentedly low level without provoking inflation as a result of close co-operation between government and trade unions. In February 1948, the latter agreed to wage restraint, which was maintained until October 1950.[37] During these two and a half years, wage rates rose by only 5 per cent while retail prices rose by 8 per cent. That such a policy could be maintained successfully was due to the widespread recognition of the needs of national reconstruction, and in particular for more exports and capital investment. For spending in these areas held the promise of future growth and rising living standards, which the defence spending that was to displace it in the early 1950s clearly would not.

Domestic economic success was accompanied by substantial progress towards British goals in Europe. The Marshall Plan fuelled economic recovery in Europe, while simultaneously funding British overseas military commitments. The Brussels Treaty of 1948 and the creation of NATO in 1949 contributed to the political stabilization of Western Europe. West Germany was firmly integrated into an American-controlled economic system, defeating Soviet hopes for a sympathetic, or at least demilitarized, buffer state. All this was achieved without increases in military costs, there being a widespread feeling that the Soviets were unlikely to invade Western Europe, given the enormous problems of recovery they faced at home. Even the 1948 Soviet blockade of West Berlin, in retaliation against currency reform in West Germany, had only a slight effect on Britain's defence budget, which was temporarily raised.

However, the simultaneous success of the British state in both domestic and international policy, despite its limited resources, could not last. It had retained too many military obligations. When it was asked to deliver on these in 1950, it could only do so by sacrificing domestic economic progress.

3. Rearmament and rethink: the early 1950s

In mid 1950 the British state appeared to have fulfilled the ambitious objectives of the wartime political consensus. In marked contrast to the years after the First World War, the transition to peace time had been achieved without mass unemployment or factory closures. The economy seemed set on a high growth path, and the Welfare State, together with (male) full employment, had brought tangible rewards to the working class, and weakened the appeal of more radical policies. Simultaneous with this economic success, the state had been able to achieve most of its international objectives. The defeat of socialism in Western Europe, and its economic and political stabilization within a capitalist framework, owed much to Britain's efforts. And Britain had successfully balanced this European commitment with a continuing involvement in the affairs of its colonies and ex-colonies in Africa and Asia. Britain was still a 'power to be reckoned with' in the world. Even the psychological impact of Indian independence was blunted for a while by the transmutation of Empire into Commonwealth.

To maintain these multiple commitments required a defence budget which, as a proportion of national income, was greater than that of any other European country. Even the US spent a smaller proportion of its income on defence in 1950.[1] However, at the time, this relatively high defence burden still appeared to allow a substantial level of economic growth. The temporary factors in Britain's success – the lack of foreign competition and the reliance on war stocks for military equipment – were either ignored or not fully understood.

It was fully understood, however, that Britain's Great Power status was now entirely dependent on the continuing co-operation of the United States. It was American finance and military might that held Western Europe together. And Britain's imperial role outside Europe – its colonies and bases, the overseas sterling area, trade preferences – existed only by consent of a US government anxious to have a reliable ally against communism. Were the 'special relationship' to be terminated, Britain would be forced into fundamental, and uncomfortable, reappraisal of its foreign policy. To avoid a break with the US was thus a precondition of Britain's continuing world role.

Dependence on the 'special relationship' made the UK exceptionally vulnerable to the American demands for rearmament made in the latter half of 1950. In the crisis atmosphere of that period, the Labour government sacrificed prospects for domestic economic growth in an effort to influence and placate the US government. When a choice had eventually to be made between the domestic and international objectives of the post-war consensus, the commitment of Britain's leaders to a Great Power role came first.

War fever and NSC-68

Two major blows to American power and prestige came in 1949. They had stood by helpless while a Communist regime took power in China and, in August of that year, came the first report of a Soviet atomic bomb being successfully tested. In response to these events, President Truman had ordered work to begin on the 'super' (or hydrogen) bomb, and had called for a major review of US security policies by his officials.[2] The result was National Security Council Memorandum 68 (NSC-68), drafted by a group under Paul Nitze and adopted in April 1950. It proposed a rapid military build-up to counter the supposed Soviet threat, and suggested that the US could afford to devote up to 20 per cent of its GNP on security expenditures, even in peacetime.[3] The document marked a shift in foreign policy as significant as the 'containment' policy inaugurated by the Truman Doctrine speech in March 1947. That policy, which had led to the Marshall Plan and the formation of NATO, was now thought insufficient. The imminent emergence of Soviet nuclear power, it was argued, required a massive new military spending programme.

In June 1950, however, the US Administration could not be sure that Congress would approve the tripling of military spending that NSC-68 proposed. The invasion of South Korea on June 25, 1950, widely believed to be the precursor to a general Communist offensive by the Soviet Union and China, effectively solved this problem. In President Truman's view:

> The attack upon Korea makes it plain beyond all doubt
> that Communism has passed beyond the use of subversion
> to conquer independent nations and will now use armed
> invasion and war.[4]

Massive US military budget increases were soon approved by Congress. From $15 billion in 1950, military spending rose to $22.3 billion in 1951 and a remarkable $44 billion in 1952. Within two years, the defence budget rose from 5.9 per cent of GNP to 17 per cent.[5]

This war fever in the United States led to increasingly insistent demands on its European allies, and on Britain in particular. In response, a British army brigade was sent to Korea and, on July 26, the government announced that an additional £100 million was to be spent in 1950–1 on military equipment.[6] These commitments, however, were seen as totally inadequate in Washington. On the day of the Commons debate on these initial measures the US approached the British government with an appeal for much bigger increases and a demand that the answer be forthcoming within ten days. On August 4 the British reply was ready. A new three-year programme, which brought total spending to £3,400 million over three years, was announced, which added no less than £1,100 million to previous plans. This increase was, however, made conditional on direct US assistance of some £550 million.[7]

Within a few weeks it became clear that the US was unwilling to provide this £550 million. Pleas from Foreign Secretary Bevin went unanswered despite the Cabinet's view that the Americans should be told that: 'the usefulness of this country would be seriously jeopardized if it ceased to be economically viable as a result of shouldering the full defence programme.'[8]

Throughout this period, the British government was unconvinced by US arguments that the Soviets were about to start a major war. The prime motive for Britain's massive defence spending increases was to influence United States policy, not to deter the Soviet Union. The UK's main concern was that a lack of visible support of United States policy in the Far East might strengthen those American political forces arguing for a shift of forces from Europe to the Far East, or for a 'Fortress America' concept. Britain therefore sought to ensure that the Korean war did not escalate to an all-out war with China, as the US Commander in Korea, General MacArthur, wanted. When North Korean forces were in retreat in autumn of 1950, Britain suggested, without success, that the United Nations troops (predominantly American) stay clear of the Chinese border.[9] When the Chinese responded by launching a counter-offensive, driving US troops onto three South Korean beachheads, Attlee continued to urge caution on the increasingly emotional Americans. While American opinion appeared to be moving towards accepting a new world war as inevitable, the ubiquitous Paul Nitze reported that: 'It is not possible to hold the United Kingdom in line for early hostilities with the Soviet Union.'[10]

Concern with the direction of American policy now led to a British decision to demand an immediate summit meeting between the two countries. The subsequent meeting between Attlee and Truman (on December 4) took place as their forces in Korea appeared about to be driven into the sea. There was growing alarm in Britain at remarks from the American president which suggested that he was considering the use of the atomic bomb to avert such a defeat. His view, as conveyed to Attlee at their meeting, that China was a complete satellite of the Soviet Union, that the situation 'looked very dark to him' and that 'the only way to meet communism is to eliminate it', could not have eased British concerns. Indeed Attlee went out of his way, in reply, to argue that the Chinese had legitimate fears for their security and were not Soviet puppets. It would be wrong for the West, he argued, to spread the conflict as it could only help the Russians were the US fully engaged in Asia.[11]

Whether or not Attlee's intervention was important, it was seen to be so at the time. Truman did not authorize use of atomic weapons, and in 1951 General MacArthur, who had advocated extending the war to China, was sacked. The price was heavy however. The American Secretary of State, Dean Acheson, insisted that, despite the economic burden of rearmament, further increases in defence spending by the British were needed. With the agreement of the British military chiefs he argued that the 'only way we can do anything with NATO is for the US and the UK to go ahead and act and force the others to follow'. Warning that 'there was a feeling in Washington that the British were not doing all they could do', Acheson stressed his government's view that 'we were so near the edge of the precipice that secondary points must be sacrificed'.[12]

Faced with this pressure, the British Cabinet believed that it had no alternative but to agree to a further increase in defence spending to £4700 million over three years – effectively a doubling of annual defence spending in the space of two years.[13] The government clearly believed that the needs of the domestic economy must take second place to Britain's commitment to the Atlantic Alliance. To have refused the request for higher defence spending would have threatened Britain's position as the 'loyal lieutenant' of the US. As one minister commented: 'None of us was taking the American alliance for granted.'[14] Until 1950 Britain had retained its continuing status as a Great Power at relatively low cost. Now it was forced to pay the full price.

The cost of rearmament

Rearmament dealt a body blow to the British economy. Between 1950 and 1952 industrial production rose by less than one per cent – after a thirty per cent rise between 1947 and 1950. Fixed investment stagnated, and civilian investment fell. Inflation rose from 3 per cent in 1950 to 12 per cent in 1951. And a balance of payments surplus of £300 million (1950) became a deficit of £400 million (1951).[15] Britain was having its first post-war experience of simultaneous inflation and stagnant output – 'stagflation' as it later became known.

A 56 per cent increase in real defence spending within two years (see Table 5) would have produced considerable strains on the economy in any circumstances. The greatest damage came, however, from the concentration of the increased spending on production and research. The £4,700 million plan announced in January 1951 envisaged a doubling of military production expenditure in 1951–2. By 1953–4, it was planned, the country would have quadrupled its annual output of tanks and combat aircraft.[16] Even after the 'stretching' of this programme, introduced later by Winston Churchill's government, defence spending on armaments and engineering products rose from £186 million in 1950–51 to £524 million in 1952–53; and on research and development from

£71 million to £124 million.[17] By contrast, expenditure on pay for civilian and military staff rose from £310 million to £429 million – a relatively modest 38 per cent increase.

Table 5   Defence Spending 1950–56

	1950–1	1951–2	1952–3	1953–4	1954–5	1955–6
£ million (cash)	777	1,110	1,404	1,364	1,436	1,405
As % GDP	5.8	7.5	8.7	7.9	7.8	7.1
£ million (1984–5 prices)	8,558	11,234	13,329	12,571	12,989	12,195
Change		+31.3%	+18.6%	–5.7%	+3.3%	–6.1%

Source: see Appendix.

The emphasis of the expanded defence programme on equipment was due, not only to the requirements of rapid rearmament, but also to the low level of equipment spending in the late 1940s. As we have seen in our account of that period, Second World War surplus stocks enabled the services to delay re-equipment and concentrate their resources on maintaining a large number of overseas commitments. By 1950, most of the weapons and stores left from the war had worn out or had become obsolete. Indeed even *Tribune*, in March 1950, argued that 'the time has now come when a considerable re-equipment programme can no longer be avoided.'[18] Accelerated preparations for the possibility of a conflict with the Soviet Union made such modernization and restocking even more necessary. The short-term economies of previous years had succeeded in concealing the long-term cost of Britain's military commitments.

With unemployment at only 1½ per cent and factories working at or near full capacity, the increase in defence production could only take place with the transfer of resources from other uses. In practice this meant that exports and investment would bear the brunt of the sacrifice since:

> the industries which will have to carry out most of the
> increased defence orders, the engineering and metal using
> industries, are the very ones on which we have relied to
> make the biggest contribution to exports and to industrial
> equipment . . . our task is to turn over progressively to
> defence production sections of the engineering industry,
> especially those producing aircraft, vehicles, radio and
> radar equipment, and machine tools . . . This will
> inevitably reduce the exports of these industries,
> particularly now when labour and materials are so
> scarce.[19]

The effect of rearmament on British industry was increased by the government's insistence that almost all the armaments required should be manufactured domestically. The disruption to industry and to long-term growth prospects could have been considerably reduced were some weapons to have been imported from the US. For Britain to depart from the principle of military self-sufficiency was, however, unacceptable at that time. It was too closely related to its status as an independent Great Power to be sacrificed in pursuit of economic objectives.

In 1950, the metal-using industries were responsible for two-fifths of all UK exports.[20] British industry's position in these markets was immediately adversely affected. Countries such as Germany, Japan, Switzerland, Sweden and Italy all gained ground due to the limited nature of their own defence programmes. While Britain shifted its factories into arms production, its competitors moved into its traditional markets. Spare industrial capacity and unemployment enabled Germany and Japan to take full advantage of markets abandoned by Britain.

Japan was granted, on American insistence, entry into traditional British markets in South-East Asia. Forbidden to rearm itself, its exports were fuelled by the demand for war materials and grew by 61 per cent in one year. It even sold steel and ships to Australia, at prices substantially higher than Britain's, because of the latter's inability to meet new orders.[21] Meanwhile, West German industrial production also expanded rapidly as occupation controls were lifted and idle factories were set to work. Its exports of steel, heavy capital goods and machine tools were particularly successful, quadrupling between 1950 and 1953.[22]

In the late 1940s British economic success had been aided by the lack of serious competition from the defeated Axis powers in crucial markets. The re-emergence of these nations in world markets now further exacerbated the problems created for Britain by its rearmament programme. The early 1950s marked the beginning of a long period of declining competitiveness, low investment and export growth, and recurring balance of payments crises. Britain's extensive military commitments overseas would continue to deepen this cycle of decline throughout the next two decades.

As a result of Korean war rearmament, Britain also plunged into short-term economic crisis. The cost of imports grew rapidly as raw material shortages fed into higher prices. The government decision to build up contingency stocks further increased the strain on the nation's gold and currency reserves. Increased import prices fed into the shops, and with a severe shortage of labour for the competing demands of the defence and civilian sectors, trade unions were able to push for higher wages in compensation. Stagnation in productivity further increased the competition for resources between labour and capital, and reduced the extra resources available for the competing demands of investment, exports, defence, and consumption.[23]

Government hopes of financing the defence programme by reductions in consumption proved difficult to fulfil. The demands on the engineering industry for arms manufacture inevitably diverted factories from export orders and capital goods production; and it proved more difficult than anticipated to turn other industries – such as textiles – to export markets in which new competitors were now emerging.

Despite its irrelevance to the provision of resources for defence production, however, the Chancellor of the Exchequer of the time, Hugh Gaitskell, was determined to include the introduction of charges for health service dentures and spectacles in his 1951 Budget. The financial savings – £25 million – were insignificant compared with the £700 million increase in defence spending. Most of his other measures were directed against investment and consumer durables competing with defence for the output of vehicle and electrical industries.[24] The health service charges were introduced only as a *symbol* of the need for austerity by ordinary people, and of the government's sacrifice of domestic aspirations for the rearmament programme. The subsequent resignations by Nye Bevan and Harold Wilson from the government, which probably contributed to the narrow election defeat in October 1951, were a direct result of that choice. The subsequent divisions between left and right in the party would return, again and again, to the issues of defence and disarmament over the next 30 years.

The Labour government had come to office in 1945 bearing the hopes of millions of citizens for a very different, and better, future. Its failure to seriously question Britain's old world role during its first years – when international politics were in unprecedented flux – ensured that those hopes remained unfulfilled. The full cost of that failure would be paid over the three decades of decline that followed.

Britain's global strategy

The resignations of Bevan and Wilson were precipitated by Gaitskell's refusal to compromise on health service charges. As their speeches at the time made clear, however, they had also become increasingly critical of the rearmament programme itself, arguing that it would be unattainable because of shortages of skilled workers, raw materials and machine tools.[25] Within months of its October 1951 election victory, the new Conservative administration accepted this argument, and agreed to stretch the £4,700 million defence programme over more than three years. Winston Churchill himself, the new Prime Minister, admitted that the Labour government's plans were 'utterly beyond our economic capacity to bear'.[26]

As war fever subsided, and economic difficulties were given greater prominence, the Conservative government ordered further cutbacks in order to reduce the damage done to exports and investment by defence's demands on the engineering industry. The 1952 Defence White Paper argued that:

Since the [£4,700 million] programme was started the economic position has seriously deteriorated and severe measures have had to be taken in the civil sector of the economy. About 80 per cent of defence production consists of products of the metal-using industries which are responsible for about two-fifths of our exports. In the light of this and other factors . . . it has been necessary to adjust the defence programme . . . reducing the immediate burden the programme will place on the metal-using industries.[27]

As a result of these cutbacks, defence spending rose less quickly than planned, and the workforce engaged in defence production fell from a peak of 900,000 in 1952 to 850,000 in 1953. Yet, as is so often the case with defence 'cuts', their result was only to reduce the increase in spending. The proportion of national income taken by defence rose from 5.8 per cent in 1950–51 to 8.7 per cent in 1952–3 before falling to 7.9 per cent in 1953–4. If the Attlee government's programme had been fully implemented, these proportions could have risen to 10 per cent in 1952–3 and 11 per cent in 1953–4.[28]

The conflict between military and economic strength, which the rearmament programme had highlighted, persuaded Churchill that a major review of defence policy was necessary. The Chiefs of Staff were asked to undertake this review, taking particularly into account the economic constraints on defence and the future role of nuclear weapons. The result was the Global Strategy Paper, which the Cabinet subsequently adopted without significant amendment.[29] It played an influential role in persuading the West to base its defence on the threat of the immediate, and widespread, use of nuclear weapons in the event of Soviet aggression. By bombing centres of population and industry on a massive scale, it was argued, the enemy could be forced into accepting defeat. The objective would be to prevent a war from occurring through Soviet fear that aggression would bring

instantaneous and overwhelming atomic air attack. It was especially imperative for the Allies to make clear the intention to use the atomic bomb immediately. To carry out this policy the Allies would have to give priority to the air striking forces and to maintain the quantitative superiority of those forces.[30]

To compensate for the alleged insufficiency of NATO conventional land forces, 'tactical' nuclear weapons were also recommended. These would provide additional firepower at low cost, and thus allow modification of the over-ambitious NATO targets for conventional forces adopted in Lisbon in early 1952. According to the British Chiefs of Staff, these targets were based on 'a modernized conception of the 1914–18 war' and their implementation would be 'an economic impossibility, a logistic nightmare and a strategic nightmare'.[31] NATO should instead rely primarily on the use of atomic weapons, and correspondingly reduce its conventional force levels in Europe.

By reliance on instantaneous nuclear retaliation, the Global Strategy Paper hoped to reduce non-nuclear military costs. In Europe, nuclear superiority would permit NATO to reduce conventional forces to little more than a 'tripwire'. Elsewhere, military commitments could also be reduced. The utility of the Middle East as an avenue for Soviet attacks on the southern flank of Europe would be thrown into question, given the assumption that a European war would be nuclear and short. And it was believed that nuclear weapons could also deter Communist 'aggression' in Asia. The 1955 Statement on Defence argued that 'the existence of the nuclear weapon may discourage overt armed intervention by the Communist powers such as occurred in Korea.'[32]

Increased reliance on nuclear weapons, however, did not prove to be a panacea for Britain's difficulties. The continued commitment to Great Power status ensured that few economies in the military budget were possible. First, with the West becoming more reliant on nuclear weapons, an independent British nuclear force became an increasingly indispensable part of being a 'world power'. Secondly, the retention of British colonies and bases in Africa and Asia continued to take a substantial part of the military budget. Thirdly, the main threat to perceived British interests in Europe came not from the Soviet Union but from the possibility of a renewal of Franco–German rivalry. Substantial British conventional forces had to be promised to NATO to avoid this possibility. Finally, the power of certain interest groups, together with the conservatism inherent in military thinking, ensured that forces and concepts with no clear purpose in the new strategy were, nevertheless, retained at considerable cost. We now look at each of these four factors in turn.

The British bomb

Before 1952 the commitment of the government to an independent

British nuclear force was by no means clear. In 1949, it had appeared willing to sacrifice independence in weapons manufacture for a stock of American bombs – possibly as few as twenty – in British custody.[33] It was only after the Global Strategy Paper that the government finally acceded to strong Royal Air Force pressure for a British-made strategic nuclear bomber force. That force – consisting of the Vulcan, Victor and Valiant bombers – would cost £600 million over 15 years.[34] It constituted a major additional cost – over and above Attlee's £4,700 million programme – in a review that was intended to reduce the burden of defence spending.

Soon after the go-ahead for the V-bombers, Britain tested its first atomic device at Monte Bello in the Pacific on October 3rd, 1952.[35] Although not yet usable as a bomb, the successful test strengthened the government's determination to have its own nuclear force. When the United States exploded the world's first hydrogen bomb one month later, the British soon resolved to follow suit. As the key thinker behind the Global Strategy Paper and Chief of the RAF, Sir John Slessor was to argue:

> If we were to leave to any ally, however staunch or loyal,
> the monopoly of an instrument of such decisive importance
> in the stupendous issues of war and peace, we should sink
> to the level of a fourth-rate power.[36]

Amongst the 'fourth-rate powers' which, Slessor believed, would find it 'manifestly uneconomical, indeed impossible' to reproduce the nuclear bomber forces of Britain and the United States was France which, within a few years, was to overtake the UK in economic strength and itself become an independent nuclear weapon state. The even more industrially powerful Germany and Japan do not merit a mention. Lord Cherwell, Churchill's close adviser, spoke for many when he voiced his deep dislike of any prospect that Britain might 'rank with other European nations who have to make do with conventional weapons.'[37]

The nuclear weapons programme, including associated bombers and missiles, may have consumed up to 20 per cent of the defence budget in the 1950s, though this proportion fell in the 1960s.[38] Its main economic impact was not, however, directly financial. It was in the illusion which it fostered that Britain remained a first-class power with world interests and responsibilities, and with a privileged access to, and influence upon, the American government. As long as British leaders remained convinced of this, repeated efforts to halt long-term economic decline would inevitably lead to failure.

Imperial burdens

The independence of India in 1947 made remarkably little immediate difference to British military thinking. The loss of the hub of the British Empire had made an anachronism of the string of bases and colonies from the Mediterranean through the Gulf, East Africa and the Indian Ocean to Malaysia and Singapore. Their primary military purpose had been the defence of the approaches to India. Much of the cost of policing them had been met from the Indian exchequer using Indian soldiers.[39] Yet the resistance to change was too strong to allow the loss of India to interfere with the continuation of the Empire. Sir Oliver Franks, British ambassador to Washington from 1948 to 1952 (and recently chairman of the Franks Commission on the Falklands), reflects the dominant mood of policy-makers at that time:

> we assume that our future will be of one piece with our past and that we shall continue as a Great Power. What is noteworthy is the way we take this for granted. It is not a belief arrived at after reflection by a conscious decision. It is part of the habit and furniture of our minds: a principle so much one with our outlook and character that it determines the way we act without emerging itself into clear consciousness.[40]

Nor did the introduction of nuclear weapons into Britain's forces allow savings in East of Suez expenditure, as the Global Strategy Paper had thought possible. The government could not use the threat of nuclear weapons to combat guerrilla warfare. Indeed, Britain did not have an effective A-bomb of its own until after the 1956 Suez operation. The government had argued that nuclear weapons could be used in future 'limited' wars on the Korea model.[41] But it could not deter peoples determined to fight colonial rule through guerrilla warfare and terrorism. In 1955, three years after the Global Strategy Paper, there were still 372,000 service personnel overseas (of whom only 80,000 were in Germany)

– as many as there were in the late 1940s.[42]

An explanation of the continued presence 'East of Suez' must be based primarily on Britain's reluctance to give up a potent symbol of its Great Power status, reinforced by its role as part of the West's defences against communism. The suppression of the Malayan rebellion, which at its peak in 1951–2 involved 50,000 troops,[43] could, it was argued, show the US that the UK was also making a major contribution to stemming alleged Chinese expansionism in Asia. Together with its 10,000 troops in Korea, this commitment probably gave Britain a degree of influence on US policy in the Far East which it would not otherwise have exerted. The success of Foreign Secretary Anthony Eden in persuading the US to accept the partition of Vietnam at the 1954 Geneva Conference was widely attributed to this 'special relationship'.[44] British influence proved of some value in this case, however, only because deep divisions already existed within the US government. And, for this limited diplomatic achievement, Eden found himself obliged to make further British military commitments to the region by becoming a signatory of the South-East Asian Treaty Organization (SEATO).

The most expensive of Britain's imperial commitments in the early 1950s, however, was the Suez land base. Built in the late nineteenth century to protect sea communications between the Mediterranean and the Indian Ocean, it had a symbolic importance for the British Empire perhaps second only to India itself. Ministers in the late 1940s were told by their advisers that 'its abandonment would be the greatest disaster that had ever occurred in this country',[45] and military leaders fought a rearguard action to preserve it. It was also the key British military installation in the Middle East, with assets then valued at between £500 and £700 million – between £5 billion and £7 billion at today's prices.[46]

Despite its dubious military value in an atomic war – made clear in the Global Strategy Paper – Britain attempted to hold on to Suez for as long as possible partly in an attempt, it appears, to influence the Egyptian government. As a result, the Egyptians were antagonized still further. In 1951 attacks on British personnel and property began on a large scale. Thereafter, 80,000 troops were stationed in Suez with the sole purpose of defending themselves and the base from attack.[47] The Egyptian government argued that their presence made their country more vulnerable to Soviet attack, rather than defending it, as the British claimed. Their consequent demand for a total withdrawal of British troops was reluctantly granted in October 1954. As the Anglo-French invasion two years later was to demonstrate, however, Britain had not yet forsaken the use of military force to influence Egyptian politics.

Despite the loss of India, then of Egypt, the services continued to seek a permanent base in the Middle East. For the next decade they were to trek from one country to another seeking a 'stable' political environment in which to base their military power. In the early 1950s, Haifa was offered by the Israelis but eventually rejected because of the possible Arab reaction. Instead, it was decided to transfer headquarter facilities to Cyprus from Suez and build a major base there. As the growing internal strife in that island made such a plan increasingly impractical, attention switched to Kenya and, finally, to Aden.[48] The apparatus of Empire plodded unthinkingly on, adapting to circumstances but failing to question what its purpose was. It would be another 15 years before the deadweight which it imposed on the British economy was to be removed. The crippling effect of imperialism on the national political psyche would persist for many years after that.

The German problem

British policy towards Europe in the 1950s was an uneasy balancing act, which has not been fully resolved even today. The commitment to remaining a world power, with a 'special relationship' with the United States and neo-colonial responsibilities in Africa and Asia, precluded a whole-hearted commitment to Europe. Yet, at the same time, the government recognized that the only possible military threat to the British Isles came from the domination of the European continent by a single hostile power. This was an inescapable result of geography and had been a central consideration in British strategy for centuries.

Moreover the 'special relationship', on which Britain's Great Power status was clearly dependent, required not only a British contribution to policing the less developed areas of the world. It also required that Britain play a leading role in United States' plans for Western Europe's integration into the world capitalist order. Britain was required to be the leading advocate of US foreign and economic policy within Europe as part of the price of American acceptance of its own continued role on the world stage.

In order to fulfil these potentially conflicting requirements, Britain found itself forced to increase its military commitment to Europe even as its relative economic power continued to dwindle. For the first time in several centuries of European diplomacy, the government agreed, in 1954, to station forces – four army divisions and a tactical air force – permanently in continental Europe. This commitment contradicted the Global Strategy Paper, which had questioned the value of maintaining substantial conventional forces in Europe, and had recommended reliance on immediate use of nuclear weapons against a major Soviet offensive.

However, the 1954 troop commitment was not made in response to a more pessimistic analysis of the Soviet threat. Indeed, with the death of Stalin, there had been a considerable thaw in East-West relations. Its purpose was to prevent a revival of Franco-German rivalry, and the disintegration of NATO that this might bring.

After the outbreak of the Korean war, The US had insisted that West German rearmament would be required in order to give Europe a chance of slowing a Soviet advance. The French, still as suspicious of the Germans as of the Russians, were dismayed by this prospect. In October 1950, they put forward the Pleven Plan for a European Army, to which each country should contribute forces in the smallest possible units.[49] The maximum international integration of the armed forces would take place, thus preventing the re-emergence of German militarism. The foundation for a Western European federal state would have been laid, and national military forces effectively ended.

Britain, however, refused to commit its forces to the European Defence Community (EDC) though it supported its formation by the continental nations. Its commitments to an independent nuclear force and to a worldwide military role made it impossible for it to surrender national sovereignty to a supra-national European body. As Foreign Secretary Eden argued:

This is something which we know, in our bones, we cannot do ... For Britain's story and her interests lie far beyond the continent of Europe. Our thoughts move across the seas to the many communities in which our people play their part, in every corner of the world. These are our family ties. That is our life: without it we should be no more than some millions of people living on an island off the coast of Europe, in which nobody wants to take any particular interest.[50]

Partly as a result of Britain's position, the mood in France too began to turn against the Pleven Plan. The French, like the British, had a long history of imperialism which had had a profound effect on domestic politics. If Britain's world role and nuclear status prevented its military integration into Europe, it was argued, did not the same argument apply to France? Moreover, with Britain on the sidelines, France could not be sure that the EDC might not, in time, become dominated by the economically more powerful Germans. In August 1954, a combination of the nationalist Left and the Right in the French National Assembly rejected the EDC and precipitated a major crisis.[51]

The possibility of German rearmament, and the twelve divisions which it could provide to NATO, was once again thrown into doubt. The defence of Western Europe was widely thought to be impossible without these divisions. In retrospect this analysis may appear unduly pessimistic. The Soviet Union's military strength had been consistently overestimated since 1945 with no serious account being taken of the likelihood of rebellion in its satellite nations in the event of war.[52] Also, the meaning of large troop numbers was doubly questionable given the US plans for 'massive retaliation' with nuclear weapons in the event of a Soviet conventional attack.[53] Nevertheless, despite their declared policy, in practice politicians' thinking was still dominated by their experiences of the Second World War. The size of armies on the ground continued to be of enormous symbolic and psychological importance.

To solve the crisis caused by the rejection of the EDC, Eden proposed a new formula for German rearmament. Germany was to contribute land and tactical air forces to NATO, permanently committed to its military command. It was prohibited from producing its own nuclear, chemical and biological weapons, and its army limited to a maximum of twelve divisions. In order to secure French acceptance of this arrangement, Britain pledged to maintain substantial forces on the Continent, and undertook 'not to withdraw those forces against the wishes of the majority of the Brussels Treaty Powers, who take their decision in the light of the views of the Supreme Allied Commander in Europe.'[54]

The agreement was a diplomatic achievement for the British government, enhancing its prestige and overcoming traditional antagonisms between France and Germany. It signified the UK's wish, derived from its self-image as a world power, to be responsible for Europe but not part of it. This wish was to be further reflected in its refusal to join the European Economic Community in the mid 1950s, whose economic success was to be underpinned by the political stabilization that the agreements on defence ensured.

Yet throughout the discussions on these agreements, there appears to have been remarkably little consideration given to the financial aspect. Until 1954 the Germans had been required to meet all the local expenditure of the British garrison in Deutschmarks out of the budget for occupation costs. But, with full sovereign status in 1955, and German rearmament, this arrangement ceased. Thereafter the British Army of the Rhine constituted, in effect, a growing subsidy by Britain of the West German economy and balance of payments.[55] Once again the government's concern for its perceived international responsibilities overrode national economic interest.

Broken-backed warfare

The importance of political prestige and military conservatism were evident in the reluctance to abandon Suez and in the requirement for large ground forces in Europe. The strength of these factors, and the power of established institutional lobbies, was also demonstrated in the success of the Royal Navy in resisting economies at this time.

In the Global Strategy Paper discussions, Sir Rhoderick McGrigor, First Sea Lord, had insisted on the need to plan for the possibility that conventional forces, particularly navies, might be required to wage hostilities even after all nuclear weapons on both sides had been used.[56] The relevance of this scenario – called 'broken-backed' warfare – was doubtful even in 1952, when, in the view of the Chiefs of Staff, 'an atomic attack would leave the USSR too devastated to continue waging full-scale war'.[57] The deployment of hydrogen bombs was to consign it to total oblivion within a few years. Nevertheless it did serve its main purpose – justifying the retention of a substantial surface fleet. By the time it fell out of favour, the Navy had found other ways to legitimize its role – the possibility of limited wars East of Suez, and, later, 'flexible response'. For several years in the mid 1950s, however, 'broken-backed' warfare served to defeat proposals for cuts in naval forces which would have little contribution to make to massive nuclear retaliation.

The adoption of 'broken-backed' warfare was a response to the Royal Navy's concern for self-preservation; and soon vanished when alternative justifications could be found. The Navy's success in obtaining resources relied, not on military strategies, but on its enormous symbolic importance in British politics. For those reared to administer an Empire based on British naval supremacy, a reduced or abandoned surface fleet would have been an admission that Britain could no longer regain that past status. Such an admission was not yet acceptable.

4. Fall from grace: 1957-68

The mid 1950s saw the economic 'miracles' in Japan and Western Europe in full swing, with Britain finding itself falling increasingly behind. While continental Western Europe's production grew by 47 per cent between 1952 and 1957, Britain's rose only 22 per cent.[1] This economic failure led to increasing concern at the costs of defence, with Harold Macmillan himself one of the strongest critics. In 1956, while Chancellor of the Exchequer, he declared that:

> for every rifle that our comrades in Europe carried we were carrying two. If we were to follow the European example, we would save £700 million a year. If only half of these resources were shifted into exports the picture of our foreign balances would be transformed. If the other half were available for investment, there would be less critical comment about our low rate of investment compared to many other countries.[2]

Eden, having succeeded Churchill as Prime Minister, was also convinced that: 'Effort must be transferred from military preparations to the maintenance and improvement of our political and economic position.'[3] His view was supported by an official review, prepared by both military and civilian officials, that concluded that 'since the war the United Kingdom had attempted too much in too many spheres of defence, which had contributed to the economic crisis which every administration had suffered since 1945.'[4]

These economic sacrifices did at least appear to have some diplomatic pay-off. It was thought that the prompt response to the US's rearmament calls in 1950 had prevented the emergence of a strong 'Asia first' lobby. Foreign Secretary Eden's successful efforts in 1954 had strengthened NATO, and thus the link between the US and Europe, by resolving differences over German rearmament. He had, in the same year, prevented (or at least postponed) American military entanglement in Indo-China by supporting a compromise with the Vietminh. These diplomatic achievements were widely seen, not only as contributing to Britain's long-term security, but also as enhancing its prestige in the world. Perhaps that was so. It is unfortunate that nobody whose voice could be heard had asked *what prestige is for*. Britain paid dearly in economic performance for the 'special relationship'. The benefits proved much less substantive or long-lasting.

Suez and Sandys

In November 1956 the failure of the Suez invasion temporarily dispelled many of the illusions of the early 1950s about Britain's real international status. Britain was forced to cease fighting, when the invasion was near to victory, by financial and diplomatic pressure from the US,[5] which made it clear that Britain's 'independence' was in practice dependent on its support. The fragility of Britain's claims to Great Power status, and even to a meaningful special relationship, was dramatically brought home.

The Suez debacle suggested that even a high level of defence spending was no guarantee of military success. As a result it threw foreign policy into confusion and prompted renewed thinking inside and outside government. Eden resigned as Prime Minister and his successor, Harold Macmillan, spoke for a general consensus when he emphasized the need for further defence economies in his first television address.[6] A major review of defence policy was ordered and the new Minister of Defence, Duncan Sandys, himself an advocate of economies, announced its results in a White Paper in April 1957. Conscription would be phased out by 1962 and the size of the armed forces reduced from 690,000 to 375,000. Several equipment projects were cancelled and the size of land and air forces in Germany reduced. Britain would soon have its own independent hydrogen bomb, and it was argued that this would restore the country's lost pride and military credibility. Increased 'tactical' nuclear firepower would compensate for reductions in conventional forces in Europe and Asia. *In toto*, the White Paper estimated that over £200 million would be saved on the planned 1957/8 military budget, and further sums in later years.[7]

The White Paper noted that:

Over the last five years, defence has on an average,
absorbed 10 per cent of Britain's gross national product.
Some 7 per cent of the working population are either in
the services or supporting them. One-eighth of the output
of the metal-using industries, upon which the export trade
so largely depends, is devoted to defence. An undue
proportion of qualified scientists and engineers are
engaged in military work. In addition the retention of such
large forces abroad gives rise to heavy charges which place
a severe strain upon the balance of payments . . . it is
impossible to escape the conclusion that Britain has been
bearing a disproportionately large share of the total
burden of Western defence.

The economies announced, however, would reduce these costs:

It can safely be assumed that the new plan, when it is fully
implemented, will further appreciably reduce the burden
on the economy. Above all, it will release skilled men,
including many badly needed scientists and engineers, for
employment in civilian industry. Both exports and capital
investment will gain.[8]

With hindsight, however, the 1957 White Paper proved to be
less radical than such a presentation may have suggested at the
time. For it was little more than a continuation of trends started in
1952 by the Global Strategy Paper, and further elaborated under
Churchill and Eden. It represented a further attempt to retain the
status, while reducing the costs, of being a world power; and it
suggested that nuclear weapons would enable Britain to fulfil these
dual objectives. The attempt proved a failure. Economies in
conventional defence proved less than had been hoped. Increased
reliance on the US for maintenance of the 'independent' nuclear
force did not greatly reduce the effects of that force on national
psychology. And, throughout the remaining years of Conservative
government, high defence spending contributed to further economic decline.

The 'biggest change'?

The 1957 White Paper described itself as 'the biggest change in military policy ever made in normal times'.[9] The reality was rather less spectacular. The economies announced were directed mainly towards curbing the growth in defence costs, rather than securing substantial reductions. After an initial fall in 1957–8, due in part to the costs of Suez the year before, spending remained steady before starting to rise again from 1960–1 onwards (see Table 6). By 1963, the government was speculating whether the target increase of $3\frac{1}{2}$ per cent per annum would be sufficient to meet military requirements.[10]

Table 6 Defence Spending 1956–64

	1956–7	1957–8	1958–9	1959–60
£ million (cash)	1,525	1,430	1,468	1,476
As % GDP	7.2	6.4	6.4	6.0
£ million (1984–5 prices)	12,508	11,297	11,217	11,135
Change	+2.6%	–9.7%	–0.7%	–0.7%

	1960–1	1961–2	1962–3	1963–4
£ million (cash)	1,596	1,689	1,767	1,792
as % GDP	6.1	6.1	6.1	5.7
£ million (1984–5 prices)	11,841	12,096	12,293	12,167
Change	+6.3%	+2.2%	+1.6%	–1.0%

Source: see Appendix.

Like the Global Strategy Paper before it, the Sandys review was attempting to reduce the costs of Britain's military commitments without questioning the commitments themselves. This approach could yield only limited savings. Even the trauma of Suez could not convince Britain that it had lost, and could not afford to regain, the international status it had enjoyed for more than a century. Indeed such was the government's commitment to the illusion of that status that the 1957 cuts fell most heavily on those forces related to defence of Britain and its European allies. Emphasis on nuclear weapons, operations outside Europe, and the alliance with the US actually increased.

The biggest reductions were made in the forces for defence of Europe. The government announced a reduction of the British Army of the Rhine from 77,000 to 64,000 in 1957–8 and a further cut to 55,000 in 1958–9. The Second Tactical Air Force in Germany was reduced by half in numbers within one year, while a similar reduction was made in the light bomber force based in England but assigned to NATO. Finally, the government abandoned plans for more advanced fighter aircraft and made deep cuts in Fighter Command, whose role was to be confined to defence of British and American nuclear bomber bases. Missile defences would in due course, it was planned, replace even this limited function.[11]

The government justified these cuts by emphasizing Soviet conventional superiority in Europe, and arguing, in accordance with the doctrine of 'massive retaliation', that NATO would be forced to resort to nuclear weapons at an early stage of any conflict. In such a conflict, large conventional forces would be redundant, as would fighter defences. Even if a new Battle of Britain was able to take a heavy toll of Soviet bombers, some would get through, and:

It must be frankly recognized that there is at present no means of providing adequate protection for the people of this country against the consequences of an attack with nuclear weapons.[12]

Massive retaliation was, however, meeting increasing resistance from NATO officials, who argued that conventional forces alone could at least 'force a pause' against a Soviet conventional attack, and delay escalation to nuclear war. The Soviet Union's nuclear strength was now growing rapidly and by the early 1960s, it would be able to destroy targets in the US itself. As a consequence, American pressure for more conventional 'options' also grew and a retreat from the extremes of massive retaliation began. When

Macmillan attempted to cut BAOR (British Army on the Rhine) to 45,000 in 1959, there was strong opposition from other NATO members who pointed to Britain's obligations under the 1954 Treaty.[13] He was forced to withdraw his proposal, and the number has remained at around 55,000 ever since.

The British government's support for 'massive retaliation' was justified by the supposedly overwhelming Eastern superiority in conventional forces and by the inevitability of a major war 'going nuclear' at an early stage. Two other factors, however, were probably of greater importance. The first was the belief that a war in Europe with the Soviet Union was most unlikely. Since the death of Stalin, there had been a marked thaw in East-West relations. The first summit meetings since the Cold War began had been held, and in May 1956 the Soviets had announced reductions in their armed forces by 1,300,000 men.[14] British leaders believed the Soviet threat sufficiently remote for it to be reasonably safe to rely on nuclear weapons. This not only helped to reduce defence costs and release resources for other uses. It also symbolized US and UK leadership – as the only nuclear powers – within NATO. By contrast, a 'No First Use' or 'minimum deterrent' policy would have reopened debate about the structure of power within NATO, and on Germany's role in particular. As long as Soviet attack remained extremely unlikely, cautious Western leaders preferred not to disturb the economic and political stability which they had enjoyed in the previous few years.

Secondly, the British government believed that the greatest threat to its own interests, and Western interests in general, came not from Europe but from insurgency and small-scale wars in the Third World. Emphasis on capabilities for operations outside Europe was therefore increased in the years following the Sandys review. Britain's appetite for a world policing role appeared unaffected by the Suez setback. Instead it reinforced the determination to rebuild the 'special relationship' with the US, and to correct the deficiencies in conventional forces which the Suez operation had revealed.

The increased importance placed on the world role at the expense of Europe became even more evident in the early 1960s. As Britain's direct economic interests in the Middle East and Asia declined, American concern to retain an ally in its anti-Communist crusade grew. Paul Nitze, now Assistant Secretary of Defense for

International Security Affairs, told a British audience that the Kennedy administration was more concerned that Britain maintain its troop numbers east of Suez than that it do so in Germany.[15] With the Americans becoming increasingly entangled in Vietnam, the pressure on Britain to retain forces in Asia grew still further. British leaders, pleased by the renewed American acceptance of their world role, were happy to oblige.

The renewed emphasis on limited wars in the Third World was encouraged by service interests under threat. At the start of the 1957 Review, Sandys had told the Royal Navy that 'broken-backed' warfare was no longer relevant in the age of the H-bomb. The role of the surface fleet as a whole, therefore, including that of its capital ship, the aircraft carrier, must be in some doubt. Unless he heard convincing arguments to the contrary, he warned, naval forces would bear the brunt of the forthcoming cuts.[16]

The Admiralty responded to this threat immediately by abandoning 'broken-backed' warfare and becoming a leading advocate of global interventionary forces – a role for which aircraft carriers were clearly suited. It mounted a major campaign to ensure that supporters of Britain's world role made their voice heard in favour of the carrier; and by the time the Review was completed, it had been saved. Indeed, the conversion was so dramatic that the White Paper's section on 'Sea Power' held the carrier's role in modern conditions to be 'increasingly significant'.[17]

The RAF was also able to use the East of Suez role to justify new equipment programmes. The 1957 review had been sceptical about the future role of manned aircraft, and several important aerospace projects had been cancelled. As it became clear over the next three years that its strategic nuclear force – the V-bombers – would also, in due course, be replaced by missiles, the RAF turned to East of Suez to justify a whole series of new projects – the TSR2, the P1154, and the HS681.[18] The aerospace industry was amongst the first to welcome the temporary reprieve that these projects represented.

There is little doubt that the expression of these service interests reinforced the commitment to an imperial role during this period. Its importance should not, however, be exaggerated. Senior officers, like their political masters, genuinely believed that Britain had a responsibility to contribute to stability and anti-Communism in the Indian Ocean area.[19] Their sectional interest only served to strengthen a consensus that already existed for retaining an important symbol of Britain's continuing 'greatness'.

The costs of Empire

The Sandys doctrine proposed to retain Britain's military commitments East of Suez but to fulfil them at a reduced cost. The large, and inefficient, conscript army, together with the string of army garrisons, would be replaced by tactical nuclear weapons and an expanded capability for rapid airlift of troops to troublespots.

The emphasis on use of nuclear weapons in the Third World, already part of Global Strategy Paper concepts, was further increased. The White Paper included nuclear bombers based in Cyprus in the forces available for defence of the Middle East against Communist infiltration, and it was announced that British nuclear weapons would be available for defence of South-East Asia.[20] Indeed Macmillan went so far as to argue that 'the end of conscription must depend on the acceptance of nuclear weapons.'[21]

More resources were also spent on RAF Transport Command in a further attempt to police the same commitments with fewer soldiers. When some of the cost of reliance on an airfield reserve – such as those of large stockpiles and long-range aircraft – became more apparent, the hope of securing further reductions in defence spending was quietly shelved. Tactical nuclear weapons and rapid airlift proved not to be the cheap panaceas which wishful thinking by the government had suggested they could be.

Nor did it prove possible to make major savings in spending on bases and associated facilities. The end of conscription meant that pay and conditions had to be considerably improved in order to attract volunteers, especially with conditions of full employment at home. Increased reliance on airlift could not avoid the need for garrisons to protect refuelling and storage bases, and costs were further increased by Foreign Office insistence on expensive permanent structures at overseas bases. Prefabricated accommodation would, it was argued, be seen as temporary, and would increase local pressure for withdrawal.[22] By 1967 it was costing £257 million to keep 160,000 men overseas – as much, after allowing for inflation, as the £190 million that had been needed for 320,000 ten years earlier.[23]

Finally, service pressures for more sophisticated ships and

planes for East of Suez operations had a sound grounding in military reality. Third World nations such as Iraq and Indonesia were acquiring increasingly sophisticated weapon systems from the Soviet Union and elsewhere. If Britain was to retain a credible conventional force in the area, it had no alternative but to follow suit. As the sophistication of weaponry increased, costs rose too, with a new Lightning fighter costing seven times as much in real terms as a wartime Spitfire. The pre-war aircraft carrier *Ark Royal* had cost just over £3 million. The 1955 version cost over £21 million.[24] Britain was finding that it could not be a world power 'on the cheap'.

The independent deterrent

Central to the 1957 Review was increased reliance on Britain's own nuclear weapons. As we have seen already, it was hoped that this would relieve the burden of defence commitments, not only in Europe but also in Asia. Britain could thus remain a world power, yet still release much-needed resources for its domestic economy.

It was not to work. Nuclear weapons proved unusable in Third World conflicts, and increasing scepticism in NATO about 'massive retaliation' limited economies in Europe. Moreover, the British nuclear force proved to be expensive in its own right, taking up between 10 and 20 per cent of the total defence budget, according to whether or not one includes in the total the cost of the fighters and missiles assigned to defence of the bomber bases.[25] Moreover, indirect effects were probably greater than these direct costs. The attainment of independent nuclear status in 1956, and the first H-bomb test in 1957, enabled the political establishment to ignore Britain's economic and political decline and put the humiliation of Suez behind them. As Denis Healey put it, the government had needed a 'virility symbol' to compensate for 'the shock of having their military impotence exposed at Suez'.[26]

The independent nuclear deterrent fostered the costly illusion that Britain remained one of the world's leading powers, and prevented a more radical reappraisal of British foreign policy as a whole. And, with H-bombs and V-bombers at last coming off the production line, Randolph Churchill expressed a widespread viewpoint when he argued that:

> Britain can knock down twelve cities in the region of
> Stalingrad and Moscow from bases in Britain and another
> dozen in the Crimea from bases in Cyprus. We did not
> have that power at the time of Suez. We are a major
> power again.[27]

Even Nye Bevan, upon his appointment as Labour's Foreign
Affairs spokesman, succumbed to the general consensus and
argued that Britain should retain its nuclear weapons as a
negotiating card.[28]

Despite the considerable investment in the V-bombers, however,
Britain soon found itself unable to keep up with the superpower
nuclear arms race. Increasingly sophisticated missiles, delivery
systems, etc. were increasingly beyond the capacity of its technological and economic resources. Paradoxically, the government
was obliged to seek access to American weapon systems in order to
retain a force whose function was to emphasize Britain's independence from American dominance.[29] This paradox reached its height
with the 1962 Nassau agreement between Macmillan and President
Kennedy, in which the United States agreed to supply its most
advanced nuclear technology – the Polaris missiles – to Britain. In
return Britain's Polaris force would be 'used for the purposes of
international defence of the Western Alliance in all circumstances'
except 'when Her Majesty's Government may decide that supreme
national interests are at stake.'[30]

The agreement was welcomed by President Kennedy, who had
recently successfully pulled through the 'eyeball-to-eyeball' Cuban
missile crisis, and was now anxious to avoid a crisis with a major
ally over what, in comparison, was a minor issue. Failure to obtain
Polaris could, Macmillan had warned, have led to the fall of the
London government, and its replacement by an anti-American
Conservative leadership determined to reassert Britain's independence.[31] Kennedy clearly felt that the close co-operation between
the two nuclear forces would minimize the possibility that there
would be any circumstances in which Britain would feel obliged,
or able, to use its nuclear missiles without American approval. To
avoid such a small and hypothetical risk Kennedy was unwilling to
jeopardize the alliance with the UK.

The agreement also suited Macmillan. It reduced the cost of
maintaining a nuclear force, which had been threatening to get

beyond the country's reach, and ended the growing unease in the Tory party. At the same time, it preserved a powerful symbol of Britain's international status and of its privileged relationship with the US. By preserving a symbol of Britain's status, however, Nassau also reinforced illusions. These were particularly evident in the emphasis the government placed on the seat at the 'top table' which nuclear weapons gave it. According to one author,

> It was perhaps unfortunate . . . that Britain played a leading part in the nuclear test ban negotiations of 1958 to 1963 . . . [it] had the effect of fostering in Britain hallucinations of world power no longer justified by realities . . . it entrenched the British illusion that, however much the country's physical strength had fallen, its moral influence remained pre-eminent.[32]

Finally, Nassau reinforced the fears of continental European countries, especially France, that a Britain in the European Community could prove to be an American 'Trojan Horse'. It was not unnoticed that a major strategic agreement had been reached in days with the US, but that in the EEC entry talks Britain had already spent many months seeking extra concessions for Commonwealth products. The perception that Britain's leaders had divided loyalties played an important part in de Gaulle's decision to veto UK membership a month later.[33] It would be a further decade before, at last, Britain would succeed in entering the Community.

Never had it so good?

The 1957 review failed to reduce significantly the burden of defence on the economy. Between the Sandys review and the last year of Conservative administration (1963/4), real defence spending rose by almost 8 per cent and, as a proportion of national income, fell only 0.6 per cent. The commitment to a world role – and consequent spending on nuclear and East of Suez forces – ensured that British defence spending remained well above the levels of its European neighbours. Yet it was continued despite a clear awareness of the burden it imposed on the domestic economy.

In the late 1950s and early 1960s, that economy was the object of increasing concern. The members of the newly formed European

Economic Community (EEC) were experiencing rates of growth which could no longer be explained away by economists as a delayed recovery from war. Between 1951 and 1960, British industrial production grew by 32 per cent, while that of Western Europe grew by 86 per cent.[34] By the early 1960s, France and Germany had both overtaken the UK in national income per head for the first time in more than a century. A flood of articles, books and speeches began to appear on Britain's failure to join this economic miracle.

This debate drew attention to two central features of Britain's economic problem – first, its recurrent, and damaging, balance of payments crises, and, secondly, the low proportion of national output devoted to investment. These two features were interlocked by a series of 'vicious circles'. The government's response to a sterling crisis was to cut back on domestic production, particularly on investment. In the upswing, the consequently low level of past investment ensured that the trade balance would rapidly worsen again, thus precipitating a further external crisis. Governments were unwilling to restrain consumption further – mainly for electoral reasons – or cut defence spending. In the short term, it was easier to cut back on investment.

The debate of the early 1960s led to an increased emphasis on government intervention in industry and a sustained expansion of the economy in order to break through these vicious circles. The National Economic Development Council (NEDC) was established in 1962, and a target of four per cent annual growth was set for the 1960s. Even the Federation of British Industries (as the CBI was then called) pressed the government to adopt the state capitalist methods which appeared to be working successfully in France.[35] At the same time, Chancellor Reginald Maudling attempted to coax investment and exports onto a higher growth path by reflating the economy and disregarding the short-term balance of payments implications. These attempts were a failure. Britain's relative decline continued, and the cycle of sterling crises and low investment intensified. It is clear that the overseas commitments of the British state were among the most important factors in explaining this failure.

As a result of the Maudling experiment, the Labour government that took over in October 1964 faced a severe economic crisis. It proved to be ill-equipped to tackle it. The most immediate problem it faced was the balance of payments. The latest forecasts suggested that the 1964 deficit would be £800 million – the largest ever in peacetime.[36] The Maudling 'dash for growth' had run into the constraint that had halted every upswing in the previous decade – the inability of the economy to, simultaneously, achieve a satisfactory rate of growth and balance the external account.

Britain's defence commitments in Europe and Asia bear a major responsibility for this problem. Since 1958, net military spending overseas had increased by 90 per cent, and accounted for one third of the record payments deficit in 1964. Other components of official spending overseas, closely linked with British imperial commitments, also contributed. *Excluding* these government transactions, the British economy was in deficit by only £66 million in 1964, and would not return to deficit until 1973.[37] The balance of payments deficits in the 1960s were thus a direct result of Britain's commitment to the trappings of a world power, of which the most important were the large overseas military presence and the priority given to sterling's reserve currency role. Chancellor of the Exchequer James Callaghan himself acknowledged in 1965 that:

> There would not have been a sterling crisis if we did not have to bear so much of the burden of defence abroad. We would have restored our balance of payments if we had not had to bear this heavy load.[38]

The Labour government, like its Conservative predecessors, was well aware of the consequences of high military spending for the domestic economy. With defence taking a proportion of national income no greater than it does today the 1965 National Plan argued that:

> at home, the defence effort pre-empts a large part of the productive potential of some of the most important and technologically advanced industrial resources and is a large user of skilled and unskilled manpower . . . As a nation we spend as much on defence as we do on investment in industrial plant and machinery . . . The defence programme now uses some 35–40 per cent of national research and development expenditure and about one-fifth of the qualified scientists and technologists

> engaged in it . . . externally, the defence effort presses hard on our balance of payments. In 1964–5 £262 million of the defence provision was direct overseas expenditure; this is more than we can afford.[39]

An additional, and growing, concern was the resource cost of maintaining a large and uncompetitive aircraft industry. Sustained mainly by military contracts, the industry was consuming 35 per cent of total industrial R&D funds, yet produced only 4 per cent of national exports.[40] In 1962, it was estimated, more than a quarter of all the mathematicians, one-sixth of the mechanical and other engineers, and one-tenth of the physicists working in manufacturing were in the aircraft industry.[41] Yet shortages of these skilled personnel in other sectors were acute, and played an important part in constraining productivity growth.

Himalayan frontiers

The new Labour government that took office in 1964 remained firmly committed to the overseas role for Britain which Attlee and Bevin had established in the late 1940s. It was to take four years of deepening economic deficits, and the abandonment of many of its ambitious goals for social reforms and industrial modernization, before the most expensive and obsolete aspects of that role were finally, and reluctantly, abandoned. The failure to tackle these problems in 1964 contributed to its economic failure, which in turn led directly to defeat in the 1970 election. And, even after the decision was finally taken (in 1968) to withdraw most forces from East of Suez, Britain retained a defence burden considerably greater than other middle-ranking powers. The instinct for 'greatness' had been tempered, not ended.

The personal commitment of Labour's leaders to Britain's 'greatness' precluded the adoption of policies which could halt its decline. It became rapidly clear that economic prosperity continued to take second place to Britain's external commitments. Decisions made in the first few weeks of the government clearly reflected this priority. The most crucial of these was Wilson's personal decision not to devalue the pound despite the widespread international view that it was 10–15 per cent overvalued.[42] His decision was strongly influenced by his determination to maintain sterling's role as a reserve currency and the influence with the United States and the Commonwealth which, it was believed, it brought. Once devaluation was ruled out, the government was forced to resort to the remedies of the Stop-Go cycle it had condemned so often in opposition.[43] Deflationary measures were introduced which ensured that the National Plan's target of four per cent annual growth was obsolete even before it had been published. The decision to maintain sterling's value at $2.80, together with the burden of excessive military spending, were further consequences of the state's commitment to an illusory world role. Together they ensured the failure of Labour's plans for industrial growth.

Labour's commitment to a world military role was, if anything, marginally greater than that of Conservative leaders. Harold Wilson appears to have been convinced that the Commonwealth was a new power bloc that could challenge, or at least intercede between, the superpowers.[44] He was suspicious of the Common Market and argued for a shift of defence resources away from Europe. Indeed the only foreign exchange savings in the defence budget mentioned in the National Plan were a result of 'offset' arrangements reached with the German government. He made the government's priorities clear in December 1964:

> whatever we may do in the field of cost effectiveness, value
> for money and a stringent review of expenditure, we
> cannot afford to relinquish our world role – our role
> which, for shorthand purposes, is sometimes called our
> 'East of Suez' role.[45]

Moreover, the government quickly demonstrated that it did not believe, contrary to its pre-election claims, that Britain's nuclear force had ceased to be independent. New Defence Minister Denis Healey easily convinced the Cabinet that the Polaris missile submarine programme should go ahead. The critics – who at that time included Lord Chalfont – had to be content with a cut in the number of submarines ordered from five to four.[46] Furthermore, in response to the first Chinese nuclear explosion, which took place as Labour assumed office, the government agreed to offer a nuclear 'umbrella' to non-nuclear India.[47] In remarkably imperial rhetoric, Wilson asserted that 'our frontiers are on the Himalayas and in the standard of living of the people of India.'[48]

These aspirations to Great Power status were sustained by a

United States which welcomed a compliant junior partner to share the burdens of its 'policing' activities. Sterling's reserve currency role, the military presence in the Far East, a relatively cheap nuclear force – all these were dependent on US backing. The 'special relationship', in its essentials, meant that Britain would be allowed to continue with its costly imperial commitments provided that its foreign policy remained consistent with that of the US. Wilson's attempt to use the special relationship to influence US policy – through interceding between North Vietnam and the US – was dismissed as 'talking claptrap' by President Johnson. And even Denis Healey regarded Wilson's hopes of using Britain's presence in Asia to prevent superpower polarization as 'fanciful and misplaced'.[49]

The continuous defence review

The Labour Party's defence policies in 1964 and 1965 were not significantly different from those that could have been expected from the Conservatives. They shared a belief in Britain's world role, in the utility of independent nuclear weapons, and in the special relationship with the United States. When faced with economic crisis, they continued to believe that they could reduce military capabilities while leaving world commitments unchanged. Duncan Sandys had sought to solve the same problem by increased reliance on nuclear weapons. The attempt had been a failure. Labour leaders now appeared to believe that superior management of the defence budget would enable them to succeed where the previous 13 years of Conservative administration had failed. It took three years of economic crisis and a series of 'long term' defence reviews before the government reluctantly conceded that it too had failed and that Britain's permanent military capability East of Suez would have to be abandoned.

The conversion of Labour leaders to withdrawal from East of Suez over the next four years was a reflection of broader shifts of opinion in the British elite. Growing concern at the serious nature of the country's economic crisis was reinforced by questioning of the political gains obtainable from a permanent military presence in the Indian Ocean. The experience of the US in Vietnam added to this scepticism. Labour MPs anxious to protect social services from cutbacks were joined by business interests concerned to prevent cuts in investment and profits. Even the Conservative Party, now led by ardent 'European' Edward Heath, urged a shift of military priorities from Asia to Europe.

Faced with this broad consensus of opinion, defence was forced to take a major share of the successive rounds of public spending cuts. At first these cuts were only in capabilities. As the government moved from one review to the next, however, the attempt to retain a major military role in Asia became increasingly less credible. Commitments began to go, culminating in the January 1968 decision to pull out most remaining troops from the Far East by 1971. Although the process was a more or less continuous one we can identify four discrete phases: first, savings were made by cancelling several expensive aircraft projects inherited from the Conservatives, and agreeing to import cheaper American planes instead. The second phase led to the Defence Review of February 1966, in which the government announced the eventual demise of the Royal Navy's aircraft carriers, and consequently accepted certain limitations on operations East of Suez. Thirdly, the 1966 sterling crisis led to further demands for defence cuts which culminated in the 'final review' of July 1967 and the announcement of an eventual withdrawal from East of Suez. Fourthly, devaluation later that year led to an acceleration of withdrawal and to the cancellation of the order for the F-111 aircraft originally allocated to East of Suez operations. Each of these phases will now be briefly discussed in turn.

When Labour took office in 1964, defence spending was set to rise, under Conservative plans, by around 4 per cent annually for the next six years – from a little under £2,000 million in 1964–5 to £2,400 million (at 1964 prices) in 1969–70. One of the new Cabinet's first decisions was to agree that those plans should be curtailed sufficiently to reduce 1969–70 spending to £2,000 million – only slightly above the level at that time.[50] Thereby, it believed, the proportion of GDP (at factor cost) devoted to defence could be reduced from 7 to 6 per cent, thus increasing the resources available for exports, investment and growth. Even this modest reduction in the defence burden, however, assumed that the National Plan's 4 per cent output growth target would be met – an assumption which proved to be hopelessly over-optimistic.

The £2,000 million figure was arbitrary and chosen without any real consideration of the possible implications for commitments and programmes. The best defence made of it was that it was no more arbitrary than the Conservatives' previous ceiling of about 7 per cent of gross national product. Yet the events of the next three years would demonstrate that it was both too low to permit the retention of a credible presence East of Suez and too high if that role were to be wound up.[51] It thus demonstrated very clearly the reluctance of the new government to match its aspirations for world status to financial reality.

The new Defence Minister, Denis Healey, set in motion a series of studies – a 'defence review' – to determine how best to meet the £2,000 million ceiling. The cancellation of the fifth Polaris submarine was announced almost immediately, followed closely by the cancellation of the P-1154, HS-681 and TSR-2 aircraft projects. Savings of £1,200 million over ten years would be made, he estimated, by buying less expensive planes from the US.[52]

The growing cost of maintaining Britain's uncompetitive aircraft industry had made some such move inevitable. When, partly due to pressure from Rolls Royce, the government decided that the imported Phantom jets must be fitted with a British engine and other British equipment, the plane doubled in cost as a result.[53] If manned aircraft were to remain feasible – and the RAF in particular had a strong interest in ensuring that they did – the principle of independence in arms manufacture would have to go.

The government also made it clear, however, that it remained strongly committed to Britain's world military role and implied that the additional £200 million savings still needed to meet the £2,000 million target would have to come from forces in Europe. The 1965 White Paper argued that NATO strategy should be revised in order to reduce the financial burden it imposed; and specifically mentioned the balance of payments burden of forces in Germany.[54] It remained sceptical of the development – favoured by US Defense Secretary McNamara – of defence options for NATO that did not rely on early use of nuclear weapons.[55] In line with US global policy at that time, Britain argued that the immediate 'threat' to the West came primarily in the Third World, not in Europe. Accordingly, it was argued, cuts if required should be made in the latter.

In practice, however, major cuts in the British contribution to NATO were not possible. The provisions of the 1954 Treaty, together with the revival of interest in EEC membership, ruled out steps which could lead to a major diplomatic rift with the rest of Western Europe. At the same time, political opinion within Britain began to move rapidly against the government's East of Suez policy. In August 1965, the Parliamentary Labour Party called on the government to speed up defence cuts, a demand backed up by the Party conference the next month.[56] The Liberal leader, Jo Grimond, argued that 'if Britain's peacekeeping role East of Suez had led to two major wars and a revolution in Aden, the sooner it was stopped the better.'[57] And most dramatically, Enoch Powell, the Conservative defence spokesman, questioned the value of Britain's military role in Asia and Africa, and pointed to the commercial success of countries, such as Japan and West Germany, who maintained no such overseas bases.[58]

Despite this chorus of dissent, however, the government continued to insist on Britain's world military role. The 1966 Defence Review admitted that Britain's economic interests in the Middle East and Asia would not alone justify heavy defence expenditure. It argued, however, that:

Britain shares with other countries a general interest in seeing peace maintained, so far as possible, throughout the world. It is this interest above all which justifies our military presence outside Europe.[59]

Such sentiments were, and are, felt widely by many British people and most of their leaders. Yet they are, in practice, a psychological legacy of imperialism, with no place in a world of sovereign states with the right to self-determination. As Ho Chi Minh argued in 1954:

Suppose we Vietnamese – together perhaps with the Indians – proposed ourselves for a peace-keeping role in Europe. What would you Europeans think?[60]

The widespread opposition to the costs of Britain's world role, however, did mean both that any increase in the ceiling on defence spending was effectively precluded, and that any additional cuts required to keep costs below the ceiling would have to come from East of Suez. The government's Defence Review, published in February 1966, accepted these premises and achieved the necessary economies by abandoning plans to order a new generation of aircraft carrier – the CVA 01 – and announcing that existing carrier forces would not be replaced.[61] To keep one carrier permanently stationed in the Far East, with another available within two weeks, would have required a minimum force of three ships, plus support vessels. This would cost £1,400 million for production and deployment over ten years – about £8,400 million at today's prices.[62] This expenditure – equivalent to the planned capital cost of the Trident programme twenty years later – could not be accommodated within the defence budget without unacceptable cuts in other areas. It therefore had to go.

The government attempted to minimize the effects that this decision would have on its East of Suez commitments. It argued that aircraft operating from land bases would be able to replace most of the functions previously fulfilled by carrier-based aircraft. Fifty F-111A aircraft were to be ordered from the US for this purpose. In addition, the government accepted that, while Britain should retain a major presence outside Europe, its forces would not undertake major operations of war except in co-operation with allies.[63] Moreover, these operations would clearly be more dependent than before on the assistance of the diminishing number of nations willing to provide bases and overflight rights to British forces. Despite these restrictions Healey was able to proclaim, with a remarkable lack of foresight:

> We have no intention of ratting on any of our commitments. We intend to remain and shall remain fully capable of carrying out all the commitments we have at the present time, including those in the Far East, the Middle East and in Africa and other parts of the world. We do intend to remain in a military sense a world power.[64]

In effect, the government was proposing a policy of remaining a Great Power 'on the cheap'. Capabilities for extra-European wars would be cut while commitments were retained. It was this operating principle that had sustained the morale of British rulers during their long retreat from world power. Yet now it was no longer enough. The decision to phase out the carrier force meant that Britain's capability for unaided operations East of Suez was more severely limited than the government admitted. It marked the beginning of the end of the East of Suez saga.

The Defence Review of 1965–6 was, however, soon overtaken

by a series of events which were to lead to a new Review and further curtailment of overseas military commitments. First, and most importantly, in July 1966 Britain experienced yet another major sterling crisis. With devaluation still ruled out as an option, the government was forced to respond to the pressure on sterling by announcing a major package of public spending cuts, tax increases and a statutory freeze on wages and dividends – measures which marked the end of the National Plan's hopes for growth and were responsible for widespread public disillusionment with the government.[65] One of the immediate steps to be announced was a £100 million cut in military and civil spending overseas. This was followed by intensified pressure for a fresh Review which would bring total defence spending well below the original £2,000 million target and question in particular the high foreign exchange costs of bases overseas.

Secondly, a US-backed military coup had installed an aggressively anti-Communist government in Indonesia which quickly ended the policy of 'confrontation' with Malaysia. This relieved the pressure on Britain's forces in the Far East, who had been committed in support of Malaysia, and appeared to promise substantial financial savings. And it accelerated a reappraisal of the need for the costly military presence in Malaysia and Singapore. Scepticism as to the value of military bases in the Middle East was also increased by the forced departure of troops from the major British base in Aden as the radical National Liberation Front moved to take total control of the country.[66]

Thirdly, the General Election in March 1966 had brought a large number of new Labour MP's into Parliament, many of whom wished an acceleration of defence spending cuts. They were joined in their opposition to the East of Suez presence by a powerful 'European' lobby, including Home Secretary Roy Jenkins. Imperial commitments, it was argued, were preventing Britain from adjusting to its new status as a medium-rank European power. Indeed, the French veto in 1963 – repeated in 1967 – was based largely on the view that Britain still saw itself as an Atlantic and world power.

Finally, increasing numbers of businessmen began to openly question the expense of Britain's world role. William Davis, in the *Financial Times*, reported that:

> It has irked bankers for a long time that governments have
> not, apparently, been willing to risk a showdown on
> defence expenditure . . . The raw materials, machinery and
> skilled labour devoted to it annually could be used to
> boost our exports. And the foreign currency spent on US
> bombers like the F-111A, or the maintenance of troops in
> Germany, makes a hefty dent in our balance of payments
> . . . the need to economise cannot really be doubted. No
> country, however well meaning, can play a star part on the
> world stage if its economy and currency are consistently in
> trouble. And trouble is inevitable if we try to do too
> much.[67]

Despite this growing pressure for a rapid pull-back, Healey
proposed to cut military spending to £1,850 million, but refused to
make an equivalent reduction in overseas commitments. 'Intellectu-
ally,' he argued, according to one report, 'it might seem to be easier
to reduce spending by cutting the East of Suez commitment
altogether but our allies would never allow that.'[68] He proposed
that Britain could maintain 'penny-packages' of troops throughout
the world, yet appeared to underestimate the possible costs of
backing up these commitments should conflict break out. As
Richard Crossman recorded shortly after joining the crucial
Cabinet subcommittee on Overseas Policy and Defence:

> I never suspected that when I got inside O.P.D. and
> discovered what was actually being done by those
> colleagues it would be so crude, so unskilful – a futile
> attempt to remain Great Britain, one of the three world
> powers, while slicing away our defences.[69]

By early 1967, even strong American pressure could not stop
further cutbacks East of Suez. In April, according to Crossman,
most of the Cabinet 'wanted no military presence in the Far East at
all and were determined not only to get off the mainland but to
withdraw our naval and air forces from anywhere East of Suez.'[70]

The government was forced to respond, albeit reluctantly, to
this pressure. In July 1967 a new Review announced that it was
planned to withdraw altogether from bases in Singapore and
Malaysia in the middle 1970s, and that total service strength would
be cut by 75,000 by the same date. However, the Review was

non-committal on Britain's future role in the Persian Gulf, and argued that 'we cannot assume that, once we have left Singapore and Malaysia, we shall never again have to use our forces in the Far East.'[71] For this possibility, a special military capability would be retained in Britain, naval forces would continue to be deployed in the Far East, and the possibility of new bases in Australia and the Indian Ocean would be examined. The option to return East of Suez, even after withdrawal in 1973–7, was still very much open. And the military was keeping open the possibility that a future Conservative government might reverse the situation.

The 1967 Review concluded: 'We have been working continuously for almost three years on a major review of defence ... This Statement marks the end of that process.'[72] Scarcely had its decisions been digested, however, than they were overturned by a fresh economic crisis. On 18 November 1967 the pound was devalued and further savings in government spending were demanded by the Treasury. Defence spending was cut by £100 million in 1968–9, the planned staging base in the Indian Ocean was abandoned, and significant further cuts in naval capability were ordered.[73] The results of the July Review were thrown into the melting pot yet again as a further round of cuts were required.

Devaluation was, in effect, an admission that the economic policies of 1964–7 had failed. The government had failed to tackle Britain's structural problems, preferring to rely on short-term expediency: a tendency clearly reflected in the string of inconclusive defence Reviews. The Cabinet was now demoralized and divided, and Harold Wilson's leadership under threat.

It was in an atmosphere of political crisis, therefore, that the final decision was taken to withdraw from East of Suez. Yet it was only by the narrowest of majorities, and adroit tactical man-oeuvring, that Harold Wilson and Chancellor Roy Jenkins succeeded in forcing through complete withdrawal from East of Suez by 1971, together with cancellation of the F-111 order. It is clear that without severe and repeated financial crises – over and above the underlying problems of long-term economic decline – this decision would never have been taken. Until the last moment leading Ministers continued to believe that it could be avoided by sleight of hand or a sudden improvement in the economy.

The crucial vote on the F-111 was decided by Wilson's casting vote, with the 'right-wing junta' of George Brown, Denis Healey,

Michael Stewart and James Callaghan voting in favour of keeping it.[74] Wilson fended off their challenge by arguing that, in the general public spending cuts to be announced in January 1968, the Party could not be kept together without right-wing 'sacred cows' being slaughtered as well as left-wing ones. The raising of the school leaving age and the restoration of prescription charges were necessary, it was argued, because '£40 million saved on prescription charges is worth £140 million anywhere else because of the impression it makes on the bankers.'[75] To get this package through the Parliamentary Labour Party it would have to be 'balanced' by a clear commitment to an early withdrawal from East of Suez. And given that decision, it was unconvincing for Healey to argue, as he did, that the F-111 was now essential for European defence when, only two years before, he had presented it as the mainstay of the East of Suez role.

Too little, too late

The decisions taken in January 1968 were a genuine turning point in British defence policy. They marked an end to the attempt to maintain a permanent military presence in Asia, and a reluctant acceptance of Britain's reduced status in world affairs. And they achieved substantial savings in defence costs, with 1969–70 spending £200 million below the original target of £2,000 million at 1964–5 prices.[76]

Table 7   Defence Spending 1964–71

	1964–5	1965–6	1966–7	1967–8	1968–9	1969–70
£ million (cash)	1,909	2,056	2,115	2,254	2,232	2,204
As % GDP	5.6	5.7	5.4	5.5	5.0	4.6
£ million (1984–5 prices)	12,412	12,779	12,591	13,043	12,317	11,534
Change	+2.0%	+3.0%	−1.5%	+3.6%	−5.6%	−6.4%

Source: see Appendix.

Despite this progress, however, Britain continued to spend a higher proportion of its national income on defence than any other Western European country. Its relative economic position continued to deteriorate, with the gap between itself and its industrial competitors widening each year. Britain was stepping down one rung in the prestige ladder when it should have been stepping down two or three. Defence cuts in the 1960s kept rough pace with the decline in Britain's relative economic position. But they failed to go far enough to correct the initial inequality in defence burdens, which had persisted since the 1940s, and which had contributed substantially to that economic decline. The 'turn to Europe', which the 1968 decision symbolized, did not lead to the burden of defence spending being reduced to European levels.

The 1968 Defence White Paper had estimated that defence spending would fall to £2,014 million at 1968 prices (about £1,700 million at 1964–5 prices) by 1972–73.[77] Denis Healey went further and predicted that, by the end of 1972, the defence budget would have been cut by one-third in real terms.[78] If these targets *had* been met, Britain's defence burden would have been reduced to the same level as that of France. In reality, despite these ambitious targets and the programmes of major defence 'cuts' on which they were based, defence spending in 1972–3 was as high in real terms as in 1964–5.[79] The succession of reviews had, once again, succeeded only in curbing defence spending growth, not in reducing its total demand on national resources.

5. Yearning for redemption: the 1970s

With the 1968 decision to withdraw most forces from East of Suez, it became declared policy to concentrate defence effort on Europe. The debate on the relative importance of this commitment compared with those in the Middle East and Asia appeared to have ended, and the reality of Britain's reduced international stature at least partially conceded. Despite this, however, Britain's defence burden continued to be greater than that of other European countries. The decline in its relative military strength had been matched by that in its economic power. After 1969, the defence burden ended its slow decline of the 1950s and 1960s and stabilized at 4.5–5.0 per cent of national income for the rest of the decade. At the same time, relative economic decline intensified and, with the onset of generalized world recession in 1974–5 and 1979–81, threatened to turn into absolute decline. The 1970s saw Britain fall from average European levels of income to the lowest position with the exception of Italy.[1] Between 1973 and 1982, national income increased by only 0.6 per cent per annum (including North Sea oil), and manufacturing output fell by 18 per cent.[2]

A new role in Europe?

A unique opportunity to restructure British defence policy had been lost in 1967–8. Despite the view of successive governments that high defence spending had severely impeded economic progress, withdrawal from East of Suez was not accompanied with proportionate cuts in the resources allocated to defence. Instead, it was decided to transfer most East of Suez forces to new NATO roles. The 1968 White Paper announced that:

> As we withdraw our forces from their stations overseas
> and concentrate them in Europe, we shall be able to make
> a larger contribution to the Alliance.[3]

Consequently, almost all the forces created specifically for extra-European operations were transferred to NATO command. The Royal Marines and assault ships for amphibious warfare in the Indian Ocean would now give NATO an improved mobile capability on its northern and southern flanks. The Army units that were to make up a strategic mobile reserve for use in the Far East were now to be transferred to NATO duties. The transport aircraft needed for rapidly reinforcing East of Suez operations would now strengthen Army mobility in Europe.[4] And the shock which F-111 cancellation caused in the RAF was ameliorated by purchase of a further twenty-six Buccaneers, and later by an extension of the V-bombers' service life. Together these would enable Britain to retain a medium-range nuclear strike force until the Multi-Role Combat Aircraft (MRCA) came into service in the 1980s.[5]

The failure to reduce Britain's defence burden in the 1970s was a result of a complex mix of factors. Military and industrial interests dependent on a high defence budget continued to have a major say in decisions on strategy and procurement. Political leaders continued to hold an image of Britain's influence in world affairs that was out of proportion with its economic strength. Finally, Britain retained important 'Great Power' military capabilities – notably forces for worldwide intervention and an independent nuclear force. Together, these factors ensured that the savings from East of Suez withdrawal were relatively small and insufficient to reduce UK military spending to the level of its main industrial competitors.

The NATO strategy of 'flexible response', newly adopted in 1968, was now used to justify conventional roles in Europe for British forces displaced from Asia, and made investment in sophisticated weapon systems for these new roles necessary. In 1957, the government's enthusiastic support for a strategy of 'massive retaliation' in Europe – and thus downgrading of conventional forces – had forced the services to justify new equipment programmes by their 'limited war' roles in the Third World. Now that this rationale was no longer available, enthusiasm for conventional force roles in Europe rapidly revived. The popularity of 'flexible response' in Britain owed as much to the military's 'flexibility' in preserving its budget intact as to any reassessment of the scenarios for a future war with the Soviet Union.

By emphasizing the need for a 'balance' between conventional, theatre nuclear, and strategic nuclear forces, flexible response was able to justify improvements in all three. Moreover, despite a drastic change in the declared role of the armed forces, the structure of the three services, and the budgetary balance between them, remained remarkably steady. Force requirements appeared to determine 'strategy' rather than vice versa. The Army was able to acquire more sophisticated conventional and tactical nuclear weapons for its role in Central Europe and to retain its strength there at or above the level of the early 1960s. Despite its growing costs in foreign exchange, proposals for reductions in BAOR became less popular now that an alternative Army role East of Suez was no longer feasible. The 'danger' of American disillusionment with Europe – which had previously necessitated British military support in the US's world policing role – now made cuts in British forces in Germany politically unacceptable.

Even the decision to phase out aircraft carriers proved to be less radical than it had at first appeared. One of the three carriers, HMS *Hermes*, was due to be phased out in 1971, according to the 1967 Review.[6] Instead it underwent a series of expensive refits before serving as a 'Anti-Submarine Warfare/Commando Carrier' in the 1982 Falklands War. The decision to phase out a second carrier – HMS *Ark Royal* – as soon as East of Suez withdrawal was complete (1971) was reversed, and it remained in service, at considerable cost, until 1978.[7] Most importantly, the government permitted new naval programmes – the through-deck cruiser, the Type 42 destroyer, and the Type 21 and Type 22 frigates – to go ahead,[8] despite the widespread view that surface ships were of dubious value in a major war in the North Atlantic. This continued emphasis partly reflected the commitment of the naval lobby to an interventionary role in the Third World. For these 'out-of-area' operations, a surface fleet was still necessary. More importantly, it reflected the remarkable success of the Senior Service in defending its most treasured equipment programmes. When 'broken-backed' warfare was abandoned in 1956–7, the Navy had become a vigorous advocate of the need to prepare for limited wars outside Europe. Now that this imperial role was no longer politically acceptable, a new *raison d'être* was required. One naval historian perceptively described the process:

it was announced that the East of Suez role would be wound up *in toto* by 1971 . . . where, however, did this leave Britain's conventional forces in general and the navy in particular? As had happened ten years before, the very role of a navy was doubtful. *Again, however, a new strategy came to the rescue.* Carrier escorts East of Suez became the basis of anti-submarine warfare and anti-aircraft forces in the Atlantic.[9]

The new enthusiasm for the possibility of conventional defence in Europe from 1968 onwards was partly a result of objective changes in the military situation. In particular, the Soviet Union had now obtained, for the first time, a secure second-strike nuclear capability, bringing the deterrent value of massive retaliation into even greater doubt. 'Flexible response' addressed this problem by increasing the emphasis on conventional defence, while continuing to modernize nuclear forces. It was a formula that was to prove popular with those who were seeking a role for existing forces in Europe. After almost two decades in which conventional forces played a minor role in plans for general war with the Soviets, at last a strategy existed which could justify a wide range of force improvements. It appeared to pass unnoticed by most of those concerned that the simultaneous integration of tactical nuclear weapons into NATO forces would make a prolonged conventional war – on land or at sea – extremely unlikely.[10]

Despite the rundown of the major Far East bases, therefore, defence spending rose significantly in the early 1970s. The Conservative Party, more committed to the military than Labour, and returned to office in 1970, accelerated some existing programmes and started others, increasing defence spending by 10 per cent in three years (see Table 8). The maintenance of a 'general capability' for overseas intervention, together with regular exercises East of Suez, helped to satisfy the strong imperial lobby in the Tory Party and the armed forces.[11] At the same time, the government managed to avoid direct involvement in further Third World conflicts. The American experience in Vietnam was demonstrating the high costs of, and lack of benefits from, entanglement in Asia. And the successful British application for EEC membership reinforced the reluctance to be distracted by further imperial operations. While a general capability for overseas intervention was retained, the NATO role was emphasized.

Table 8 Defence Spending 1969–75

	1969–70	1970–1	1971–2	1972–3	1973–4	1974–5
Defence spending (£ million cash)	2,204	2,503	2,828	3,092	3,484	4,164
As % GDP	4.6	4.7	4.8	4.6	4.7	4.7
Defence spending (£ million 1984–5 prices)	11,534	12,128	12,547	12,680	13,311	13,327
Change	−6.4%	+5.1%	+3.5%	+1.1%	+5.0%	+0.1%

Source: see Appendix.

While explicit commitments outside Europe were now relatively few, however, the armed forces, and in particular the Navy, continued to regard their world role as important. It was argued that it was important for Europe to give the US support in its global policing role. And Britain's imperial tradition, as reflected in the structure of its armed forces, made it the best country, it was further argued, to fulfil this function on behalf of Western Europe as a whole.[12] Conveniently, it was thought, Britain could use its residual world role to strengthen its position within Europe. In practice, as in the 1950s and 1960s, the effect was probably the opposite. Britain's 'special relationship' with the United States continued to be a cause of friction between itself and its neighbours through the 1970s.

However, the October War of 1973 – like the Suez crisis in 1956 – was to demonstrate Britain's inability to influence US policy when it mattered. The 'special relationship' did not prevent President Nixon from ordering nuclear bombers in Britain on to a 'Defcon Three' alert without prior consultation with the host government.[13] As in the Cuban missile crisis of 1962, the leaders of 'Great' Britain were forced to stand by while the two superpowers engaged in a dangerous game of nuclear brinkmanship. The considerable resources expended on the independent nuclear force and on overseas capability did not appear to produce a greater influence for Britain than that possessed by its less heavily-armed, but more prosperous, European partners.

Britain's diminished status had already been demonstrated by its exclusion from the strategic arms limitation talks on nuclear weapons between the US and the Soviet Union. The contrast with the 1950s and early 1960s – when the UK at least had a place at the 'top table' – was readily apparent. The independent nuclear force had long since ceased to provide Britain with any significant influence in international affairs, though it did help to perpetuate the assumption that it was still a Great Power. Defence and foreign policy continued to be based on a belief, often subconsciously held, that Britain was a minor world power, rather than a medium European power. Ten further years of economic decline were to do nothing to alter this belief.

Labour's phoney cuts

It was not long, however, before economic crisis once again intervened in defence spending plans. The 1973 October war in the Middle East led to a quadrupling of the world oil price, and to a major economic crisis.[14] Public spending cuts were announced, including an immediate 5 per cent cut in planned growth in defence spending for 1974–5.[15] It was clear that the severity of the crisis would mean further cuts in later years. Before the Conservative government could consider the long-term implications for defence, however, it became a victim of that crisis itself. Rather than make concessions to the miners, considerably strengthened by the oil price rise, Prime Minister Heath called a General Election, which he lost narrowly.

The incoming Labour government was elected on a manifesto pledge to 'progressively reduce the burden of Britain's defence spending to bring our costs into line with those carried out by our main European allies.'[16] Faced with declining output and accelerating inflation, and under pressure from increasingly influential left-wing elements within the Party, it seemed that it would be forced to make substantial cuts in military spending.

The results of the 'comprehensive defence review', when announced in March 1975, did not, however, reflect this serious economic situation. Indeed, although the Labour Party at grass roots appeared to have moved to the left in the early 1970s, its leaders now proved, if anything, less capable of making major changes in defence policy than in 1964–70. After the Review, defence spending in real terms would still rise for two more years (to 1976/7) and remain steady thereafter.[17] And most of the £4,700 million (in 1974 prices) 'savings' announced were in the levels of spending provisionally planned for the 1980s,[18] levels which would, in the event, be restored by Mrs Thatcher after 1979. Barbara Castle records in her diary for 6 March 1975 that David Owen 'keeps telling me the cuts are phoney and that, if only someone would let him loose on the programme, he could make big reductions.'[19]

The government was only able to give the appearance that it was fulfilling its manifesto pledge by a statistical sleight of hand. By assuming an implausible increase in the future economic growth rate over past levels, it claimed that the defence burden would be reduced from 5.5 per cent to 4.5 per cent of GNP,[20] thus bringing it *ten years later* 'more into line' with major European allies. It was therefore hardly surprising that the *Times*, guardian of ruling class values, compared the March 1975 plans favourably with the Conservatives' short-term economies in 1973.[21] The armed forces and weapons companies had feared that the cuts might have been much more severe. They could now breathe a collective sigh of relief.

Large sections of the Labour Party, however, were not impressed by the Review and pressed for larger cuts in defence spending. The important Defence study group of the party's National Executive suggested that a further 20 per cent cut in planned defence spending was needed to fulfil the Manifesto target.[22] A growing number of left-wing MPs – 75 by 1977 – defied the Government whip and voted for larger cuts in Parliament.[23] And Denis Healey, now Chancellor of the Exchequer, urged much larger, and immediate, cuts in defence in order to release resources for an export-led economic upturn from 1977 onwards.[24]

With cuts in public spending as a whole starting to bite, Healey argued, defence must take its fair share. His proposals would have meant a cut of £500 million per annum in the defence budget – effectively doubling the savings achieved by the Review, though still far short of the Manifesto commitment. These proposals were, however, defeated. The predictable fury of the Chiefs of Staff was reinforced by a rebellion by the Manifesto group of right-wing Labour MPs, who wielded disproportionate power due to the government's slender parliamentary majority.[25] The employment implications of further cuts also enabled the military lobby to recruit support from key union leaders with considerable influence within the Party. Even some left-wing MPs, it was reported, were supporting large cuts in the defence budget as a whole, while pressing for equipment orders in their own areas.[26] Despite evidence that a transfer of resources into productive spending would create more jobs, not fewer, the employment argument was used to great effect to gain support for defence spending within the Labour movement. Its desire to retain jobs – whether useful or not – was exploited by the military lobby within the Party. It was conveniently ignored that cuts not directed at the defence budget would need to be made in education, health and the social services with even greater employment consequences.

More important than the jobs argument, however, was the continued commitment of most Labour leaders, and much of the liberal establishment, to an international role for Britain greater than its economic status would suggest. One of the more cogent presentations of this argument came from journalist Andrew Wilson – later author of the *Disarmers' Handbook* – in an *Observer* article in May 1976:

> Another point which must surely engage members of the Labour Party – and anyone else who wants to preserve our liberal influence in international affairs – is the loss that would be caused to Britain's standing in NATO by any further diminution of our defence effort . . .
>
> Britain continues to fill key posts in NATO, such as Command of the Northern Army Group, which came to her as a senior founder member of the Organisation . . . Although the West German Government has never sought to fill these posts with German officers, it is unthinkable that it would not do so if Britain were to reduce the Rhine Army, and the strength of our naval and air commitments, on the scale of a £1,000 million defence cut. Is this what the Labour Executive really wants?[27]

Like its predecessors, the government appeared to believe military strength led to political influence. Once more, it attached more importance to this strength than to the needs of the domestic economy. Britain, after all, still had a 'responsibility' to restrain countries – such as the US and Germany – with a supposedly less cautious or humane military outlook. The potential for arrogance and self-deception in such a position, stated so baldly, is clear. Nevertheless it continued to play a major role in justifying Britain's disproportionately large military establishment.

The 1975 Review did mean, however, some further contraction in Britain's East of Suez commitments. The remaining forces in Malaysia and Singapore would be withdrawn and a rundown in the Mediterranean fleet undertaken. Some of the forces originally designed for imperial policing – and awkwardly transferred to duties in NATO after the 1968 decision – would be phased out.[28] These moves represented a new stage in the drawn-out process of retreat from Britain's imperial commitments. Significant capabilities for 'out-of-area' operations, however, were retained, particularly in the Royal Navy. And no attempt was made to tackle the other symbol of the nation's Great Power pretensions – the nuclear force – despite its escalating cost.

Cuts in remaining Mediterranean and East of Suez commitments, however, only accounted for a small proportion of the savings announced in 1975 and 1976. Most savings – particularly those made after the Defence Review – came from short-term measures that had serious consequences for the current effectiveness of the armed forces. Training facilities, maintenance and ammunition were cut, while the budget for equipment escaped relatively unscathed.[29] Between 1974–5 and 1978–9, equipment spending rose by 29.5 per cent, after allowing for inflation. Spending on personnel, by contrast, fell by 8.0 per cent and that on other items – such as repairs, stores and buildings – fell by 20.0 per cent (see Table 17 in Chapter 7). This pattern could not be continued. Sophisticated tanks and aircraft were breaking down for lack of spare parts. Gunners at the Royal Artillery's main range at Larkhill in Wiltshire were rationed to firing two Blowpipe anti-aircraft missiles a year.[30] RAF Phantom crews were allowed to fire on average less than one live air-to-air missile a year; flying training had to be severely limited due to shortages of aviation fuel. The chairman of the US Joint Chiefs of Staff, General George

Brown, described Britain's forces as 'pathetic'.[31]

Cuts of this nature were bound to be reversed. Their disproportionate effect was leading to growing discontent in the armed forces. As new weapon systems came into service, more funds would be needed to maintain, operate and train on them. If it was unwilling to cut major equipment programmes, the government could not expect to restrain the defence budget to zero growth for long. The strain would simply be too great.

This was clearly recognized by the Labour government as early as 1976. It emphasized that cuts in spending for 1977–8 and 1978–9 were dictated solely by the short-term economic outlook, and did not reflect long-term plans.[32] With the advent of North Sea oil in the early 1980s, it was optimistically believed, economic growth would pick up and the defence budget could be increased to make up for the temporary cuts in previous years. The government thus felt able to agree, in May 1977, to implement NATO's target of 3 per cent annual real increases in the defence budget, subject to the provision that 'for some individual countries economic circumstances will affect what can be achieved'.[33] With rising oil revenues, the government at that time did not expect this provision to be applicable to Britain. According to Labour plans, defence spending would be increased by 3 per cent in both 1979–80 and 1980–1, and further increases in later years were clearly possible. It is unlikely that a Labour government would have continued with the 3 per cent commitment, faced with the subsequent economic recession and the need for further public spending cuts. Nevertheless it is important to note that the increased levels of defence expenditure in the first years of the Thatcher government were largely a result of decisions taken by its Labour predecessor. What was exceptional was the commitment to retain these inherited plans despite falling national output.

A tale of three projects

The 1975 Review demonstrated clearly that, in order to implement long-term cuts in defence spending, equipment programmes must be cancelled. There is an underlying trend for equipment costs to escalate as new technologies make weapon systems more sophisticated and push unit costs ever higher. Only by periodically cutting back on the number of major programmes can arms spending be

Table 9   Defence Spending 1974-9

	1974-5	1975-6	1976-7	1977-8	1978-9
£ million (cash)	4,164	5,346	6,158	6,787	7,455
As % GDP	4.7	4.8	4.8	4.5	4.4
£ million (1984-5 prices)	13,327	13,649	13,885	13,459	13,365
Change	+0.1%	+2.5%	+1.7%	-3.1%	-0.7%

Source: see Appendix.

kept under control. Otherwise the equipment budget will rise steadily – as it did between 1974-5 and 1978-9 (a 30 per cent real increase). In the long run, perhaps, different technologies will allow the development of cheaper ways of producing the same (or better) weapon systems. Such alternatives, however, do not yet exist, and have proved irrelevant within the time frame of most defence reviews.

This point was well understood by Roy Jenkins in 1968. In his role as Chancellor of the Exchequer, he rejected Defence Secretary Healey's offer to find equivalent cuts elsewhere in his budget if he were allowed to retain the order for the F-111 aircraft. [34] Jenkins made clear that lasting cuts in defence spending required cuts in defence equipment programmes. Healey was defeated.

The same argument was equally valid in the debate in late 1975, for which the two Labour leaders now found themselves playing different parts. To implement the £500 million annual cut Healey – now Chancellor – was proposing, and which Roy Jenkins, now Home Secretary, opposed, would clearly require the cancellation of several major projects. Indeed Healey made it clear that it was now his view that the defence industry was too big and that he would welcome major cancellations of arms contracts in order to release scarce skilled labour for the next economic upturn. [35]

The Cabinet rejected Healey's proposals. A cut of the magnitude proposed would almost certainly have required the cancellation of the three major projects which were symbols of Britain's continued attachment to its imperial and nuclear roles – the through-deck cruiser, the secret Chevaline project and the Multi-Role Combat

Aircraft (MRCA). The government was unwilling to cancel any one of them. Consequently the contribution that defence could make to the Chancellor's public spending cuts was severely limited and, as we have already seen, proved to be temporary in nature.

Yet all three of these projects, whose dubious rationales we shall shortly examine, could have been stopped in 1975 at a relatively modest cost. Each project had been conceived in outline in the late 1960s and had incurred substantial R & D costs in the early 1970s, allowing the first realistic total cost estimates to be made in 1974 or 1975. It was an indication of the conservatism of Harold Wilson's second administration that considerations which had justified the cancellation of TSR-2 and CVA-01 in 1965–6 were not judged sufficient to allow the cancellation of their successors – MRCA and the through-deck cruiser – in 1975–6, despite the increased severity of the country's economic crisis.

If these projects had been cancelled, and associated savings made in support costs, Britain's defence burden could have been reduced to nearer the level of the higher spenders amongst its European NATO allies. A real break could have been made with its imperial past, and funding of the defence budget put on a basis more compatible with the resources available from the domestic economy. A major step could have been taken towards ending the attachment to symbols of Britain's past glory, and a greater concentration on its future prosperity. Instead, like the two previous post-war Labour governments, the 1975 Cabinet was unwilling to abandon Britain's claim to the military status of a Great Power. The remainder of this chapter will look in more detail at the three projects mentioned, each of which has had important repercussions for defence policy in the 1980s.

From cruiser to carrier

In 1966, the Labour government had cancelled the CVA-01 carrier programme – a decision further strengthened by the 1968 decision to withdraw from East of Suez. As Healey argued in 1969:

> While it was a difficult judgement to decide against the carrier forces for maritime operations East of Suez, once we had decided to withdraw from major military responsibilities in that area in the middle 1970s, I do not believe that the decision was easy to contest.[36]

Healey's decision provoked considerable concern within the Royal Navy. It would not only weaken the Navy's capability for operations outside the North Atlantic. It also deprived it of a 'flagship' – central to the traditions and structure of the surface fleet. After the retirement of the existing carriers in the 1970s, the Navy feared that it would be reduced to a force consisting of submarines, minesweepers and a depleted number of surface ships – a fate which the admirals would do a great deal to avoid. It would be faced with the perceived humiliation of relying entirely on the RAF for air cover.

This situation was remedied by two developments. First, as we saw earlier in this chapter, the Royal Navy was able to retain two carriers – *Hermes* and *Ark Royal* – throughout the 1970s which Healey had originally planned to scrap by 1972. Second, there was the 'through-deck cruiser' project, later to become the 'ASW (Anti-Submarine Warfare) cruiser' and finally the 'ASW carrier'. This was effectively a mini-carrier, fulfilling most of the functions previously intended for the cancelled CVA carriers, in particular the role of fleet flagship. The design had rapidly evolved from a 12,579 ton vessel carrying six Sea King helicopters to a 19,000 ton giant with accommodation for fourteen. This in turn provided the Navy with a ready-made capability for handling the Harrier vertical take-off and landing aircraft.[37] It was then but a short step for the Navy to argue that it could now retain its own force of fixed-wing aircraft and prevent the assumption of an RAF monopoly when the old carriers were finally phased out.

Despite the powerful naval lobbying for the project, however, it was not until April 1973 that the Conservative government placed the order for the first of the cruisers – HMS *Invincible*.[38] Even at this stage the government refused to commit itself to ordering Sea Harriers. It was left to Roy Mason, Labour's Defence Secretary, to announce the purchase of the first batch of Sea Harriers in May 1975, only months after a supposedly cost-cutting defence review.[39] The total cost of the new carrier programme, including aircraft and support vessels, was estimated at £2,360 million over 20 years – £6,100 million at 1984–5 prices.[40]

The only way that the expenditure on this programme could be justified was as part of a 'general capability' to intervene in Third World conflicts against militarily inferior forces. With the number of British land bases continuing to diminish, the importance of sea power for such operations would, in many ways, be increased. Although most major ships would deploy in the NATO area in peacetime, the government made clear that they could 'deploy world-wide as allied or national interests require'.[41]

It is remarkable how the carrier – the symbol of Britain's imperial capability – was retained through the defence review. For many in the Royal Navy, the view that Britain still had military roles outside Europe was vindicated by the Falklands operations. Britain would have been unable to win the 1982 war had Denis Healey's decision to abandon the carriers been implemented.[42] As long as Britain continued to insist on the right to conduct such operations, the imperial structure of the Royal Navy remained relatively secure from further cuts.

Staying in the nuclear club

In January 1980, Defence Secretary Francis Pym announced that the Chevaline programme to update Britain's Polaris missiles was nearing completion, at an estimated cost of £1,000 million.[43] For more than a decade, it had been one of the best-kept secrets in government. Reviews of its progress had been made by a ministerial subcommittee and, it appears, most members of the Cabinet were unaware of its existence. The only indication of the expenditure in the money voted by Parliament for defence was a footnote to Vote 2 of the estimates: 'including provision . . . for expenditure on some nuclear supplies and services not separately identified for security reasons.'[44]

The initial studies for a Polaris improvement programme had begun in 1967. However it appears to have been mid 1973 before the government decided to go ahead with the Chevaline project and rejected the possible alternative of buying Poseidon missiles from the US.[45] This decision, confirmed by the Labour government in early 1974, was influenced by the public controversy in both the US and UK which a decision to purchase Poseidon would have meant. Given the Labour Party's 1974 manifesto commitment that they did not 'intend to move to a new generation of strategic nuclear weapons',[46] this would have proved embarrassing. Chevaline could be kept secret in a way which Poseidon could not; and, even if it were revealed, could plausibly be represented as merely an improvement on the present generation of missiles.

By 1975, however, the project appeared to be getting into deep trouble. Even for a government strongly committed to maintaining Britain's nuclear force, its justification was becoming increasingly doubtful. At a time when the whole defence budget was under scrutiny, the cost of the programme was getting out of control. The estimate of total cost made in 1972 had been £175 million. By March 1976 this had risen to £388 million (again at 1972 prices), and by 1980 this would rise a further £140 million to £530 million.[47] Expressed in today's prices Chevaline has actually cost at least £2,200 million[48] – equivalent to the total estimated capital cost of the original Polaris programme.[49]

Moreover, the project was still at a relatively early stage in 1975. Only £36 million had been spent by April 1974, with a further £49 million being used over the next year.[50] A decision in 1974 to cancel the project would have meant relatively small 'sunk' costs, and substantial savings for the government over the next decade.

Finally, the military rationale for the programme, always dubious, was now virtually non-existent. Chevaline's complex system of penetration aids (or dummy warheads) aboard a manoeuvrable spacecraft had been designed specifically to overcome the Anti-Ballistic Missile (ABM) defences around Moscow. Such a capability, it was argued, given Moscow's importance to the Soviet system, added to the bargaining power which Britain possessed. Its use would almost certainly trigger the release of all remaining Soviet missiles and thus precipitate a global holocaust. This capability, it was noted, would exercise an important influence, not only on Soviet actions, but also on those of the United States.

However by 1974 it had become abundantly clear that the Soviets would not deploy an effective ABM system. The 1972 ABM Treaty with the United States, amended in 1974, ruled out further development of such systems, in recognition of the failure of both countries to solve the technical problems involved. Even without Chevaline or Poseidon, Britain's four submarines would be able to meet the 'Moscow criterion'.

Despite its rising costs and increasingly doubtful military rationale, however, the Labour government decided to continue with the Chevaline programme. Cancellation would, it was argued, lead to the British team of nuclear weapon experts at Aldermaston breaking up, with subsequent difficulties in reforming them for future work. It would have created difficulties for the Trident programme in the early 1980s if Chevaline had not kept the design scientists busy through the 1970s.[51] Since the Labour government quite clearly wanted to retain an option of replacing Polaris in the 1990s, this argument must have been a persuasive one. With little attendant publicity, the decision to continue Chevaline was a clear indication that Britain was determined to remain a member of the nuclear club, with all the implications for its perceived world status that membership imputed.

One of the most remarkable features of the nuclear debate has been government's success in consistently understating in public the costs of the British nuclear force. In addition to the secret funds spent on Chevaline, the 1974–9 government approved substantial sums for new tactical nuclear systems – Lance missiles, nuclear depth charges, and improved bombs for strike aircraft.[52] Like Chevaline spending, this money was not included in published figures for nuclear weapons costs. In the 1975–6 Defence Estimates only £58 million out of £4,548 million was identified as on nuclear forces.[53] Yet this figure was accepted uncritically by almost all commentators as representing total nuclear expenditure – to the delight of the Ministry of Defence. This myth proved to be an important factor in quelling occasional nuclear doubts felt in both the 1964–70 and 1974–9 Labour cabinets.[54] Yet, as Chevaline made clear even before the costly Trident programme, the cost of retaining nuclear weapons has been, and remains, substantial. Only by a combination of creative accountancy, government secrecy, and public gullibility has this fact been hidden for so long. It remains to be seen whether it is a myth which will influence future governments.

The Tornado project

The most expensive weapons project of all, however, was the Tornado aircraft, produced jointly by Britain, West Germany and Italy – and described by German Chancellor Helmut Schmidt as 'the greatest technological project since the birth of Christ'.[55] The total capital cost for Britain's 385 aircraft alone is likely to be at least £13,400 million[56] – 50 per cent higher than official estimates of the cost of Trident. Throughout the late 1970s and early 1980s, it has constituted most of the RAF's equipment budget, and has been one of the main contributors to the rising total defence bill during these years. For the next fifteen to twenty years, it is likely to consume a further £10,000–£15,000 million in maintenance and operational costs.[57]

Despite the enormous cost of the project, however, the military purpose of Tornado was always highly questionable. In order to justify its expense, and allow a relatively large production run, it was supposed to fulfil a number of different functions previously carried out by separate types of aircraft – thus its original title 'Multi-Role Combat Aircraft'. In the RAF, for example, it was due to replace, or has already replaced, Vulcan, Canberra, Buccaneer, Lightning and Phantom planes.[58] The attempt to give Tornado the equipment to fulfil the, often quite different, military roles of all those aircraft has been one of the primary reasons for the extremely high cost of each plane. Moreover, in some of its roles at least, it is now proving to be of little practical use. Indeed, such is the reluctance of the RAF and the Luftwaffe to use Tornado for 'close support' and 'battlefield interdiction' – two of its originally specified functions – that by 1984 plans were well advanced to produce a new aircraft for these functions.[59] In practice, the RAF now sees Tornado as fulfilling only two primary roles. First, the 220 Tornado GRIs will be used for high-speed long-range bombing missions. Secondly, the 165 F2 models, which are being produced only for the UK, will be used for long-range air defence.

Yet, upon close examination, it is difficult to avoid the impression that the emphasis given to these two roles, at least in part, is a result of the RAF's need to justify a substantial programme of re-equipment. For, if government had cancelled Tornado in 1975 or 1976, as the Labour Party National Executive Committee had suggested, and as Denis Healey's proposed cuts in December 1975 would probably have required, the independent existence of the RAF would clearly have been threatened.

The abolition of the RAF had formed the basis of a proposal by the chairman of Labour's backbench defence committee, Alan Lee Williams, in 1977. Despite his opposition to cuts in defence spending, Mr Williams had proposed that the RAF should be absorbed into the army since it 'no longer has either global or strategic responsibilities – nothing left but to defend Britain, fly anti-submarine patrols for the navy (which many NATO navies do quite well for themselves) and support the army . . . the RAF has never adjusted its psyche to this reduced role.' Moreover, Mr Williams suggested, such a proposal would cut 'spending, particularly on the most modern – and now very expensive – manned aircraft, to what is needed to do what the army needs done.'[60]

The possibility of such a fate must have added to RAF concern that Tornado must not be cancelled. The eventual decision to continue the project owed more to this pressure, combined with fear of the possible employment implications and knowledge of the political difficulties in cancelling a multinational project, than to the inherent military value of the programme.

Britain's nuclear bomber

In the 1960s, the RAF's ambitions had been shaken by the cancellation of the TSR2 in 1965 and the decision not to purchase the F111 (intended to replace TSR2) in 1968. After the failure to agree on a suitable programme to develop an alternative replacement for F111 with the French,[61] a complex series of negotiations led to an agreement on the Tornado project in early 1969. Both the air forces and the manufacturers concerned clearly hoped that, by having a collaborative project, they would be able to avoid future cancellation in circumstances in which domestic manufacture (TSR-2) and importing (F-111) had not. They were proved to be right. The complicated series of agreements between the governments and firms involved ensured that cancellation would entail very large financial, and political, penalties. Collaboration proved to be less successful in its proclaimed objective of lowering costs.[62]

Britain's requirement for the Tornado strike aircraft can be traced back to the Second World War. Ever since that time, 'strategic bombing' has been seen by the RAF as its most important mission, enabling it to decide the outcome of a war without reference to, or assistance from, naval and ground forces. In 1942–5, it took the form of saturation attacks on German cities, the most notorious of which, on Dresden, killed over 25,000 people.[63] The advent of nuclear weapons made strategic bombing, in RAF eyes, still more crucial in a future war. The primacy of strategic bombing had been the central feature of the 1952 Global Strategy Paper, and had justified the V-bomber programme in the 1950s. Even after the Royal Navy's Polaris submarines had taken over the strategic nuclear mission in 1969, the RAF remained determined to stay in the long-range nuclear game. The retention of the V-bombers in a nuclear role through the 1970s was one immediate consequence. The 220 Tornado bombers now entering service will enable the RAF to fulfil this ambition until the end of the century.

Tornado strike aircraft are 'dual capable' – that is, they can be used with either conventional or nuclear weapons. Given the sophistication of East European air defences, however, the rate of aircraft losses in a major war would be high, and the military gains low, from deep conventional strikes.[64] This will increase the pressure to 'withhold' many, perhaps most, aircraft for use in a nuclear role, as suggested recently by one RAF officer:

> In any future war in Europe, conventional attacks on traditional interdiction targets, while contributing little to the immediate battle, would probably result in significant losses of interdiction aircraft [e.g. Tornado] . . . However, should conventional defence fail, short-range interdiction with tactical nuclear weapons would probably constitute an essential element of the subsequent battle.
>
> Interdiction therefore, unlike the Dodo, is not quite extinct. But its continued survival, in a European environment, probably depends upon its ability to lay nuclear eggs![65]

Yet the military need for a British nuclear force – below the 'strategic' level but above the short-range 'battlefield' level – is very doubtful indeed. It depends initially on the probability attached to limiting a nuclear war once started. Unless it is believed that a limited, nuclear war in Europe is a significant possibility, Tornado's nuclear role is redundant. Even those who accept the necessity for a minimum independent 'deterrent' must have second thoughts on the massive sums being spent on Tornado, given the flimsiness of the premise on which it appears to be based.

In reality, the Tornado bomber is needed as much in order to protect the RAF's institutional existence, and the careers of those in it, as for its military benefits. RAF pressure for a nuclear role is, in effect, a way of maintaining its bureaucratic influence within a framework which places a high reliance on nuclear weapons. It reflects the perception that Britain's role as an independent nuclear power is necessary for its influence within NATO. As long as NATO doctrine emphasizes preparation for limited nuclear war, Britain will want its own theatre nuclear weapons involved in those preparations. Indeed, even if British leaders realized that 'controlled escalation' was a forlorn hope, there would be pressure for them to maintain Tornado's nuclear role in order to safeguard Britain's position as the number two in the Alliance.

In the last two years, under increasing pressure from the peace movements in Europe and elsewhere, NATO commanders have sought to give greater public emphasis to conventional roles for deep-strike aircraft such as Tornado.[66] In this way, it is hoped, public concern about nuclear weapons can be used to extract still greater resources for defence from limited national budgets. Additional funds would be spent on the new conventional weapons which rapid technological development is now making possible. It is argued that existing deep-strike weapon systems – such as Tornado – have at present inadequate conventional armaments, thus confining their role largely to nuclear missions. New conventional weapons will, it is hoped, remedy this position. Precision-guided weapons, with a destructive potential approaching that of small nuclear bombs, would enable reliance on nuclear weapons to be reduced.[67] The plan to equip Tornado with conventionally armed cruise missiles is one example of this apparent shift in emphasis.

It is questionable whether these new conventional systems will be accompanied by any meaningful reduction in NATO's reliance on nuclear weapons. Even if some shift is achieved, however, new conventional deep-strike weapons, if they worked, would be extremely destabilizing. They would tend to blur the distinction between nuclear and conventional war, and might give the Soviet Union the impression that NATO was seeking to acquire a capability for conventional offensive.[68] The new weapons could thus fuel a conventional arms race in what is still an unstable region – Central and Eastern Europe – and increase the danger of war by miscalculation. Whether in its nuclear or its conventional role, therefore, the Tornado bombers are likely to contribute to the escalation of tension in Europe.

Battle of Britain?

At first sight, the role of the other version of Tornado – the F2 or 'air defence variant' – is more appealing. The 165 aircraft to be purchased are intended for use in the long-range defence of the UK against Soviet bombers. These British-only Tornados have two clear (though negative) advantages over the GRI 'common version' of the plane. First, they are due to be deployed in a defensive, rather than offensive, role (though with some modifications they could probably be adapted to most attack missions). Secondly, they are not designated as 'nuclear capable' (though, again, the necessary adaptations would be relatively straightforward). However the military advantages gained from the considerable sum spent on adapting Tornado for air defence are less obvious. In 1976, when the air defence Tornados could have been cancelled with relatively little loss in 'sunk' costs, the Ministry of Defence itself believed that the new aircraft themselves were not much better than the Phantoms which they would replace, though 'the weapon system [missiles, radar, etc.] is a complete step forward.'[69]

Moreover, the Soviet bomber threat, against which Tornado F2 is claimed to be a response, appears to be less formidable than is sometimes presented. In 1957 the Sandys review had questioned the value of defences against attack by nuclear bombers since it only needed a handful of planes to get through for the entire nation to be devastated. The subsequent East of Suez withdrawal further limited the role for RAF fighter aircraft. It was not until the 1970s that the threat of Soviet conventional air attacks against military targets in the UK became the focus of attention – conveniently for Tornado. As the government admitted:

> It is not thought that any threat from the [Soviet] Backfire and Fencer forces is necessarily imminent. But it is feared that it will become steadily more serious as the aircraft are increased in numbers and improved in quality. The new emphasis on air defences [reflected in Tornado F2] is designed to keep pace with that build-up.[70]

It is therefore difficult to see why such a high priority has been given to air defence over Britain at a time when, according to our government, the West would be hard-pressed to stop a Soviet attack in Central Europe. It is a good example of how the nebulous NATO doctrine of 'flexible response' can justify each and every new weapon system by reference to a series of 'scenarios', however improbable. And it is yet another illustration of the way in which the British armed forces have used that doctrine to retain the structures and forces of the past remarkably unscathed.

6. Military spending and the British economy

The connection between Britain's high level of military spending and its poor economic performance was recognized by members of successive governments in the 1950s and 1960s. In 1958, for example, Peter Thorneycroft, shortly after resigning as Chancellor of the Exchequer, argued that expenditure on British nuclear weapons was 'a questionable policy . . . Our prestige will be rated not by the bombs we make nor by the money we can spend, but by the contribution we can make to Western solvency and economic strength.'[1] And, in 1965, Labour's National Plan argued that: 'If we endeavour to support too large a defence effort, it will create economic weakness which will, in the long run, frustrate our external policy as a whole no less than our internal policy.'[2]

Despite these concerns, shared by both Conservative and Labour administrations, the series of defence 'reviews' described in previous chapters succeeded only in halting the growth in military spending. As a consequence, as Table 10 shows, the UK has consistently spent more of its national income on the military than any of its main allies (and economic competitors), with the important exception of the US (to whom the arguments of this book could be applied *a fortiori*).

The relationship between high military spending and poor economic performance is not unique to the UK. An important recent study of thirteen countries over the period 1960–79, has shown that:

> those nations spending a larger share of their gross
> domestic product on the military generally experienced
> lower economic growth than those which spent less.[3]

At one end of the spectrum, Japan had an annual growth rate of 8.5 per cent in 1960–79 and spent only 0.9 per cent of its national income on defence; at the other, the UK's rate of growth was only

2.5 per cent and its military burden 5.4 per cent.

It would be wrong to argue that the level of military burden was the only determinant of growth. France, for example, has managed to combine a relatively high growth rate with high military spending. Nevertheless it does appear that it is an important factor – and that in Britain it has been crucial.

Table 10 Military Burden, 1950–83

	1950	1955	1960	1965	1970	1975	1980	1983
USA	5.1	10.2	9.0	7.6	8.0	5.9	5.6	6.9
UK	6.6	8.2	6.5	5.9	4.8	4.9	5.1	5.6
France	5.5	6.4	6.5	5.2	4.2	3.8	4.0	4.2
West Germany	4.4	4.1	4.0	4.3	3.3	3.6	3.3	3.4
Netherlands	4.8	5.7	4.1	4.0	3.5	3.4	3.1	3.3
Australia	3.0	3.8	2.7	3.4	3.5	2.8	2.7	2.8**
Italy	4.3	3.7	3.3	3.3	2.7	2.5	2.4	2.8
Canada	2.6	6.3	4.2	2.9	2.4	1.9	1.8	2.1
Spain	. . .	2.2	2.2	1.8	1.6	1.7	1.9	2.1*
Japan	. . .	1.8	1.1	0.9	0.8	1.0	1.0	1.0*

Notes:
1. . . . not available
   * 1982 figures
   ** 1981 figures
2. Taken from *SIPRI Yearbook* 1980, 1984.
3. Military burden is military expenditure as a proportion of Gross Domestic Product at purchasers' values.
4. The NATO definition of military expenditure is used. The UK 1984/85 defence budget is 2.3 per cent greater on this basis than on the UK government's definition (*Statement on the Defence Estimates 1984* Cmnd 9227-II, Table 2.4).
5. The countries shown are the ten largest members of the Organization for Economic Co-operation and Development (OECD). The comparison thus excludes less developed countries and members of the Soviet bloc.

Military spending has contributed to Britain's relative economic decline in three interrelated ways: first, it has taken place at the expense of investment, rather than consumption. As a result, the capacity for future production (and consumption) has risen relatively slowly. Secondly, it has used a disproportionate amount of scarce high-technology inputs. These have not been available for civilian use, and the rate of technical progress outside the military sector has been slowed as a result. Thirdly, it has harmed the UK balance of payments, both through diversion of resources from export industries, and by the high level of overseas military expenditure. This has in turn resulted in policies of economic management which have damaged investment, and thus long-term growth potential.

Military spending and investment

The main cause of Britain's low level of growth in productivity and output has been a persistently low level of productive investment. By the mid 1970s, Britain's investment per head of population was less than half the level of France and Germany and only slightly higher than in Ireland, Italy, Spain and Greece.[4] And since then the situation has deteriorated still further. Net investment (excluding North Sea operations) has declined from 5 per cent of companies' net capital stock in the mid 1960s to less than 2 per cent in the mid 1970s and below 1 per cent today. In the manufacturing sector, investment has, for the last three years, been insufficient even to cover depreciation: *net* investment has, in other words, been negative. Indeed the Deputy Governor of the Bank of England recently argued, along with most informed commentators, that sustained gains in productivity in the 1980s will require a much higher level of investment than at present.[5]

There is widespread agreement that low productive investment is the immediate cause of low output growth; and that this in turn has led to poor productivity and declining international competitiveness. There is much less agreement as to why investment has been relatively low. Two alternative arguments to that emphasized in this volume should be briefly considered.

The first argument is that the British working class was relatively strong economically during this period and was thus able to obtain a high share of wages in total output. As a result, profits were squeezed and both the means and incentive to invest were reduced. In contrast, it is argued, the experience of fascism and the defeat of the Second World War had demoralized workers in Japan, Italy and Germany. Their trade unions could thus not obtain the same share of national income as their counterparts in the UK.[6]

Furthermore, some authors argue, strong working-class organization has also slowed down the introduction of more efficient technologies and working practices.[7] As a result the incentives to invest have been reduced and the investment that has taken place has had lower returns than in other countries. The relatively strong British working class has thus both increased the share of real wages, reducing the resources available for investment, and restricted the opportunities for productivity growth, reducing the incentives for investment.

The second argument is that the formation of a Welfare State – again arguably a result of a strong working class – has led to a high level of government spending, high taxation and/or borrowing, and a squeeze on both profits and investment. This argument has gained considerable favour in recent years and remains an influential component of Thatcherism.[8]

To test these arguments against the alternative hypothesis of this book – that it is military spending that is primarily responsible for squeezing investment – a number of econometric studies have been conducted.

In a comprehensive study of data for 14 advanced Western countries during 1954–73,[9] Ron Smith found that a change in the military's share of national output tended to be associated with an equal change in the share of investment, but in an opposite direction.

A similar result was obtained by Robert De Grasse, using a different statistical test on 13 industrial countries for the period 1960–79. De Grasse concluded that there was no clear statistical relationship between growth and either wages or civilian government spending. Only military spending was associated with lower economic growth, less investment and slower productivity growth.

> One interesting finding was that there is no apparent relationship between private consumption as a share of GDP and military spending . . . Instead, to compensate for

arms spending, the slice of the pie that seems to be reduced the most is investment.[10]

This finding does not necessarily imply that in the UK lower levels of private consumption or current government spending could not have released resources for investment. It does, however, show that such a course would have needed exceptionally low levels of spending in these two categories, given the high military burden. In the event, post-war aspirations for both private goods and public services made such a course politically unacceptable, and investment was cut instead.

Slow economic growth made industrial conflict over 'shares of the cake' more intense and doomed attempts to reduce permanently the share of real wages, as the experience with successive rounds of incomes policies showed. In the public sector, cuts fell most heavily on capital projects as the share of current spending could not be reduced during a period of low growth and rising demographic and social pressures.

Arms spending and scarce resources

So far I have been discussing the allocation of expenditure between macro-economic categories – government spending, consumption, investment, military spending. In principle it is possible to switch expenditure between all these categories. In practice there are physical constraints on doing so which have reinforced the tendency of military spending and civilian investment to act as direct substitutes. They relate to the nature of modern 'arms spending', which means both spending on equipment production and on defence research and development (R & D). The military budget can be divided into two main categories – arms spending and personnel spending. As the modern battlefield becomes increasingly mechanized, the proportion going on arms has tended to increase and that on personnel has declined.

Arms spending competes directly with civilian investment for scarce resources both in the equipment production sector and in research and development. The competition for the resources of the equipment production sector was particularly important in the period after the outbreak of the Korean war in 1950, when a programme of rearmament led to arms spending almost trebling in two years – from £186 million in 1950–51 to £524 million in 1952–3.[11] The government recognized that structural factors meant that most of this burden would fall on particular sectors, as it made clear in the 1951 Economic Survey:

> The increased claims of defence are not distributed evenly over the economy, but are largely concentrated upon particular sectors – most of all upon the metal-using industries. The great bulk of the output of these industries goes to home investment and exports and only a very small part consists of consumption goods. This makes it much more difficult to shift the main burden of rearmament on to consumption. It is indeed certain that defence orders must to a considerable extent conflict with production of metal goods for export and investment.[12]

The diversion of machine tools to the defence sector resulted in a cut in civilian deliveries of about one third, despite increased deliveries from the US, and subsequently led to reductions in investment and export performance. In 1959, Denis Healey noted that Britain's engineering industry, crucial to its exports, had been 'particularly hard hit by rearmament' while its commercial rivals, especially West Germany, were not similarly hampered.[13]

In theory the high arms spending of the early 1950s could have generated a larger engineering sector, able to meet simultaneously the demands of exports, investment and military spending. In practice this was most unlikely. In the short run new capacity could not be created. A sudden increase in demand for armaments, together with insistence on domestic procurement, inevitably diverted resources from other uses. Only over a period of several years could the size and composition of the capital stock adjust to higher arms spending, but then other factors came into play. Because of the political pressure for better wages and civil public services, investment suffered most during government-sponsored 'Stops'.

After the mid 1950s the level of arms spending (once inflation is taken into account) declined to some extent, although it remained substantially higher than in most other industrial countries. The retreat from East of Suez, together with some relaxation of the policy of domestic arms production, helped to offset the tendency for the sophistication, and costs, of modern weapons to increase.

From 1974 onwards, however, the level of equipment spending began to increase again. Between 1974–5 and 1984–5, equipment spending rose from £4,162 million (at 1984–5 prices) to £7,796 million – a rise of 87 per cent after allowing for inflation.[14] Arms spending is now at its highest ever peacetime level, and appears likely to grow still further.

Probably as important as the strain on the capacity of the engineering industry was the demand for the limited resources for R & D, and in particular for first-rate research personnel. The concentration of R & D effort in the defence sector was particularly marked in the 1950s as Britain sought to keep up with the technological arms race between the superpowers. Germany and Japan were capturing one market after another in steel, ship-building, machinery, etc., while British scientists and engineers were concentrated in fields such as aircraft, atomic energy, and radar. Military R & D grew from £71 million in 1950–51 to £204 million in 1956–7. By the latter year, 40 per cent of all professionally qualified scientists and engineers engaged in R & D were working on defence projects. In 1955–56 almost 60 per cent of national R & D was financed from defence funds, and nearly two-thirds of the research done by private industry was on defence contracts.[15] At the same time the mechanical engineering industry, shipbuilding and steel had scarcely any graduate engineers in any positions before the 1960s, in marked contrast to the prominent place they held in German industry.

Increasingly, however, it became clear that Britain was unable to produce the entire range of sophisticated weapons it required, despite this enormous effort. Enormous resources were wasted on projects that were not completed. Between 1945 and 1956, 166 aircraft projects (civilian and military) were started, of which no less than 142 were discontinued, 16 had partly succeeded, and only 8 were successful – all at a cost of £1,000 million.[16] Partly as a result of such failures there was some reduction in R & D spending and some erosion of self-reliance in arms manufacture. An agreement was reached to purchase Polaris nuclear missiles from the US. And, after Denis Healey became Defence Minister in 1964, a series of British aerospace projects were cancelled in favour of cheaper imported alternatives such as the Phantom and Hercules aircraft. Withdrawal of military forces from East of Suez enabled further savings to be made in some of the forces designed for that role, such as the planned new aircraft carrier.

These savings proved, however, to be temporary and limited. The power of domestic military and industrial interests and the insistence on an increased role in NATO, together with the retention of some nuclear and out-of-area commitments, ensured that the costs of military R & D started to rise again. Between 1966–70 and 1976–79, defence R & D rose as a proportion of total R & D (public and private) from 25.6 per cent to 29.3 per cent. (See Table 11.)[17] Today the British government spends about half its R & D budget on defence, considerably more than Japan, Germany or France.[18]

Table 11 Share of Military R & D Spending in Total R & D Spending (public and private, percentage average of available years)

	1963–5	1966–70	1971–5	1976–9	1980–1*
Canada	10.6	7.2	. . .	3.6	2.7
France	26.2	22.5	18.4	19.6	23.3
West Germany	10.8	10.3	6.9	6.2	. . .
Italy	2.6	2.4	2.1	1.9	1.4
Japan	0.9	0.9	0.7	0.6	0.6
Netherlands	1.9	2.3	2.0	1.6	1.5
Spain	2.7	5.1	. . .	3.3	. . .
Sweden	34.2	27.3	15.2	14.2	. . .
UK	34.5	25.6	28.9	29.3	28.0
USA	40.6	31.2	27.7	25.4	23.8

Source: Mary Acland-Hood, 'Statistics on military research and development expenditure', in *SIPRI Yearbook 1984*, Table 6.4.
Notes: . . . not available
* provisional figures

In the 1980s, Britain's high level of arms spending continues to deprive civilian industry of the scarce skilled personnel that are necessary for technical innovation, productivity growth and efficient investment. The opportunities lost are particularly costly in growing new areas such as 'information technology'. A recent report from the National Economic Development Council has argued that 'One of the most critical issues of all [in the information technology industry] is the availability of skilled manpower . . . Too often contracts are being lost and employment opportunities for the less skilled are being lost with them, because of the lack of a few key engineers.' The report advocates a long-term industrial strategy and 'the use of public procurement to support the information technology industry in the civil field rather than predominantly in defence.'[19] Yet it is precisely in such high technology areas that Britain's arms budget is increasingly concentrated.

'Spin-off'

An important argument for arms production has been that there will be 'spin-offs' benefiting technical progress in civilian products. It is an argument which can clearly be countered by pointing out that it would almost certainly be possible to use R & D resources more effectively were they to be applied directly to the advance of civilian technology. Chance by-products of military R & D can at best reduce, not eliminate, the cost to the civilian economy.

In the period we are considering, however, there are two further important objections. The first is that some investment in 'spin-off' civilian sectors has itself been an uneconomic use of resources and thus a further cost, not a benefit, to the economy. The second is that modern military technology has increasingly diverged from civilian technology, and therefore the scope for spin-off has been reduced.

The British aerospace industry produces both military and civilian products, and provides a good example of 'negative spin-off'. The production and export of civilian aircraft and parts depends to some extent on knowledge and skills acquired in military production, and vice versa. This has meant that considerable subsidies have been given for the maintenance of the civil aerospace industry, the funds provided for the survival of Rolls Royce and the cost of Concorde being two good examples. In a 1976 report to the Department of Industry, N.K. Gardiner estimated that over £1,500 million (at 1974 prices) of government finance had been invested in *civil* aerospace since 1945 for a return of under £150 million.[20] Despite these subsidies, however, the enormous economies of scale in the aerospace industry ensured that the US, with its much larger investments, would remain supreme in world markets. Other medium-sized nations, such as Germany and Japan, avoided aerospace, concentrating their research efforts in products in which they had a greater long-run comparative advantage.

The allocation of R & D resources to the nuclear power programme provides another powerful example of the disadvantages of 'spin-off'. The nuclear industry began with military objectives – the provision of fissile material for British atomic and hydrogen bombs. By the 1950s the comparative advantage in nuclear technology was used to justify a large investment programme in nuclear power generation. Despite an initial lead, however, Britain was unable to compete successfully with the much larger American nuclear industry; and the economic viability of nuclear power in future seems increasingly under question. Without the initial impetus provided by the race to build the A-bomb, it is doubtful whether Britain would have invested as much as it did in this dangerous and inefficient industry.[21] Yet, despite this record, the Department of Energy in 1981–2 spent £172 million on atomic energy out of a total R & D budget of £216 million, compared with less than £1 million for solar energy, and only £500,000 for energy conservation.[22]

The need to maintain and develop civilian products, in which other nations have a clear comparative advantage, so as to build or keep a capacity for military production, thus constituted an indirect cost of arms spending and defence policy, and resulted in the concentration of R & D in a relatively small number of sectors.

The second objection to the spin-off argument rests on the proposition that modern military technological development increasingly puts an emphasis on custom-built, highly sophisticated, low volume production in direct contrast to the emphasis on high volume inexpensive products for civilian markets. The Geddes report on the shipbuilding industry, for example, found that:

The community of interest between naval and civil ship research workers can be exaggerated. Naval research is to a large extent concerned with obtaining extreme performance from ships at a cost per ton greatly in excess of that

> practicable for a merchant ship. The problems involved in
> this are different from those involved in research aimed . . .
> at reduction of sea transport costs.[23]

In the 1980s a sector where, *a priori*, one might expect considerable spin-off potential is electronics – an industry whose success is thought by many to be essential for future economic prosperity. Yet UK civilian electronics perform relatively badly in most of the sectors where world markets are growing fastest and where there are the greatest opportunities for growth in the future.

The Japanese by contrast have proved most successful in civilian electronics – TVs, radios, video-recorders, etc. – by adapting innovations that came initially from military research in the US, such as solid-state integrated circuits, and turning them into marketable products. British firms – with their emphasis on military products – have not fared so well. The Ferranti microprocessor, for example, was developed for the UK Ministry of Defence and has found new commercial uses. Sciberras argues that:

> This focus on specialized devices for custom markets,
> where Government is the major customer, will further
> entrench UK firms in market areas which are a diminishing
> stimulus for technical innovation with widespread
> applications.[24]

This argument may apply with equal force to the increasing problems the US faces in international markets. As Lester Thurow, an economic adviser to the 1984 Presidential contender Gary Hart, has argued:

> If the brightest engineers in Japan are designing video
> recorders and the brightest engineers in the United States
> are designing MX missiles, then we shouldn't find it
> surprising that they conquer the video-recorder market.[25]

Finally, the economic difficulties created by high levels of arms spending are not confined to developed capitalist countries. This is particularly evident for the Soviet Union, which spends a much greater proportion of its national income on defence than any major Western nation. Indeed Britain's 1984 Defence White Paper recently contended that:

It has been estimated that [Soviet] military requirements absorb a third of the output of the important machine-building and metal-working sector. The defence industries thus deprive the civil sector of scarce resources, particularly skilled manpower. Unlike the West, there is little spin-off from technical advances in the defence sector into the civil economy, and this pre-emption of key resources for defence thus inhibits general economic development.[26]

The implication that Britain can avoid the consequences of arms spending, yet the Soviets cannot, appears to owe more to wishful thinking than to serious economic analysis.

The arms trade

Successive governments have claimed that the export of armaments constitutes a valuable spin-off from Britain's investment in its arms industry. Whatever else one might think about the wisdom or morality of such a trade, it must be conceded that some benefit to Britain's balance of payments does accrue because of the £2,400 million of annual military exports.[27] The hidden costs of this are, however, substantial. Given the scale of resources devoted to arms production, the return is relatively poor. Italy, with a level of defence spending less than 40 per cent that of the UK, had a roughly equal share of the world arms market in 1979–83. And France, whose total defence budget is comparable to Britain's, exported two and a half times as much during the same period.[28]

In recent years the real value of arms sales has increased with a substantial stepping up of sales efforts under the Conservatives. By and large, however, British arms remain uncompetitive on world markets. The military shipyards are particularly unsuccessful, despite substantial direct subsidies and concessionary finance to purchasers. The main 'market' appears to be Hong Kong.[29] In aircraft, Britain's sales have found it difficult making headway against US competition, with some notable exceptions such as the Harrier jumpjet. Indeed the existence of a protected domestic market may, in some cases, actually reduce the pressure on British producers to increase competitiveness, while it can also provide, in others, a source of R & D finance and initial orders.

Nor is the government able to recover a significant proportion of its outlay on defence R & D by spreading the costs over total production, domestic and export. The Royal Ordnance Factories' exports often fail to cover fixed overhead costs. And a government levy on commercial exports of defence equipment, intended to recoup such outlays, yielded only £9 million per year in the 1970s.[30]

Despite the modest returns involved, however, there is constant pressure on government to seek further exports in order to keep arms factories in work between domestic orders. As a result, particularly under the present administration, there is an eagerness to sell weapons overseas that can often act directly against Britain's own defence interests. There is an increasing tendency to ask for weapon designs to be geared to the needs of Third World markets in addition to its own requirements. The additional costs to, and/or reduced efficiency of, Britain's own armed forces are a hidden cost of this policy.

In addition, exports to areas of potential conflict often lead to unfortunate results. Some of the most advanced weapons used by Argentina in the 1982 Falklands War were British-supplied. And the possibility of the Iran-Iraq conflict disrupting Western oil supplies does not appear to have been considered when Britain agreed to sell massive quantities of arms to both sides in the past. It is unclear what advantage the UK, or the West in general, has in the proliferation of the most modern weapon systems throughout the Third World. Yet that is the direct result of current 'liberal' arms sales policies.

Finally, while arms exports may provide a limited plus for the balance of payments, this is outweighed (for arms exports as a whole) by their economic and political costs. A truer measure of their cost can only be obtained by asking: how would the volume of exports be changed if the resources used were redeployed elsewhere in the economy? Since over a quarter of total R & D (government and civilian) is spent on defence, yet only $3\frac{1}{2}$ per cent of visible exports are provided, it would be surprising if the answer was favourable for the arms trade. It is clear that the existence of a British arms industry cannot be justified by the contribution it makes to the balance of payments. At best, arms exports offset only a small part of the costs of that industry. More probably, they add a further burden, and contribute Britain's part in the rapid militarization of the Third World.

Military spending and the balance of payments

Until the advent of significant revenues from North Sea oil, balance of payments crises were a recurrent, and apparently inevitable, feature of the British economy. Even General Elections sometimes appeared to depend on the latest trade figures – as was evident in 1970. The balance of payments dominated government economic planning from 1945 until 1978–9.

The most important long-term effect of these crises was on investment and growth. A short 'Stop-Go' cycle became established in which any economic upswing was soon interrupted by a balance of payments crisis. These were sometimes a result of a current account deficit caused by rising imports, sometimes because of speculative capital flows. The response of governments was invariably to slam on the economic brakes, hitting particularly hard (at least after 1950) at the investment goods sector. Thus any deficit in the balance of payments had two undesirable effects: first, it caused an immediate loss of output in the economy several times its size. Secondly, it reduced the incentives for domestic investment, which in turn led to higher overseas investment, and, in future years, lower exports and less import substitution. These trends, for their part, then created the conditions for the next crisis. A cycle was created which caused tremendous damage to the economy yet was initiated and fuelled by relatively small external deficits.

Military spending indirectly affected the balance of payments by (i) diverting production from industries – such as engineering – whose production could otherwise have been used for export, (ii) reducing the rate of modernization in civilian sectors, thus harming their long-run international competitiveness in both domestic and overseas markets. A study, in 1973, suggested that there was a statistical relationship between high military spending and low export growth. It concluded that:

> high military expenditure reduces export availabilities in the machinery and transport equipment sector where chances for export expansion have been above average. This brake on the most expansive sector dampens export growth in general. A slow-down in GNP growth follows from this.[31]

In Britain, high arms spending reduced the availability of resources for the modernization of civilian industry. Partely as a result, it lost one market after another to foreign competitors and its share of world trade fell rapidly, as Table 12 shows. It is of interest to note that, as with productivity, Britain's relative decline appears to have slowed down in the 1930s and 1940s. Some of the rapid growth of German and Japanese market shares in the 1950s may be explicable in terms of the under-utilization of productive resources in 1950, combined with the after-effects of war, but continually high levels of industrial investment were a more important ingredient.

Table 12 Shares in the value of world exports of manufactures, 1899–1983 (percentages)

	1899	1927	1937	1950	1960	1970	1980	1983
United Kingdom	33.2	22.9	21.3	25.5	16.5	10.8	9.7	8.0
France	...	...	...	9.9	9.6	8.7	10.0	8.8
West Germany	...	...	...	7.3	19.3	19.8	19.9	19.0
Japan	...	...	...	3.4	6.9	11.7	14.8	18.7
United States	...	...	...	27.3	21.6	18.5	17.0	17.1

... not available
Sources: London and Cambridge Economic Service, *The British Economy, Key Statistics*, London 1970; *National Institute Economic Review*, February 1984.

Nor has the decline in Britain's external competitiveness halted. Although North Sea oil has temporarily hidden the underlying trend, a return to some form of stop-go cycle in the late 1980s appears to be a near certainty. The current boom in manufactured imports in recent years, combined with little or no real net investment at home, ensures this will occur. The limited growth in arms exports can do little to offset this trend. Indeed, by absorbing resources needed for potentially viable civilian sectors, it may make things even worse.

In addition to these indirect effects, there was, and is, the direct effect of overseas military spending. First, Britain maintained bases in the Middle and Far East for part or all of this time which were costly in foreign exchange – Suez, Aden, Singapore, Hong Kong, etc. Secondly, its forces were almost continuously engaged in 'limited' counter-insurgency conflict in the Empire, and also in occasional larger wars. Finally, as a result of the commitment in 1954 to maintain permanently a substantial peacetime force in West Germany, a considerable proportion of the British Army and Air Force is stationed in that country, adding further to foreign exchange costs.

Together, these overseas commitments have added a considerable burden to the balance of payments which has only been partially offset by the US forces stationed in Britain, defence aid from the US in the mid 1950s, and 'support costs' paid by Germany up to 1957. The claim made by Ministers to have covered the costs of Britain's forces in Germany through the 'offset arrangements' – now terminated – was misleading. Offset was only an undertaking to buy a certain amount of goods in Britain, not a direct contribution of Deutschmarks to the UK government. It may be assumed that at least some of the purchases specified as being made under this arrangement would have been made without it, and that an additional proportion merely diverted British production from other export markets.

The UK deficit on overseas military spending contrasted with the substantial surpluses of countries – such as Germany and Japan – which benefit, economically at least, from the presence of foreign troops. British spending in Germany alone, some £957 million in 1984–5, constitutes a substantial transfer from the balance of payments of a weak industrial nation to that of its main European competitor.[32] Indeed, an examination of the statistics shows that government overseas expenditure – of which military spending has been the most important component – may in itself help to explain Britain's persistent balance of payments crisis. Table 13 shows that for the period 1958–81, Britain had an accumulated commercial surplus of £16,710 million offset by a government deficit of £30,330 million. Of this, £9,790 million was the deficit in military spending overseas. Although part of the government deficit was accounted for by aid to less developed countries, Britain's record in this area was by no means exceptionally generous. It is in military spending that Britain had a particularly large deficit.

Table 13   The UK Balance of Payments, 1958–81

	'Private' balance (£m)	'Official' balance (£m)	Of which military spending (net)	Overall balance (£m)
1958	+558	−410	−143	+148
1959	+367	−479	−137	−112
1960	+76	−533	−188	−457
1961	+605	−541	−209	+64
1962	+625	−611	−231	+14
1963	+549	−661	−239	−112
1964	−66	−689	−268	−755
1965	+420	−683	−268	−263
1966	+698	−682	−282	+16
1967	+242	−646	−267	−404
1968	+266	−676	−266	−410
1969	+1,201	−972	−271	+229
1958–69	+5,541	−7,583	−2,769	−2,042
1970	+1,450	−969	−286	+481
1971	+1,945	−940	−299	+1,005
1972	+207	−844	−323	−637
1973	−432	−1,067	−375	−1,499
1974	−1,203	−1,301	−489	−2,504
1975	+93	−1,758	−549	−1,665
1976	+865	−2,087	−664	−1,222
1977	+3,164	−1,443	−753	+1,721
1978	+1,382	−3,426	−731	−2,044
1979	−554	−2,894	−850	−3,448
1980	+2,549	−2,736	−851	−187
1981	+1,703	−3,282	−851	−1,579
1970–81	+11,169	−22,747	−7,021	−11,578
1958–81	+16,710	−30,330	−9,790	−13,620

Sources: W.A.P. Manser, *Britain in Balance*, London: Penguin 1971, p.29; *Economic Trends, 1982 Supplement*, London: HMSO 1983, Tables, 128, 129, 140; *United Kingdom Balance of Payments, 1965; United Kingdom Balance of Payments, 1964*–74; United Kingdom Balance of Payments, 1982, London: HMSO (various dates).

Table 13 Continued / . . .

Notes:
1. 'Private' balance = visible trade balance + invisible balance (excluding general government) + overseas investment in UK private sector – UK private investment overseas.
2. 'Official' balance = invisible balance (general government) + overseas investment in UK public sector + net official long-term capital.
3. Military spending (net) = cost of stationing troops abroad + other military services – receipts from US forces in Britain – private expenditure by US forces in Britain.

Even after withdrawal from most extra-European commitments by the early 1970s, military spending abroad remained substantial. In 1984–5 estimated net military spending overseas is £1,369 million, which comfortably exceeded the net government contribution to the EEC (£375 million in 1984–5) over which there has been considerably more controversy.[33] As North Sea oil revenues decline, and Britain faces renewed balance of payments problems, overseas military spending is likely to become a major political issue – as it did during the 1976–7 sterling crisis.[34]

The effect of high overseas military spending on the long-run rate of growth is difficult to estimate, given the complex interrelationships between investment, exports and the stop-go cycle that are involved. Nevertheless it is clear that Britain's operational military spending abroad had a severe impact on the supply of scarce foreign exchange which reinforced that of equipment and R & D spending on industrial export potential. The defence burden must bear much of the responsibility for Britain's perennial balance of payments problems, and the consequent enforced economic slowdowns.

The costs of the world role

There is thus considerable evidence that Britain's high level of military spending since the Second World War has been an important contributory factor in its relative economic decline. As important as the direct effects of military spending, however, have been the indirect effects of a foreign policy that has consistently given preference to the attempt to retain a world role above domestic economic performance. Indeed, Samuel Brittan, in a seminal study of post-war Treasury policy, concluded that:

> the excessive 'overseas' orientation among the upper reaches of British policy-makers . . . gave priority to the maintenance of a world role the country could no longer carry . . . While British leaders rushed from capital to capital on self-appointed international peace-keeping missions, the rest of the world was more conscious of the rustle of their begging bowl, their utter dependence on the USA, their repeated humiliation by de Gaulle . . . The best that governments can do to help people recover a healthy patriotism and sense of national pride is to concentrate on the welfare of the inhabitants of these isles.[35]

This priority has been reflected in a number of ways – the commitment to sterling's reserve role, the high levels of overseas investment, the failure to join the European Community at an earlier moment, and, not least, the high level of military spending.

Sterling's reserve currency status in the post-war period was closely linked to both high military spending and high levels of overseas investment. In the heyday of the Pax Britannica, it had been a source of economic benefit to Britain. However, as the Empire began to disintegrate under pressure from both the US and the USSR, sterling increasingly became a 'Negotiated Currency', defined thus because the issuing state had to offer special inducements to its holders.[36] The inducements which Britain offered far exceeded in value any direct benefits it received from the continuing existence of sterling balances. These inducements included military commitments, economic aid and preference in overseas investment. Their purpose was primarily political, rather than economic, deriving from the state's desire to retain and enhance Britain's world role through its relationships with the Commonwealth and the US. Each type of link – membership of the Overseas Sterling Area (OSA), military spending, economic aid, and continued investment – enhanced the others in various ways. Without one of them, such as military spending, the others would have been much diminished.

Yet the burden imposed by sterling's role had been recognized, as early as 1952, by Harold Macmillan. In his memoirs he records that 'Many of us began to ask ourselves whether Great Britain could ever become a going concern again if she continued to carry the whole burden of operating a banking as well as a trading system, and shoulder all the obligations of sterling as an international currency.'[37]

The strength of the political commitment to sterling's world role, often at the expense of domestic economic policy, was perhaps most clearly reflected in Harold Wilson's obstinate refusal to devalue sterling in 1964–7, despite the widespread consensus of opinion that it was overvalued. This refusal effectively destroyed the National Plan's aspirations for economic development, and thus Labour's hopes of an industrial revival.

A particularly damaging consequence of the world role was the continuing export of capital on a massive scale. During 1946–59 the outflow of British capital amounted to £4,000 million, most of it to OSA countries.[38] This was an annual rate of £280 million, or between a quarter and a third of domestic net investment. The export of capital on this scale was actively encouraged by the government despite the long-run damage to domestic growth and its contribution in the short run to balance of payments deficits. Without a military presence to protect British overseas investment, the level of capital flow would have been considerably lower. There appears to be a clear falling off in UK investment in areas where British military withdrawal took place.[39] Thus overseas military spending not only directly hurt the current account but indirectly ensured a deterioration in the capital account.

Nor was the British military commitment confined to the maintenance of bases. Inevitably it also involved participation in a series of limited conflicts, some of which proved extremely costly, including those in Malaya in 1951–2, Kenya in the mid 1950s, Cyprus, Kuwait and East Africa. One of the most expensive conflicts was a result of an arrangement in 1957 with Malaya that it would remain in the sterling area in exchange for a continuing British military presence and other economic links. Partly as a result, anti-colonial resentment increased and Britain found itself involved in the 'confrontation' of 1963–6 which cost £260 million per annum and at its peak in 1966 involved 60,000 British service personnel.[40] This arrangement, costly though it was, only delayed the rundown in sterling reserves which Malaysia eventually undertook in the late 1960s.

The existence of large sterling balances, particularly in several Middle East countries not part of the British Empire, contributed to the illusion in the War Office that overseas military spending was not costly to the balance of payments. Once such balances were exhausted, bases were usually soon removed – as in Egypt in 1954.[41]

The continued existence of sterling balances in the 1950s and 1960s was itself one cause of UK balance of payments crises. A rundown of, say, Australian sterling reserves due to fluctuations in its exports could lead to a run on the pound in foreign exchange markets, precipitating domestic deflation in the UK quite unrelated to its own balance of trade. If the British government had negotiated an end to sterling balances at an earlier date, together with an end to related global military and political commitments, the balance of payments would have been more stable and the stop-go cycle thus more manageable.

Overseas military spending, therefore, was an essential component of a set of interrelated circumstances which resulted from a failure to adjust to the political disintegration of the British Empire and the diminished economic strength of the UK. Without it, the level of overseas investment would have been lower and the Sterling Area would have been wound up sooner – both of which could have done the domestic economy no harm.

Finally, Britain's commitment to the Empire and Commonwealth, and to a world role, meant that it was unwilling to enter the European Community in its formative years, when it could undoubtedly have played a major role in shaping its policies. When the government did decide to apply in 1962, its reluctance to abandon its Atlantic and Commonwealth links played the major role in de Gaulle's veto. Five years later, the EEC Commission's *Opinion* on Britain's second application presented by future French premier Raymond Barre, argued that:

the accession of the United Kingdom to the Community would raise economic and financial problems which will have to be examined in depth.

Experience has shown time and time again that in the United Kingdom there is a recurrent conflict – much more serious than elsewhere – between achievement of a growth rate comparable to the annual average attained . . . in most other industrialised countries, and the need to balance external payments.

. . . the difficulties [of the British economy] in fact seem to be mainly structural in origin, and stem either from defects in the distribution of productive resources . . . or from the economic, monetary and financial burdens inherited from the country's past, the Second World War and the country's international position in the postwar world.[42]

The experience of recent years has demonstrated that the British government is not yet ready to remove these inherited burdens. Indeed, as Chapter 7 will show, there has been a sustained effort to increase them.

7. The Empire strikes back: the 1980s

The Thatcher government, elected in May 1979, has broken with the consensus policies of the 1970s, and appears to be engaged in an attempt to restore Britain to its past 'greatness'. In pursuit of this objective, the most sustained peacetime increase in defence spending since 1945 has been accompanied by an increased emphasis on the independent nuclear deterrent, on the 'special relationship' with the US, and on reviving Britain's military role outside the NATO area.

Defence spending under the Conservatives

The rise in defence spending in the early 1980s is the largest since 1945, with the exception of Korean war rearmament in 1950–2. Between 1978–79 and 1985–86, defence spending in cost terms is planned to rise by 29.6 per cent, an increase of 3.8 per cent per annum.[1]

As a result, Britain has over-achieved the NATO target of 3 per cent real annual growth, and the gap between the UK military burden and that of its European allies has widened further, as Table 14 shows. In 1983, Britain is estimated to have the second largest military budget in NATO, and the fourth largest in the world.[2]

Britain's 1977 commitment to the NATO target was based on the assumption that rising revenues from the North Sea oil fields would enable the government to reach, if not surpass, the $2\frac{1}{2}$–3 per cent per annum long-term growth rate of the economy. If such an assumption had been proven correct, a 3 per cent per annum real growth in defence spending would not have led to a significant increase in the military burden. It is unlikely, however, that any Labour government would have continued with the commitment to the 3 per cent target, faced with the subsequent economic

Table 14   NATO Defence Burdens 1979–83

	1979	1980	1981	1982	1983
Belgium	3.3	3.3	3.5	3.4	3.4
Denmark	2.3	2.4	2.5	2.5	. . .
France	3.9	4.0	4.2	4.2	4.2
West Germany	3.3	3.3	3.4	3.4	3.4
Greece	6.3	5.7	7.0	7.0	7.1
Italy	2.4	2.4	2.5	2.6	2.8
Netherlands	3.2	3.1	3.2	3.2	3.3
Norway	3.1	2.9	2.9	3.0	3.1
Portugal	3.5	3.5	3.5	3.4	3.4
Turkey	4.3	4.3	4.9	5.2	4.9
NATO Europe (excl. UK)	**3.6**	**3.5**	**3.8**	**3.8**	**3.8**
UK	4.7	5.1	4.9	5.1	5.6

Source: NATO Review, No. 6, 1983, Table 11.
Notes:
1. 'Defence Burden' is defence expenditure as percentage of gross domestic product at purchasers' values.
2. 1983 figures are estimated.
3. Also see Appendix for technical discussion.

recession. The government expenditure plans of January 1979 had assumed that GDP would increase by 14.5 per cent between 1977 and 1982. In the event, GDP only rose by 3.7 per cent.[3]

It is remarkable how badly Britain performed economically during this period. In 1978 Britain was still importing a net 900,000 barrels of oil per day; today it is exporting a net 600,000 barrels per day, and is the world's fifth largest oil producer. Oil and gas has risen from 1.9 per cent of GDP in 1978 to 6.5 per cent in 1982.[4] Yet total output and profits have slumped; unemployment has more than doubled; and many manufacturing industries are on their knees. Rather than provide the resources for increased domestic investment, North Sea oil has been used to finance record levels of overseas investment,[5] higher unemployment, and a growing defence budget.

The combination of rearmament with economic recession has

meant that the proportion of national income devoted to the military has increased considerably – from 4.4 per cent in 1978–79 to 5.2 per cent in 1983–4 (see Table 15). This represents a return to the level of the late 1960s, when Britain still had considerable military commitments East of Suez. It demonstrates clearly the much higher priority given to defence by this Government compared with any of its recent Labour or Conservative predecessors.

Table 15   Defence Spending 1978–87

	1978–9	1979–80	1980–1	1981–2
£ million (cash)	7,455	9,178	11,182	12,607
As % GDP	4.4	4.5	4.8	4.9
£ million (1984–5 prices)	13,365	14,090	14,474	14,859
Change	–0.7%	+5.4%	+2.7%	+2.7%

	1982–3	1983–4	1984–5	1985–6	1986–7
£ million (cash)	14,408	15,716	17,031	18,060	18,660
As % GDP	5.1	5.2	5.2	5.2	5.1
£ million (1984–5 prices)	15,922	16,462	17,031	17,324	17,210
Change	+7.2%	+3.4%	+3.5%	+1.7%	–0.7%

Source: see Appendix.

To some extent, the economic effects of these plans have so far been concealed by the rise in North Sea oil revenues, which has enabled the government to pay for the higher defence budget without equivalent increases in taxation or borrowing. Nevertheless it has still found it necessary to accompany the 27 per cent increase in defence spending with cuts of 6 per cent in education spending, 61 per cent in housing and 14 per cent in overseas aid (as Table 16 shows). And the historical relationship between defence spending and investment still appears to hold good. As happened time and again during the 'stop-go' cycle in the 1950s and 1960s, public capital spending has been cut more than current spending. While defence spending rose 27 per cent, and other current spending rose 9 per cent, between 1978–9 and 1984–5, government capital spending fell by over 23 per cent in the same period.[6]

Table 16 Public expenditures in cost terms by programme 1978/9–1984/5

	1978/9 (£m)	1984/5 (£m)	Change (£m)	% Change
Defence	12,183	15,448	+3,265	+26.8%
Social Security	26,713	33,747	+7,034	+26.3%
Health and Personal Social Services	12,067	13,987	+1,920	+15.9%
Education and Science	12,602	11,839	−763	−6.1%
Scotland, Wales and Northern Ireland	11,917	12,227	+310	+2.6%
Industry, energy, trade and employment	6,486	5,088	−1,398	−21.6%
Law, order and protective services	3,306	4,446	+1,140	+34.5%
Transport	4,342	3,966	−376	−8.7%
Other environmental services	3,611	3,130	−481	−13.3%
Housing	5,803	2,264	−3,539	−61.0%
Agriculture, Fisheries, Food and Forestry	1,320	1,857	+537	+40.7%
Overseas Aid	1,162	997	−165	−14.2%
EEC net contribution	1,220	340	−880	−72.1%
Other spending	4,124	3,902	−222	−5.4%
Adjustments	—	1,370	+1,370	
Planning total	**106,857**	**114,606**	**+7,949**	**+7.2%**

Source: Cmnd 9143–1, Table 1–14, HMSO.
Note: 1982/83 prices.

The cost of higher defence spending has thus been lower investment in public services, in building, and in manufacturing, rather than greater restraints on current consumption. If defence spending had been held at its 1978–9 level in real terms, an extra £3,300 million would have been available in 1984–5 for other uses. The increase in the defence budget over the last years would, if used elsewhere, have been sufficient (in theory at least) to restore all the cuts in government capital spending. Alternatively it could have been used to quadruple the overseas aid budget, or to finance an 85 per cent increase in child benefits.[7] For those who are unconvinced of the case for the size of the present defence budget, the argument that 'there is no money' for productive and socially useful purposes is clearly fallacious.

Moreover, military spending continues to have a disproportionate effect on the economy as a result of its intensive use of key scientific and technical resources. Despite continued shortages of skilled personnel in high technology industries, a growing proportion of the defence budget is being devoted to research, development and procurement. Of total R & D (private and public) 28.0 per cent is now spent on defence, a greater proportion than in any of Britain's main European allies.[8]

Yet there has been little 'spin-off' from military technology. Despite the increasing sophistication of British defence products, civilian products continue to lose out in international competition. The results are only too clear in declining industries such as vehicles and steel. But they are as important for the growing sectors such as telecommunications and consumer electronics. It is not entirely coincidental that the nation that spends less than one per cent of its national income, and only 2.3 per cent of government R & D funds, on defence – Japan – is overtaking the United States and Europe in a growing list of high-technology products.[9]

The military-industrial sector continues to be protected from international competition, with the government insisting on a 'Buy British' policy for the armed forces. The determination to retain self-sufficiency in arms manufacture is in clear contrast to the relative lack of effort in other industries – such as telecommunications, steel or civilian electronics – which some would consider to be equally 'strategic'.

Finally, it is interesting to contrast the continual controversy over the contribution to the European Economic Community (£500 million net in 1983–4) [10] with the lack of debate over the foreign exchange cost of the forces kept in West Germany. In 1984–5 the net cost in foreign exchange of military spending overseas was £1,369 million, of which £957 million was local defence spending in the Federal Republic of Germany (FRG).[11] A continuing transfer of this magnitude from the UK to the FRG's balance of payments is bound to further weaken the British economy.

Restoration or fall?

The increase in defence spending in the early 1980s has been accompanied by clear shifts in foreign and defence policy. The reluctant retreat from world power status of the previous decades has been halted and there has been a cautious reassertion of the principles on which defence policy was based in the 1950s and early 1960s. The process of withdrawal from a global role has been halted, and a new emphasis put on 'out-of-area' capabilities. Government now appears to place greater importance on the 'independence' of Britain's strategic nuclear force, rather than its role as a 'contribution to NATO'. And Mrs Thatcher's strident anti-Soviet rhetoric has contributed to a revitalization of the Anglo-American 'special relationship'. We now examine each of these shifts in turn.

East of Suez revisited

The first of these changes in the emphasis of defence policy is perhaps the most surprising. In the late 1960s the government renounced its 'special capability' for intervention outside Europe, and the Conservatives made little effort to revive it in 1970–4. Though Britain still possessed a considerable general capability for intervention, particularly in the Navy, the emphasis in official statements throughout the 1970s was on NATO roles. Since 1979, however, the new government has ordered the reconstruction of a specialist capability for independent intervention outside Europe, and has made clear its renewed willingness to help the US in world policing 'responsibilities'.[12] It has justified this new departure in policy by arguing that, although the Soviet threat in the Third World is less severe in its direct effect on British security, the likelihood of a conflict there is much greater. And supposed Soviet 'gains' – such as in Angola, Vietnam, and Afghanistan – need to be countered, it is argued, by increased Western military deployment and, if necessary, intervention.[13]

This argument is similar to that used in the early 1960s to justify an increased emphasis on East of Suez commitments at the expense of NATO. And, as at that time, the progress of the Soviet Union in the Third World is a secondary consideration in deciding its popularity. It has more to do with the resurgence of support for an imperial role in the political establishment and the concern, particularly in the Navy, for the preservation of its surface fleet. The experience of Empire, it is argued, gives Britain a special right (and duty!) to intervene in the affairs of less developed nations in order to protect Western interests. In the words of the 1981 Defence White Paper,

> it [is] increasingly necessary for NATO members to look to Western security concerns over a wider field than before, and not to assume that these concerns can be limited by the boundaries of the Treaty area. Britain's own needs, outlook and interest give her a special role and a special duty in efforts of this kind.[14]

The unwillingness of political and military leaders to accept the end of Empire was considerably strengthened by the 1982 Falklands War. Not only did it demonstrate the 'need' for a Royal Navy capable of intervening far from home. It also showed very clearly the considerable capability that Britain already possessed. A force of 28,000 men and over 100 ships – including most of the Royal Navy's most modern vessels – was able to move 8000 miles and successfully defeat a reasonably strong Third World military power.[15] The ability to project power in this way could clearly be useful in interventions against unfriendly regimes elsewhere in the less developed world.

Certain forces have already been earmarked specifically for out-of-area commitments. One Army brigade of 5,000 men has been equipped as a small-scale rapid-deployment force, prepared to fly at short notice to troublespots around the world.[16] The RAF is purchasing new Tristar tanker aircraft and modernizing its long-range Hercules transport aircraft in what could be the first stage in the restoration of the force level that was run down with withdrawal from East of Suez.[17] And the government has made clear that it intends to make particular use of the new 'Invincible' carriers in out-of-area deployments.[18]

Perhaps the main symbol of the new policy, however, has been the increased naval deployment outside NATO waters. Since the start of the Iran-Iraq war in 1980, a patrol of two warships has been maintained in the Indian Ocean, ready to intervene, in support of the US Navy, if Western oil supplies or friendly regimes appear to be threatened. [19] During 1983, as the Lebanon crisis continued, a naval task force more powerful than that sent to the Falklands took part in Exercise 'Display Determination' in the Eastern Mediterranean.[20] Increasingly it appears that a large proportion, sometimes more than half, of Britain's major surface ships can be deployed on such exercises without serious consequences for NATO defences.[21] With several other ships tied up on permanent duties in the South Atlantic, Caribbean and Indian Ocean, Britain's North Atlantic defences now often consist mainly of submarines, patrol aircraft and smaller surface vessels.[22] The Navy's surface fleet is seeking to regain its traditional role of asserting British power throughout the world. The government's expansive view was summarized by John Stanley, Minister of State for the Armed Forces:

> There is no doubt at all that worldwide – and particularly perhaps in the Caribbean, Africa, the Gulf and as we are seeing right now with our current task force deployment to the Indian Ocean, South Pacific and the Far East – the visible presence of a Royal Navy ship serves . . . British interests very well.[23]

NATO has expressed relatively little concern at the dispersal of the British fleet throughout the globe, despite the fact that Britain contributes 70 per cent of NATO's maritime forces in the Eastern Atlantic. For NATO maritime defences now depend increasingly on submarines and land-based aircraft. Large surface ships are extremely vulnerable to attack by cheap, but effective, guided missiles. For defence against a sophisticated opponent their presence is of doubtful military value. The next Battle of the Atlantic, if there is one, will be won or lost under the ocean.

Moreover, the US (and to a lesser extent other NATO members) support Britain's renewed enthusiasm for an imperial role. The Americans are putting enormous resources into their own interventionary forces, with plans for a 600-ship navy and a powerful Rapid Deployment Force.[24] They welcome the political benefits that possible British help in Third World conflicts would bring – provided, as before, that it is support rather than advice which is offered. The US bitterly regretted Britain's refusal to send troops to Vietnam in the 1960s. The new British interest in threats to Western interests 'out-of-area' may promise a more receptive response next time around.

The return to an imperial role clearly has dangers for the Navy. Were a future government ever to feel that an out-of-area role was neither necessary nor desirable, the surface fleet could be pruned drastically without significantly affecting NATO's Atlantic defences. The Navy would be unlikely to survive the second retreat from East of Suez as well as the first. Its leaders probably feel, however, that they have no alternative. As John Nott's 1981 cuts made clear, the surface fleet has a limited future in a Europe-only role. [25] Much more than the other two services, the Royal Navy's future is bound up with Britain's world role, just as it was the instrument of its imperial might in the past.

The holocaust factor

In addition to reviving the world policing role, the Conservative government has also focused increased attention on the other symbol of Britain's Great Power status – its strategic nuclear force. Although operationally independent, governments since 1964 have publicly described it as simply a 'contribution to NATO'. Even the 1970–4 Conservative administration did not depart from this formula. It may seem ironical that Mrs Thatcher's government has proved much more open on its nuclear weapons programme than previous Labour governments.[26] Yet it is a direct consequence of the greater importance which it attaches to the political and military value of the independent British 'deterrent'.

For, in contrast to the tepid justifications of the past, the government now proclaims that the independent nuclear force is one of the 'main pillars' of its defence programme,[27] and it has devoted considerable effort to win approval for its decision to order the Trident system as a replacement for Polaris/Chevaline in the mid 1990s. The decision to opt for the most sophisticated, and powerful, system available – and reject options such as cruise missiles – is itself an indication of the priority given to the nuclear force. It has similarities with the increased emphasis put in the 1957 White Paper on the 'independent deterrent'. Then, as now, it has been used to show that Britain is still a major military power despite its economic difficulties. Moreover, the government is keen to stress, as in 1957, that spending on Britain's own nuclear weapons is more likely to deter a Soviet invasion of Western Europe than an equivalent amount spent on strengthening conventional forces in Germany.[28]

Yet this proposition depends on the assumption that British nuclear weapons could conceivably be used, not only to retaliate against an all-out nuclear attack, but also as a response to a Soviet conventional attack on Western Europe. And it assumes that there are circumstances where the British could use nuclear weapons while the Americans hesitated. The insanity of these conceptions is not diminished by the probability that British attacks on major targets within the Soviet Union would trigger strikes by the two superpowers, both on each other and on Britain. The use of the independent nuclear force would bring about not only the destruction of the British Isles and the Soviet Union, but possibly the extinction of the human species itself. Such a capability can have no rational military purpose.

However, in the world in which we live, this is not necessarily an obstacle to the purchase of new, considerably more powerful, weapon systems, such as Trident. Rather, it appears, an ability to destroy the world enables Britain's leaders to believe that it is still a world power. In their eyes at least, the possession of nuclear weapons keeps Britain a notch above more prosperous states such as Germany and Japan, and on a par with its traditional rival, France. Though increasing numbers of ex-colonial states in the underdeveloped world will acquire nuclear weapons over the next couple of decades, they are unlikely to acquire a capability which rivals Britain's Trident system in its destructiveness. The nuclear symbol of Britain's world status will thus be secure from rivals for many years to come, providing comfort for leaders faced with the intractable and dull problems of continuing economic decline.

The Auld Alliance

Ever since the Second World War Britain has depended on its alliance with the US to maintain the status of a major power. In the 1980s, even more than in the 1950s, Britain's renewed enthusiasm for a world role depends largely on American support. And that support depends, in turn, on its acceptance of American leadership in the Western world.

Britain's renewed military interest outside Europe – after a hiatus in the 1970s – has paralleled a similar development in the US. There, the trauma of defeat by the Vietnamese led to a period of relative restraint in defence spending and reduced willingness of Congress to sanction intervention in the Third World. From 1978 onwards, however, this restraint gave way to a more belligerent attitude, helping Ronald Reagan to gain election in 1980 on a militantly anti-Soviet platform.[29] In the massive defence budget increases that have followed, particular priority has been given to Third World 'power projection' forces. Sizeable US-based forces have been reallocated from their previous NATO role to the Rapid Deployment Force set up to strengthen US military power in the Gulf.[30] A further increase in the US's aircraft carrier fleet has been ordered, and it has made it clear that, in response to developments in Iran and Afghanistan, US military priorities have shifted away from Europe.

In planning for future military interventions, however, the Americans are anxious not to repeat the experience in Vietnam where, in their view, they received no help from European allies. They will welcome even the symbolic presence of these countries as a way of legitimizing their 'peacekeeping' role – as it did in 1983 in Lebanon. This US requirement neatly complements British wishes for a renewed role in world 'peacekeeping'; a role which, without US support, would be impossible to sustain.

Similar advantages are evident in the nuclear field. Although much information is classified, it is clear that for Britain to have remained a significant nuclear weapons state without American help would have incurred much higher expense than it does at present – as France knows to its cost. The Trident agreement between the two countries supplies Britain with the most advanced missile technology currently available at a development cost of virtually zero.[31] These, together with what appears to be close co-operation in deployment of missile submarines, are clear signs of the uniqueness of the relationship between the two states. The continuing willingness of the US to grant the British certain privileges over other allies has been reciprocated by the latter's uncritical support of American intransigence in arms talks with the USSR, even when other European governments have been urging a more conciliatory position.

The emphasis on the Anglo-American alliance has also fitted in well with Mrs Thatcher's populist politics. Greater attention has been given to the military confrontation with the Soviets than by any government since the 1950s. Like Reagan, Mrs Thatcher has used the supposed worldwide Soviet threat to build a right-wing domestic political consensus. The new government has proved more sympathetic to the American concern to reassert its global superiority than to Germany's obvious wish to isolate Europe from the New Cold War and preserve some of the advantages of detente. And there has been a noticeable distancing of Britain from Western Europe, particularly in 1980 in the response to the Iranian and Afghanistan crises. Though, on other issues, it has sided with the other European powers, it is clear that the 'special relationship' continues to be a major factor in Britain's foreign policy.

The crisis which perhaps most clearly illustrated the dependence of Britain's neo-imperial aspirations upon the special relationship, however, was the Falklands War. It is now clear that the US provided Britain with considerable assistance throughout the conflict. The provision of millions of gallons of aviation fuel, Sidewinder AIM-9L missiles for Britain's Harriers, and, perhaps most important, accurate intelligence on Argentine movements and plans, all helped British forces.[32] Even the order to the submarine *HMS Conqueror* to sink the *General Belgrano* was probably communicated via a US military satellite. And, according to one US report, the US Defense Secretary Mr Weinberger offered to replace either of Britain's carriers, *Hermes* and *Invincible*, with a US-supplied ship, should one be sunk by Argentina.[33] Despite the dispatch of most of its fleet to the South Atlantic, Britain, it appears, could not have won the war without American help.

Continuing strains

Despite the substantial increases in defence spending in the early 1980s, however, there have been continuing strains in the defence budget. Additional funds have been needed simply to restore the temporary economies – in personnel, training, fuel, maintenance, and so on – made under Labour. The 1979 Armed Forces pay award of 33 per cent, for example, announced immediately after the Conservatives' election victory, was no more than was needed to restore salaries to comparable civilian rates.[34] It was clearly senseless to spend large amounts over several years training servicemen to operate sophisticated equipment, and then have them leave at the first opportunity, or take 'moonlighting' jobs.

In fact, the trend in equipment spending under the Conservatives has been little different from under Labour. In the first six years of Conservative rule (1978/9–1984/5), equipment costs have risen by 6.5 per cent annually compared with a 6.4 per cent annual increase in four years under Labour (1974/5–1978/9), reflecting the unwillingness of both parties to consider cancellations of major weapons projects. It is in other spending – on personnel, buildings and stores – that an explanation of the recent increase in total defence costs must be found. Under the Conservatives, non-equipment costs have risen by over 2 per cent annually compared with a fall of over 3 per cent annually under Labour. A relatively modest rise, considering the problems inherited from the previous government, but enough to increase the total defence bill by 27 per cent compared with less than 1 per cent in Labour's four years (see Table 17).

Even with real growth of over 3 per cent per year in the funds available for defence, however, the Conservatives have found difficulties in financing the ambitious programme that they inherited. In August 1980, Francis Pym, the then Defence Secretary, was compelled to announce a temporary moratorium on defence contracts to bring his budget within the 3 per cent target.[35] This was followed by the appointment of John Nott as Mr Pym's successor, with a brief to bring the budget under control. The new defence review that followed in June 1981, in order to make room in future budgets for Trident costs, announced major cuts in the surface fleet.[36] In a reversal of Labour's policy, Mr Nott questioned the necessity for a large fleet of sophisticated frigates,

Table 17 Defence Equipment Spending 1974–84

£m (1984–5 prices)

	Equipment Spending	Non-equipment Spending	Total
1974/5	4,167	9,160	13,327
1978/9	5,346	8,019	13,365
1984/5	7,796	9,235	17,031
Annual % change 1974/5 to 1978/9	+6.4%	–3.5%	+0.1%
Annual % change 1978/9 to 1984/5	+6.5%	+2.4%	+4.1%

Source: Annual Abstract of Statistics 1984, Table 7.2, HMSO; *Statement on the Defence Estimates 1984 Volume II,* Table 2.1, HMSO.

destroyers, and carriers in the North Atlantic. For NATO maritime defence, he argued, a smaller fleet, acting along with submarines and land-based aircraft, would suffice. Accordingly, he announced that the first of the new carriers, HMS *Invincible*, would be sold to Australia only a couple of years after entering the Royal Navy, the old carrier HMS *Hermes* (recently refitted to carry Harriers) would be scrapped, and the two assault ships *Fearless* and *Intrepid*, ideal for operations outside the NATO area, would also have to go. Most significantly he announced that the number of frigates and destroyers would be cut from 59 to 42, with 8 ships held in reserve. Plans to order more of the sophisticated new ships, and to modernize existing ones, were abandoned. Instead, it was decided to introduce a new ship, the Type 23, at a much lower cost than the ships it would replace, and with correspondingly reduced capabilities.

These cuts brought a furious reaction from the Navy lobby. The Minister for the Navy, Keith Speed, resigned in protest; and a major campaign took place in an attempt to convince government that the Senior Service remained essential for Britain's 'worldwide' interests.

Less than a year after the Nott review, however, the Falklands war came to the Navy's rescue. The war could not have been won without the two carriers *Hermes* and *Invincible*, which Nott had intended to scrap or sell. It was thus a perfect 'demonstration' of the continuing value of a sophisticated surface fleet able to operate outside the NATO area. As a result, therefore, an extra £1,000 million was earmarked for naval equipment programmes.[37] And a further £215 million was to be spent on a new Falklands military airport, which could be used as an important staging post for 'power projection' in the future.[38] John Nott was obliged, in recognition of the Navy's success, to reverse most of the 1981 cuts. The planned sale of *Invincible* was cancelled, as was the scrapping of the assault ships *Fearless* and *Intrepid*. Four Type 22 ships were to replace the ships lost in battle, rather than the Type 23s, which had been intended as a cheaper replacement. The number of frigates and destroyers would be kept at 55, at least for the time being, and existing ships fitted with a range of new weapons systems. Despite his view that Britain 'simply cannot afford yet another peripheral defence commitment', Nott was obliged to give way to the pressure generated by the war.[39]

Over and above the bonus from the Falklands war, a further development in 1982 gave the government a temporary breather in tackling the problem of rising defence costs. The 1982 decision to switch from the C4 to the D5 missile meant that total expenditure on the Trident programme would increase to £7,500 million on government estimates. It also meant, however, that spending on the project was delayed, with much less being spent in the early part of the 1980s than originally intended. Indeed John Nott conceded, shortly after the announcement, that: 'It eases the problem of the defence budget in the next two or three years, and very significantly so.'[40] By postponing this expenditure, however, the government has only postponed the budgetary crunch into the mid and late 1980s, when Trident costs are likely to be a heavy burden for the defence budget as a whole.

Prospects and problems

Indeed it now appears that the government will face increasing difficulties in financing its defence policy in the late 1980s. The new emphases in defence policy, so far relatively inexpensive, may now prove to be a growing burden. The Trident project has involved little expenditure up to 1984, but over the next three to four years that will change rapidly. Even if the increased emphasis on out-of-area operations as a result of the Falklands War does not drag Britain into further conflict, the service pressures for increased funding for interventionary forces will increase. And, finally, there are the costs of retaining a special relationship with the United States. The Americans will add their weight to those within Britain who support an increased out-of-area involvement. If the US continues to increase its own defence budget by up to 10 per cent each year, it is likely to insist that Britain also makes some attempt to follow suit. Britain may feel it needs to respond to this demand – as it did in 1950–2 – in order to prevent the US 'losing interest' in Europe and moving towards a policy of 'global unilateralism'. In particular, there is likely to be growing pressure for the UK and other NATO countries to increase the amount spent on 'emerging technologies' which, it is now claimed, could reduce NATO's reliance on nuclear weapons.[41]

Were the United States military build-up to continue into the later 1980s, however, as the present Administration plans, there may also be an acceleration of Soviet defence spending. According to the CIA, the total Soviet military budget has been growing by only 2 per cent per annum in real terms since 1976 or 1977; and procurement of new weapons, it appears, has shown no increase at all.[42] If the present level of world tension persists or increases, the Soviet leadership could decide to allocate more resources to arms production in an effort to keep up with NATO. This would allow them to increase production of modern weapons systems, which in turn would add to pressures in Britain and elsewhere for further military funds.

Moreover, pressure for growth in spending in the late 1980s is also likely to come from the escalation in the real cost of defence equipment. The Ministry of Defence has estimated that equipment unit costs increase at an annual rate, over and above inflation, of between 6 per cent and 10 per cent.[43] As new technologies are devised, there will be military and industrial pressure to add them to new weapon systems and cost escalation will continue. Between 1974–5 and 1984–5, as Table 17 shows, equipment spending has risen by 87 per cent, after allowing for general inflation. Yet, despite this increase, the number of major surface ships has fallen from 78 to 64, the number of RAF combat aircraft has only risen from 500 to 620, and the number of medium battle tanks has risen from 900 to 970.[44] As each new generation of weapons system is given the latest sophisticated technology, its cost is bound to continue to exceed that of the system it replaces.

There may need to be a further allowance made for the 'relative price effect' (RPE) – that is the extent to which defence costs (after allowing for changes in quality) rise at a rate faster than prices over the whole economy. Current defence spending plans appear to assume a future RPE of zero. Yet in 1968–79, the average RPE was 2.23 per cent; and in the last five financial years defence costs have risen at 0.8 per cent per annum faster than the national income price index (the 'GDP deflator').[45] Some part of this increase may be due to technological improvements in weapons systems which are not fully picked up as 'quality' changes, and thus appear as cost growth. But part may also be due to the relative inefficiency of the defence industry as a result of its protection from international competition. Unlike civilian industries such as steel and cars, the monopoly suppliers of defence equipment for the Ministry of Defence (MoD) do not have the same pressure to increase productivity in order to survive. The efficiency of naval procurement, in particular, appears to suffer from a cosy relationship between contractors and purchasers which they have little incentive to disturb. Recent moves towards more cost-effective procurement procedures – announced in the 1984 Defence White Paper – may alleviate this problem to some extent.[46] However, it is unlikely to disappear while the government remains committed to buying British arms, irrespective of whether they are competitive with foreign alternatives.

With this continuing cost escalation, the defence budget is certain to come under growing strain. For rising costs for each unit of equipment (per plane, ship, tank, missile) reduces the number that can be bought within a given budget. And, no matter how sophisticated individual weapons are, numbers will remain crucial in military operations. The government will be obliged to make substantial cuts in planned commitments or accept a further increase in defence spending.

When the oil runs out

During the last five years, state oil revenues have been used to finance an increase in the proportion of national income taken by public spending from $40\frac{1}{2}$ per cent in 1978–9 to 43 per cent in 1983–4, thus sheltering government from the full impact of recession.[47] These additional funds have been used to pay for the two million increase in unemployment, and for the increase in defence spending. A financial bonus of this magnitude, however, will not be available to pay for further increases in public spending in the late 1980s. Although 1984 and 1985 are likely to see a modest rise in national output, economic decline is more likely to accelerate than diminish thereafter. After 1986, it has been estimated, state oil revenues will fall by £1,000 million each year until 1990, and by a further £6,000 million by 2000.[48] Moreover, if the oil price does not keep pace with inflation, as is probable if the world economy continues to be depressed, then tax revenue from North Sea oil could plunge even more dramatically. Any increases in defence – or other – public spending will have to be financed out of increases in non-oil taxation or borrowing *over and above* that necessary to offset the loss in oil revenues.

Indeed growing pressure for curbs on defence spending in the late 1980s is already apparent. In 1983 the Ministry of Defence suffered a serious setback in the annual round of discussions on public spending. The Treasury had argued that, were national output to continue its slow growth, there would be a major problem in financing public spending in the late 1980s necessitating politically unacceptable increases in taxes or in borrowing. The main cause of this hypothetical crisis – and a clue to its bureaucratic significance – was the Treasury's generous assumption that defence spending would grow at 3 per cent annually in 'real' terms, *plus* an allowance of 2 per cent annually for the 'relative price effect'.[49]

Large increases in taxation are an unpalatable prospect for any government seeking re-election and would be particularly undesirable for the present administration. Chancellor Nigel Lawson has therefore been able to use the possibility of a public spending crisis in the late 1980s to obtain two major concessions from the MoD. First, no allowance is to be made for the increase in defence costs above the general inflation rate. Any increases that do take place in future will have to be financed out of real defence spending. Secondly, Michael Heseltine has agreed that the 3 per cent commitment cannot be continued after 1985–6, and for 1986–7 has accepted that there will be no real growth in his budget.[50] Taken together, these two concessions, if implemented, will result in a marked slowdown in the growth of defence spending. Yet they may only be the start. If the economy falters and unemployment rises, or the balance of payments goes into deficit again, there is likely to be Treasury pressure for further cuts. Given increased military commitments and continued escalation in equipment costs, the defence budget faces a severe financial squeeze in the late 1980s.

Choices to be made

If this squeeze does take place, the old dilemmas of British defence policy are likely to resurface with renewed rigour. As in successive defence 'reviews', the government will need to look again at the possibilities for savings in one or more of its main military commitments. Two commitments in particular are likely to come under intense scrutiny – the Trident strategic nuclear programme and the maintenance of a garrison on the Falkland Islands. Both are national rather than NATO commitments, linked closely with the attempt to regain Britain's past independent status despite its continuing economic decline. As such, they are vulnerable to criticism from those who place an overriding priority on commitments to Western European defence.

In the late 1980s an increasing proportion of the defence budget will be devoted to these two commitments. By 1988–9 annual outlays on Trident will reach over £1,000 million at today's prices – 6–8 per cent of the total defence budget – and remain at about that level for seven years.[51] Fortress Falklands will also be absorbing a considerable sum if present plans continue. During 1983–4 Falklands-related defence spending will, on government estimates, reach £900 million – 50 per cent more than that spent on air defence (£570 million) and over half the level of expenditure on the British Army in Germany (£1700 million).[52] Even after equipment lost in the conflict is replaced and major capital projects are completed, the garrison is likely to cost at least £400–£450 million annually to maintain.[53] Were another defence review necessary, the government will face strong pressure from NATO allies to look to these national commitments for the greatest savings.

Trident is likely to be a prime candidate for cancellation. The quoted cost of £8,700 million (at 1983–4 prices) could prove a gross underestimate, given the inflation often associated with such advanced and unproven technologies. Moreover, this official estimate excludes a number of related items – such as improved communications and support facilities – necessary for the programme; and it makes no allowance for future running costs. According to Anthony Cordesman, writing in *Armed Forces Journal International*:

> The true life cycle cost of the entire Trident force . . . from the mid 1980s – when major investment must begin – to the year 2000, will almost certainly be well in excess of 50 billion in 1983–84 pounds.[54]

Were such an estimate to be correct, Britain would be required to spend about 20 per cent of its defence budget on Trident over a period of 15 years, about the same amount as France expects to pay for its independent nuclear force. The British government has always excluded many items from its estimates of the cost of nuclear forces. It is plausible to believe that, once these items are included, Cordesman's estimate may prove nearer the truth than the official figure.

However, a Conservative government is unlikely to cancel Trident without ordering an alternative, lower-cost, replacement for the ageing Polaris submarines. Most of the alternative systems being discussed centre around the cruise missile, based either on submarines or aboard aircraft. Estimates of the capital cost of such a programme range from £2,500 million to £6,250 million at 1983 prices[55] – excluding, as does the official Trident estimate, some procurement items and all running costs. Such a force would be cheaper than Trident. However, given the continuing development of Soviet air defences, a cruise missile force might need to be updated in the 1990s, reducing further the savings from, and thereby the political incentives for, Trident cancellation.

The 'Fortress Falklands' commitment is a second possible target for spending cuts. The strains which it will impose on the defence budget in the late 1980s are considerable. First, on MoD estimates, an additional £175–200 million will be needed annually to maintain the garrison and supporting shipping in the later 1980s.[56] Secondly, some of the armed forces in theory committed to NATO will be stationed in the South Atlantic with a consequent reduction in their availability for a European crisis. Attributing their costs while on garrison duty in the South Atlantic theatre would add upwards of £200 million annually to the bill.[57] Thirdly, further long-term costs will be incurred by more rapid wear and tear, resulting in shortened lives for equipment such as the nuclear fleet submarines. Even if there is no second Falklands war, these three factors ensure that the annual cost of the garrison in the late 1980s is unlikely to be less than £400–450 million per annum. Nor can a second conflict be ruled out. If Mrs Thatcher refuses to negotiate with the new civilian regime in Argentina, her chance may be lost. Faced with domestic political problems, it is plausible that a future Argentine regime – civilian or military – may again revert to military adventure. The costs of a second Falklands war could dwarf those of the first in both human and financial terms.

Because of these factors, there is already substantial pressure on the Government to change its 'Fortress Falklands' policy. The Conservative-controlled Defence Committee of the House of Commons, in a coded criticism of government priorities, commented in 1983:

> Had the decision as to the future position of the Islands rested with us, we would have had the difficult task of reconciling the vast sums of money to be spent there with the restraints on expenditure applied elsewhere within the defence budget to meet equally important political obligations.[58]

Were a Falklands settlement reached, there would be substantial resources released for use elsewhere, particularly if it led to lower priority being given to 'out-of-area' forces as a whole. Such a policy would allow the government to renew John Nott's 1981 plans for reducing the surface fleet and leaving maritime defence in the North Atlantic mainly to a combination of attack submarines and landbased air power.

Were economies to be concentrated on strategic nuclear and out-of-area capabilities, it would resume the historic trend towards withdrawal from a global role. It would demonstrate an acceptance of Britain's status as a medium-rank European state and indicate a willingness to forgo the military prerogatives of a Great Power. At the same time it would allow Britain to retain its current strength in Germany, and thus avoid the political problems that a cut in the British Army on the Rhine would involve.

However, such a course would encounter strong resistance from those who favour a more nationalist foreign and defence policy. And, as the Falklands war demonstrated, the domestic political dividends from such a policy can be considerable. Its advocates argue that defence policy can, and should, be used to raise national prestige at home and abroad. In France, external policy has enjoyed a remarkable political consensus by its emphasis on grandeur and national independence. Given the emotional pull of Empire, a neo-Gaullist British defence policy could also, it is believed, have favourable political benefits.

A renewed emphasis on national power and glory as a means of creating national consensus might have considerable appeal to Mrs Thatcher, well aware of the electoral bonus from her 'resolute approach' during the Falklands crisis. It may also accord with her personal dedication to renewing Victorian ideals, clearly expressed in her speech at Cheltenham in July 1982:

> When we started out there were the waverers and the
> fainthearts . . . Those who believed that our decline was
> irreversible . . . that Britain was no longer the nation that
> had built an Empire and ruled a quarter of the world. Well
> they were wrong. The lesson of the Falklands is that Britain
> has not changed and that this nation still has those sterling
> qualities which shine through our history.[59]

A nationalist approach to defence priorities would tend to favour both the continuation of the Trident programme and an unyielding position over the Falklands. Possible financial benefits from ending these commitments would be outweighed by the potential political costs.

Quite apart from the domestic political difficulties involved, cancelling Trident would almost certainly invite unfavourable comparisons between the UK and France – a factor which should not be underestimated. Britain would be placed in what some would perceive as the humiliating position of having a strategic nuclear force which was demonstrably 'inferior' to that of its

European partner and historic rival. With strategic cruise missiles Britain's ability to 'stand alone' in a crisis might be questioned; and its capability to unilaterally 'trigger' a worldwide nuclear conflict would be seen to be considerably less than that of France's rapidly expanding ballistic missile submarine fleet.

At the same time a military withdrawal from the Falklands would require some form of political settlement. Whatever form it took, such a settlement would be bound to involve substantial concessions to Argentina on the question of sovereignty. It is difficult to see such concessions being made while Mrs Thatcher remains Premier.

Were the government determined to continue with both the Trident programme and with the Falklands garrison, it would create grave problems for the defence budget. With little or no growth in the resources available for defence after 1985-6, a cutback in other commitments would be required. The argument on the relative merits of other commitments would be conducted in an atmosphere of intense inter-service rivalry.

The Navy Lobby would start in a strong position as a result of the Falklands conflict and the consequent naval re-equipment announced in *The Falklands: The Lessons*. The retention of three carriers and the purchase of additional Type 22 frigates indicates that the Admiralty has, for the moment at least, won the argument for having the most sophisticated – and expensive – ships available. In addition, the Falklands commitment will strengthen the Navy's hand further in arguing for a new 'division of labour' within NATO – in which Britain would concentrate more resources on its maritime forces and on out-of-area intervention. Such a line of reasoning would find favour, not only within important sections of the Tory Party, but also from notable figures on the Opposition benches. Labour defence spokesman John Silkin and former Prime Minister James Callaghan are amongst the ex-naval officers calling for a cut in the continental commitment. As Silkin has argued:

> We need a surface fleet to fulfil our obligations to Third World nations who look to Britain, rather than the USA or the Soviet Union, for protection.[60]

Moreover, the political tide, at present, is running in favour of strengthening Britain's capability for military operations outside

Europe. Admiral of the Fleet Lord Hill Norton, recently Chief of Defence Staff, has argued, for example, that defence policy must re-establish 'our autonomy as a medium power' by giving top priority to Trident, defence of Britain itself and to global intervention forces. The increased resources needed for these commitments could, he argued, come from reducing the size of the air and land forces based in Germany since, in his view, 'all the circumstances have dramatically changed since our unnatural commitment to maintain large standing forces in Europe was undertaken.'[61].

Army supporters are likely to react angrily to such suggestions.[62] They will point out that circumstances have changed since the days of the Empire. Britain's defence is now inseparable from that of Western Europe as a whole. A reduction in UK forces in Germany would be seen as an attempt to sever this linkage and could have severe political consequences, particularly if it led to moves by the US in the same directions. Moreover, such a plea is unlikely to be sympathetically received if Britain is simultaneously spending a growing proportion of its defence budget on Fortress Falklands and Trident. On current estimates, these two commitments could cost £1,500–£1,600 million annually (at 1982–3 prices) by the end of the decade – as much as the £1,512 million budgeted for BAOR itself in 1982–3.[63] Britain could be invited, none too politely, to put its commitments to NATO before its illusions of imperial grandeur.

Rising defence costs will force the government to increase spending further in the late 1980s or review its existing military commitments. Yet, with sustained economic growth unlikely, further rapid growth in the defence budget will become increasingly popular. The government will then have to decide where its priorities lie. It will not find a decision easy. Strong political factors will make cuts to Trident and the Falklands unpopular for a Conservative government. Yet cuts in European commitments pose equally severe problems for external policy. The most probable course of action, perhaps, may be a resort to short-term economies, similar to those Labour implemented in 1975–9. Such a course would be likely to lead to severe reductions in the operational efficiency of the armed forces. The Conservatives, nevertheless, may find the hope of postponing difficult decisions until after the General Election (due by 1988) irresistible.

8. Paying for a real defence

However the Conservative government chooses to respond to the dilemmas described above it is unlikely to actually reduce the level of military spending in the late 1980s. The changes it makes will probably be 'course adjustments' rather than radical departures; and if the latter do occur, they are likely to lead to more military commitments rather than fewer. Military spending, therefore, will continue to be a substantial, and probably growing, burden on Britain's ailing economy.

The growth in arms spending, however, does not only constitute an economic problem. It also increases the risks of nuclear war and exacerbates underdevelopment and conflict in the Third World. The intense rivalry between West and East is leading to the development of nuclear 'warfighting' technologies, and contributing to the illusion that nuclear war can be fought and won. NATO plans for more powerful non-nuclear weapons could, if implemented, lead to a new and dangerous conventional arms race. And the American obsession with anti-Communism threatens to turn every local conflict into a test of wills between the superpowers.

The continued build-up of weapons by existing nuclear powers, together with their willingness to use these weapons in Third World diplomacy,[1] in turn increases the pressures on other nations to go nuclear. And Western arms exports, together with direct economic and military involvement, strengthen repressive governments, and weaken countries seeking a non-aligned path to development. In the name of fighting Soviet influence, the West encourages the maintenance of regimes with little popular support and no commitment to tackling the problems of poverty and inequality. Countries which decide to pursue more egalitarian policies often find that only the Soviet Union and its allies are willing to provide economic and military assistance. The division of the world into two armed camps appears preferable to the emergence of non-aligned countries capable of deciding their own destiny. Yet the accelerated militarization of the less developed world, to which this leads, in turn increases the danger of local conflict escalating into nuclear confrontation.

As the dangers inherent in current policies grow, however, so does the strength of opposition to them. In Britain the long period of consensus between Labour and Conservative has ended, and peace movements in many countries have mobilized millions of people in radical demands for an end to the nuclear arms race. This widespread, and growing, concern is in large part a reaction to the advent of the Second Cold War, and the increased possibility of nuclear conflict which it brings. Yet it also provides a political basis for new thinking. By bringing into question existing ortho-doxies it presents an opportunity for the development of new policies. For Britain, it is suggested, the minimum criteria for such a policy are clear: first, it must help reduce the dangers of nuclear war; secondly, it must make some contribution to progress and stability in the less developed world, without which global peace will be constantly undermined; and thirdly, it must reduce the burden of British military spending to a more acceptable level.

The remainder of this chapter will suggest a possible defence policy which a disarmament-oriented British government could realistically adopt, and which could fulfil these three objectives simultaneously. The emphasis of the discussion will be on the costs of an alternative defence policy, though its general rationale, will, hopefully, be clear. The chapter concludes with a discussion of the economic implications of an alternative defence policy.

NATO: in or out

The most pressing question of defence policy which a radical government, intent on nuclear disarmament, would need to resolve would be Britain's relationship with NATO. Two main alternatives would be available – to remain a member of NATO and seek to change its policy from within; or to withdraw from the Alliance and move towards a non-aligned role such as that of Sweden or Yugoslavia. The choice between these alternatives is complex and must depend partly on the circumstances at the time, particularly other NATO members' reactions to British proposals for change. At present, there are strong reasons for arguing that the option of continued membership is preferable, with a non-aligned policy as a 'fall-back' alternative.[2]

The first reason is that, given the international strength of the peace movement, a radical British government may be able to obtain support from other countries for major shifts in NATO policy. Belgium, Holland, Greece and the Scandinavian countries would be the most likely supporters. Under plausible circumstances, West Germany might also follow a similar path. Even in the US, public opinion has already been affected by the Freeze movement. A British initiative for phased nuclear disarmament would, at the very least, divide opinion within NATO rather than unite it in opposition, as withdrawal would certainly do.

Moreover, it is clear that British policy must seek to prevent the outbreak of a major European war, rather than simply to isolate itself from it. For were such a war to occur, Britain would be involved, whether or not it was a party to the original conflict. One or both superpowers would seek to gain control of the British Isles, if only to pre-empt their use by the other. And, even if Britain did not suffer a direct nuclear attack, fallout would ensure it suffered millions of casualties. In the fragile and small planet on which we live, only an internationalist policy makes sense.[3] The decision as to whether to remain in NATO, therefore, must be decided by considering which course of action reduces the probability of a major war – not how Britain could stay clear of such a war should it occur.

Secondly, a policy of immediate withdrawal from NATO might have unintended, and damaging, consequences, both in Europe and in Britain. In Europe, particularly if British withdrawal was followed by a reduced United States presence, Germany could decide to acquire its own nuclear weapons. Were this to happen, the situation in Central Europe would become much more dangerous. NATO was formed as much to assuage fears of a resurgence of German militarism as to counter the supposed Soviet threat. Given their continuing paranoia on the question, the reaction of the Soviets to a more assertive, and nuclear, Germany would be unpredictable, and perhaps dangerous.

Moreover, in Britain, a policy of non-alignment could, under stress, easily be transformed into a reassertion of nationalism. Powerful conservative elements of the ruling class would welcome a loosening of military ties with Europe as a way to restore Britain as an independent world power. Even important Labour politicians – such as Peter Shore – appear to base their opposition to European ties on a quasi-imperial ideology of national sovereignty.

Finally, those who support a policy of immediate NATO withdrawal must consider the probable political consequences of such a move. For it is clear that there is unlikely to be much domestic support for a pull-out unless other members attempt overt sabotage of a new government. By isolating the government from potential sympathizers in Britain and elsewhere, such a policy would invite economic sanctions and encourage covert attempts to undermine it. Since it would, presumably, be suicidal to accept Soviet aid, the government would find itself isolated both domestically and internationally. It would be forced to concede rapidly to avoid its own collapse.

A real defence policy

If NATO withdrawal is ruled out in the short term, there are at least five main commitments on which a disarmament-oriented defence policy, I would suggest, should be based.

* Spending on Britain's own nuclear weapons should be ended.
* Out-of-area intervention capabilities should be phased out.
* NATO should be pressed to reduce its own reliance on nuclear weapons, and to accept the concept of a European nuclear-weapon-free zone; and British forces in Europe should be used as a bargaining counter in order to accelerate this process.
* Increasing emphasis should be placed on defensive, rather than offensive, conventional forces.
* The commitment to national self-sufficiency in arms production should be abandoned.

Together these five commitments would allow a substantial cut in British defence spending without reducing national security. Indeed, by reducing tension between the military blocs in Europe, they would reduce the probability of war and make further bilateral reductions in military spending possible.

Fundamental to a radical defence policy must be the scrapping of *Britain's own nuclear weapons*. They serve no rational military purpose, consume considerable resources, and contribute to the illusion that Britain is still one of the world's major powers.[4] Yet their abandonment, carefully timed, could create new and powerful, political pressure for NATO to reduce reliance on nuclear weapons, and on both superpowers to reach agreement on deep cuts in their own arsenals. And, through the example of its own nuclear disarmament, the pressure on Third World leaders to acquire nuclear weapons could be at least somewhat reduced.

Cancellation of the Trident programme alone would save around £1,200 million annually (6–8 per cent of the defence budget) in the late 1980s and early 1990s. And savings on other nuclear weapons spending would be much greater than the government claims. At present, most nuclear spending in the published defence budget is indistinguishable from that on conventional forces: the only exception is £384 million for the 'Nuclear strategic force' – only 2.3 per cent of the total defence budget.[5] By skilful public relations, the government has been able to give the impression that this relatively small amount is the sum total of nuclear weapons spending at present. Yet this excludes much more than it includes. One prominent defence economist, David Greenwood, estimates that strategic nuclear spending alone amounted to 7.0 per cent of the total defence budget in 1981–2[6] – before Trident costs started to build up. If tactical and theatre nuclear forces are also included, well over £1,000 million is already being spent annually on the nuclear force; and this will rise to £2,000 million per annum by 1988. On a reasonable estimate, therefore, the scrapping of Britain's nuclear capability would save up to 15 per cent of total defence spending in the late 1980s.[7]

A new government would also save considerable money by ending the *Third World intervention role* and winding up its capabilities for out-of-area operations. The dismantling of these capabilities would not only help to end the illusions of national grandeur, and provide resources for domestic economic recovery. It would also help to alter the nature of Britain's relationship with the Third World. By ceasing to plan military intervention to protect its supposed interests outside Europe, Britain would help to strengthen international law.

As part of such a policy the regular naval patrols in the Caribbean and Indian Ocean should be ended, and commitments to Gulf states renegotiated. The policy of Fortress Falklands should be replaced by a willingness to negotiate a compromise with the Argentine government, provided the interests of the Islanders are taken into account. And the recently formed mini-Rapid Deployment Force should be disbanded. Each of these commitments could be ended without affecting NATO's defences in any way. And the completion of Britain's withdrawal from outside Europe would also allow the government to renew and extend John Nott's 1981 plan for cuts in the surface fleet. The three aircraft carriers planned could be retired or sold, and orders for new, over-sophisticated, frigates and destroyers (such as the Type 23) discontinued. A *more cost-effective maritime defence* could be provided by insisting that capabilities for extra-European (and nuclear) operations – which have pushed up the costs of existing ships – are unnecessary and undesirable. In future, defence in the North Atlantic could be based principally on a combination of landbased aircraft, hunter-killer submarines and mine barriers with existing surface ships in a progressively diminishing role.[8]

Savings in these areas alone – nuclear weapons, extra-European intervention, and maritime forces – could save 15–20 per cent of the defence budget by the end of a five year government. On reasonable assumptions, this would reduce Britain's defence burden to around the same level as that of France (4.2 per cent of GDP), and considerably nearer the European average (3.8 per cent).[9] Yet it could be achieved without affecting Britain's conventional contribution to the defence of Western Europe.

Further savings could be made to bring the total defence budget fully into line with those of other NATO members by reducing the size of Britain's land and air forces in Europe: the *British Army of the Rhine* (BAOR) and the Second Tactical Air Force. Such a course, however, may be unwise. The considerable financial costs of BAOR, in particular, need to be balanced against the political leverage on NATO policy which its presence in Germany allows. A major reduction in its size would be seen as an isolationist policy by other Europeans, and would reduce British hopes of influencing the debate within NATO on the role of nuclear weapons.

Partly in response to the pressure from the peace movements, there are now growing demands, even within establishment circles, for a new look at NATO 'flexible response' strategy. A radical British government could help to tip the balance in this argument. It could declare that it was willing to maintain BAOR at its current level, but only if NATO fulfilled certain conditions. First, it should be asked to scrap its battlefield nuclear weapons in Europe – a proposal which even the British Social Democrats support. Second, NATO should make a declaration that it would never be the first to use nuclear weapons, and agree to phase out all systems designed for this purpose.[10] Third, and as a logical consequence of 'No First Use', NATO should initiate negotiations with the Warsaw Pact on a proposal for *a European nuclear-weapons-free zone*.[11]

Such demands would encounter powerful opposition, but they would also generate considerable support. Throughout the difficult negotiations that would ensue, Britain could make clear its commitment to European defence, provided that it ceased to be based on the suicidal threat of nuclear holocaust. It could point out that, if other members were unwilling to take these minimum steps, Britain would be forced to withdraw its forces from Germany, and eventually from NATO Military Command. Given the changing mood within NATO, however, and the catalytic effect British unilateralism could have, it is at least possible that such moves may not be necessary. The result – a sizeable reduction in the risks of nuclear conflict – would be well worth the cost of retaining the BAOR.

No policy for reducing defence spending can work for long, however, unless it tackles the continued escalation in equipment costs. Without this, the savings on nuclear and intervention capabilities suggested here would soon be used up on increasingly expensive conventional weapons for Britain's European forces. It will thus be necessary for a cost-cutting government to question the need for the over-sophisticated weapons now in the pipeline. This would not only provide increased resources for the civilian economy at minimal cost to national security. It could also lessen the influence of Britain's own 'military-industrial complex' – in itself a contribution to curbing the arms race.

Measures now being introduced to increase efficiency and reduce excess profits may generate some savings. It must be emphasized, however, that the escalation in the costs of weapon systems is not simply a technological or managerial problem. Savings from these measures are likely to be severely limited unless there are also shifts in a broader policy level. Two changes, in particular, are needed to reduce growth in equipment costs substantially. The first is agreement to shift towards increasingly 'non-provocative' conventional defences. The second is a dilution of the principle of 'self-reliance' in arms manufacture. We now examine these two in turn.

A *'non-provocative' defence policy* aims to minimize the emphasis on forces that could be perceived, by a potential opponent, as offensive rather than defensive. A shift towards such a policy by NATO would help to ensure that, if measures to stop and reverse the nuclear arms race were beginning to be effective, a conventional arms race did not take its place. It is therefore likely to be favoured by a disarmament-oriented government. Indeed it is a central component of most recent proposals for non-nuclear defence.[12]

A reduction in emphasis on offensive forces would also have the important side-effect that it could considerably reduce equipment costs. The most expensive conventional weapon systems – such as aircraft carriers, battle tanks, and long-range bombers – are often those associated with offensive roles. For example, long-range bombers, such as Tornado, are designed to destroy targets deep in Eastern Europe – a mission that requires expensive capabilities for penetrating hundreds of kilometres of Warsaw Pact air defences. An increased emphasis on defensive forces would allow greater use to be made of less sophisticated, and cheaper, technologies. It would mean increased priority for anti-tank munitions instead of tanks, and for coastal protection vessels and conventionally-powered submarines instead of carrier task forces. It could reduce costs and ease tensions without diminishing the capability to deter a potential opponent from aggression.

Such a policy is directly opposite in its emphasis to the suggestions now coming from NATO that the 'nuclear threshold' could be raised by spending more on conventional 'deep-strike' weapons. These proposals, if implemented, could give NATO a capability to launch a pre-emptive first strike against military targets – nuclear and conventional – using only conventional weapons. Such a capability would be likely to convince the Soviet Union that the United States and its allies wanted a conventional capability to 'take the war' into Eastern Europe. Indeed a prominent American strategist, Professor Huntingdon, recently argued that:

On moral and political grounds, surely it is more desirable

to deter by threatening to liberate Eastern Europeans than by threatening to incinerate Russians.[13]

This is a conventional 'deterrence' capability which NATO should not acquire. Not only would it be extremely destabilizing, set off a vigorous conventional arms race, and increase the pressure for Soviet first use of nuclear weapons. It would also, as its promoters are well aware, require massive investment in new weapon systems. The cost of such systems would be considerable, as NATO's demand for 4 per cent real annual growth in NATO spending to pay for them illustrates.[14] Meeting such demands would make reductions in British defence spending impossible – even if nuclear and extra-European spending was cut back. A radical UK government should reject such proposals and insist that any measures that are adopted for improving conventional forces should be primarily defensive in nature. In this way, it can help to reduce the burden of defence spending and, simultaneously, diminish the mutual mistrust which feeds the arms race in Europe.

The second way in which equipment costs could be reduced – in addition to moving towards a non-provocative defence – would be to question the need for a policy of near-total *self-reliance in weapons production*. By agreeing to import equipment when available at a lower price from other European nations, substantial savings could be made without any loss of military preparedness. By aiding standardization of weapons between the forces of the various NATO members, moreover, such a step could also have clear military benefits.[15]

Britain's arms monopolies would, of course, fiercely resist exposure to international competition in the previously cosseted home market. But there is no military reason why Britain's defence spending should be used simply to maintain domestic arms producers in business. With the withdrawal from Empire, equipment needs are little different from those of European allies. Only if it were planning to fight a long war without allies would Britain need self-sufficiency in major weapon systems. Yet it is generally agreed that the next major war in Europe, if it occurs, would be short and fought with weapons already available. Domestic facilities for repair and maintenance would continue to be crucial. But factories for producing large numbers of new weapons over the years – such as were vital in the Second World War – would now be of little value.

The government, indeed, has implicitly accepted the merits of the argument by permitting a growing number of collaborative equipment projects, the most notable of which is the £12 billion Tornado programme. It is hard to see why military 'self-reliance' is better served by such projects than by importing arms, or by producing under licence – both of which are likely to be cheaper. If other nations were unwilling to sell weapons to Britain there would be a strong case for domestic production. Past experience suggests, however, that there would be no shortage of willing suppliers, eager to offer their products at little above marginal cost, and asking for little or no contribution to project overheads. Britain could thus obtain the equipment and spares it wanted at production cost, and allow other nations to bear a fairer share of the burden of NATO's research and development spending.

At the same time there would be some, perhaps many, areas where British companies were able to compete successfully, without massive government subsidy, for defence contracts in Britain and in other NATO countries.[16] In such cases, there would be no reason why these areas of British 'comparative advantage' should not be modestly encouraged. Without doubt, however, in many cases it would be cheaper to purchase already developed equipment from overseas. In these cases, the government should not be afraid to face up to the domestic sectional interests likely to oppose such moves. It is quite illogical, and extremely expensive, to protect domestic defence contractors – and the related nuclear power and aerospace industries – while allowing most civilian industries to go to the wall. It indicates the hollowness of government 'free market' rhetoric that it does not seem to apply to those industries – defence equipment, agriculture, etc. – to which its Party has always had close personal links.[17]

Implementing such a policy would incur some short-term political and economic costs. These should not, however, be exaggerated. The loss of political support possible amongst workers in arms industries could be considerably reduced if a coherent strategy for providing alternative employment was adopted. And the increased spending on weapons imports would be more than offset by considerable long-term economic benefit. Not only would a competitive procurement policy directly help to reduce defence spending. It would also release considerable scarce resources – in particular skilled personnel in R & D – from relatively unproductive military uses for use in the civilian sector. At present, military R & D constitutes 50 per cent of total government R & D, with nuclear power and aerospace taking up a further 12 per cent.[18] The programme of measures outlined in this chapter could reduce this spending considerably, perhaps by as much as 50–75 per cent, and certainly by proportionally more than the proposed cut in the defence budget as a whole. Employed in civilian industry, these resources are likely in the long run to more than compensate for the increased arms imports by their contribution to a more efficient civilian economy.

Perhaps the biggest advantage in a competitive procurement policy, however, would be that it would reduce the lobbying power of the domestic arms industry, its role as a monopoly supplier and its ability to argue for new equipment orders, irrespective of military merit and priority. If weapons were bought 'off the shelf', rather than having to be ordered domestically long before they come into service, there would be less scope for the 'worst-case' military planning that has helped to fund the escalation in equipment costs. And the 'follow-on principle' – the need to provide new contracts for arms manufacturers to prevent design teams being disbanded and plants closed – could be weakened.

The case of Tornado illustrates the advantages of an alternative policy very clearly. The aircraft is based on design concepts and priorities decided upon in 1969 on the basis of predictions of possible threats, and desirable responses, in the 1980s and beyond. If Britain had kept out of that project and left its choice of aircraft until the 1980s – when the planes were needed – it would have been able to choose between Tornado, its American and French rivals, and buying no planes at all, on the basis of a military assessment 13 years more up-to-date. As a result it could have increased the match between military requirements and equipment purchased, while also reducing the cost of procurement. The only loss would have been in national prestige and in the vested interests of the British companies concerned. A similar principle applied in the Future European Fighter Aircraft[19] – the project needed as a 'follow-on' to Tornado – would allow Britain to decide on how to replace its Jaguars in 1993 rather than 1983, with consequent gains in military effectiveness.

The acceptance of Britain's inability to develop and produce efficiently the full range of modern weapon systems, as it did when still a Great Power, must be an integral part of the transition to a military status commensurate with its economic strength. Combined with the other measures proposed here – scrapping nuclear and out-of-area roles, and reducing emphasis on offensive forces – such a policy could, over a number of years, reduce defence spending perhaps by a third or more. A 30 per cent cut would bring Britain's defence burden into line with the European NATO average. Moreover, the measures to reduce nuclear and offensive forces are likely to reduce tension and thus increase the probability of mutual force reductions by East and West. Should such an arms race in reverse gather steam, the financial savings available would be considerably greater, and the benefits to international security immeasurable.

Guns and butter

It is often suggested that a large cut in arms spending – such as proposed in this chapter – would create enormous economic disruption and throw hundreds of thousands of people out of work. Such a line of reasoning is grossly misleading. In reality, a cut in military spending would be an economic opportunity rather than a problem. It would release valuable resources desperately needed for investment and growth, and the transfer of resources from military to civilian purposes would create more jobs rather than fewer. Moreover, the disruption caused during the transition from one level of spending to another is usually exaggerated. A cut of 25–30 per cent in defence spending would take several years to implement and the average annual reduction in the defence budget would be no more than 5 per cent – comparable with the average increase (4.3 per cent) between 1978–9 and 1983–4.

The corollary of this, however, is that the economic benefits from a reduction in military spending will also, in the main, be relatively long-term. As skilled personnel transfer into civilian jobs, and as armament firms adapt to new products, there should be some increase in the level of non-military production. But markets lost, and capital investment forgone, over three decades of decline cannot be regained overnight. The process of restoring the British economy to health is bound to be long and difficult.

It will thus be important to ensure that defence cuts are

accompanied by measures to increase the level of investment, if long-term gains are to be maximized. The resources released from arms production would, for the most part, be particularly suitable for production of capital goods. And there appears to be no shortage of opportunities for investment, particularly in new technology industries currently suffering shortages in many of the skills which the defence sector possesses in abundance.

An important role in promoting new investment can be played by 'conversion' plans for existing arms factories. A series of such studies, carried out by workers now involved in arms production, have shown that existing skills and resources could be used to make a range of socially useful alternative products in areas as diverse as public transport, health, solar power, and deep-sea diving.[20] Government financing of such projects, even if only providing a fraction of the amount presently spent on defence R & D, could undoubtedly be a catalyst for the development of productive new technologies. This could significantly reduce the need for plant closures and redundancies, and be a concrete demonstration of the social and economic benefits of disarmament. It would thus play an important role in reinforcing popular support for the defence and disarmament programme as a whole, without which it is unlikely that a government would have the political will to complete a cut of 30 per cent in the defence bill.

To make maximum use of the skilled personnel released from the defence industry, however, will not only require changes at a factory level. There will also be a need for a substantial shakeup in the management structures of the industries involved. If the strategy for 'converted' firms is left entirely in the hands of current managers, the alternative products favoured are likely to be those which require least disruption of the methods developed for military equipment. Such a course would lead to over-sophisticated products for which there would be no market without heavy subsidies, and which would therefore minimize the economic gains from conversion. It would be foolish, for example, if superficially more attractive, to switch the teams of nuclear weapon scientists to an expanded civil nuclear programme. And the government should resist pressure to replace subsidized military aircraft by over-sophisticated civilian projects – like Concorde – which are bound to be a continuing burden on the national economy. Because of this danger, Ron Smith and Dan Smith, authors of *The*

Economics of Militarism, have argued that:

> In general, a programme of conversion should minimise upheaval as much as possible. But in the case of research, development and management, the rule is the more upheaval, the better. Design teams need to be broken up and dispersed . . . structures which maintain the current attitudes and approach of the arms industry will have to be demolished.[21]

As well as encouraging a more profitable civilian use of workers' skills such a policy will also prevent pressure from the firms concerned, when faced with difficulties in highly competitive civilian markets, for a reversion to a more cosseted military, and/or over-sophisticated civilian, government market. Defence-oriented companies, during a recent study by Sir Ieuan Maddocks, made quite clear their view that they 'were not the right kind of company'[22] to apply their high skills in civilian uses because of their lack of entrepreneurial skills, the need for shorter timescales, and the very different relationship with consumers. A major reorganization of the managements and companies concerned must, therefore, be a necessary part of a conversion programme that seeks, not simply to preserve jobs, but to create productive new civilian industries. Provided that these problems are recognized and tackled, potential gains from conversion are considerable. The transfer of many of the country's most skilled scientists and engineers into productive employment could significantly enhance the potential for productivity growth and industrial recovery.

Jobs and bombs

The employment implications of cutting defence spending are frequently misrepresented. In the 1983 General Election, for example, Defence Secretary Michael Heseltine claimed that Labour's manifesto promise – to reduce defence spending to the NATO European average – would cost 400,000 jobs. This assertion deliberately ignored the fact that the money saved in defence would create more jobs if used for almost any alternative purpose. For, because the defence sector has a greater concentration of scarce, well-paid scientists and technicians, fewer people are employed per pound spent than in civilian industry as a whole or in government service.[23] A shift of spending into other sectors would result in more jobs for the same total budget.

A recent study, using an Institute of Employment Research version of the Cambridge Growth Project model of the economy, investigated the impact of a 35 per cent across-the-board cut in military spending.[24] In 'Scenario A', it assumed that this cut was balanced by an equal increase in other public spending, half of which went on public investment in housing, schools, and so on. In this scenario, the authors estimated that a 250,000 fall in defence employment would be more than offset by a 350,000 rise in civilian jobs. Only in the unlikely event of there being no compensating rise in non-defence spending – 'Scenario B' – would total employment fall.

The net employment gains from defence cuts are a result of the increasingly capital-intensive nature of defence spending, and of equipment spending in particular. Between 1963 and 1978, employment as a result of UK defence spending fell from 1,583,000 to 1,130,000, a drop of 29 per cent, while defence spending rose from £12,167 million to £13,365 million in 1984–85 cost terms – a rise of 10 per cent.[25] Despite a 29 per cent real increase in spending, employment in the Ministry of Defence is due to fall by a further 9 per cent between 1978 and 1985.[26] Even with a rising budget, therefore, jobs in the defence sector are far from secure.

The particular economies suggested earlier in this chapter, moreover, would result in a less substantial reduction in defence employment than the across-the-board cut assumed in the Institute simulation. By retaining BAOR at its current strength, while making the biggest cuts in R & D and capital-intensive equipment programmes, it would shift defence to a more labour-intensive posture. The percentage of the defence budget spent on personnel – especially services personnel – would be likely to grow at the expense of equipment. According to recent government statistics, each £1,000 million devoted to service pay and allowances sustained 121,000 posts in the regular forces, while £1,000 million spent on defence equipment sustained only 75,000 jobs, both direct and indirect, in UK industries.[27] A shift away from equipment spending, therefore, is likely to reduce further the impact on jobs of any cutbacks. There is, therefore, no reason why defence cuts should not, rather than creating unemployment, actually make some contribution to reducing it. At any rate, it is clear that attempts to justify defence spending by reference to the number of jobs created are misplaced. An alternative low-cost defence policy would, in aggregate, create significantly more jobs. Combined with a coherent strategy for conversion and retraining, there is no reason why the vast majority of the workers directly affected should not find fruitful alternative employment in the civilian sector.

Conclusion

It is clear that Britain could reduce its military budget by at least 30 per cent by abandoning capabilities and commitments which serve little purpose in terms of national or NATO security. Neither the abandonment of Britain's nuclear weapons, nor its refusal to retain worldwide intervention forces, would diminish the ability of the armed forces to defend Britain and its European allies. An increased emphasis on non-provocative force structures would reduce tension between the blocs without diminishing substantially the capability for deterring aggression. And a policy of buying the best weapons at the lowest prices would harm only arms manufacturers unable to compete in international markets. It is quite wrong to suppose, therefore, that Britain's defences would be denuded were it to reduce its military burden to the level of other industrial countries. Such a reduction is perfectly possible within a reasonable time period, without leaving NATO, and without abandoning a commitment to sound national defence.

Cuts in military spending alone cannot cure Britain's economic malaise. Simultaneous attempts are needed to tackle other constraints on economic development, amongst which other legacies of Empire – such as the role of the City and the level of overseas investment – are also significant. Nevertheless, defence cuts can make a significant contribution by releasing considerable valuable, but scarce, resources for use elsewhere. Current defence policy is compatible with neither economic prosperity nor with national security. An alternative non-nuclear defence policy, along the lines suggested here, would enable Britain both to reduce its defence burden to a more sustainable level and to make some contribution to ending the arms race that threatens us all.

Notes and references

1. Paying for greatness

1. Eric J. Hobsbawm, *Industry and Empire*, London: Penguin 1969, p. 134; Peter Mathias, *The First Industrial Nation*, London: Methuen 1969, p. 250; Paul Kennedy, *The Realities Behind Diplomacy*, London: Fontana 1981, pp. 20–1.
2. Susan Strange, *Sterling and British Policy*, London, Oxford University Press 1971, p. 182.
3. Peter Mathias, *op. cit.*, pp. 320–334.
4. Phyllis Deane and W.A.Cole, *British Economic Growth 1688–1959*, London: Cambridge University Press 1962, p. 297.
5. *Ibid.* pp. 266–279; Eric Hobsbawm, *op. cit.*, pp. 191–192. Alec Cairncross, in *Home and Foreign Investment 1870–1913*, London: Cambridge University Press 1953, argues that 'long run foreign investment was largely at the expense of home investment, or vice versa' (p. 187).
6. Eric Hobsbawm, *op. cit.*, pp. 172–194; William Ashworth, *An Economic History of England 1870–1939*, London: Methuen 1960, pp. 138–162.
7. Paul Kennedy, *op. cit*, pp. 118–128.
8. Susan Strange, *op. cit.*, p. 182.
9. *Ibid*, p. 181.
10. Susan Strange, *op. cit.*, Chapter 2; D.E. Moggridge, *The Return to Gold, 1925*, London: Cambridge University Press, 1969.
11. Eric Hobsbawm, *op. cit.*, pp. 207–224; *Guardian*, 13 June 1984; Derek Aldcroft, 'Economic Growth in Britain in the Interwar Years: A Reassessment' in Derek H. Aldcroft and Peter Fearon, *Economic Growth in 20th Century Britain*, London: Macmillan 1969, pp. 34–54; H.W. Richardson, *Economic Recovery in Britain 1932–39*, London: Weidenfeld and Nicolson 1967.
12. Andrew Gamble, *Britain in Decline*, London: Macmillan 1981, pp. 64–79. Tom Nairn, 'The Twilight of the British State', *New Left Review*, 101–102, Feb–Apr 1977, pp. 3–61.
13. Carlo Cipolla, *The Economic Decline of Empires*, London: Methuen, 1970, pp. 1–15.
14. B.H. Liddell Hart, *Deterrence or Defence*, London: Stevens 1960.

15. Daniel Yergin, *Shattered Peace: The Origins of the Cold War and the National Security State*, London: Penguin 1980, pp. 58–60.

16. Anthony Sampson, *The Changing Anatomy of Britain*, London: Coronet 1982, p. 144. Historian Cornelli Barnett has argued that 'The Victorian public school is one of the keys to our decline, turning out by means of curriculum and the moulding influence of school life alike a governing class ignorant of, and antipathetic towards, science technology and industry' (*Times*, 30 September 1975).

17. Paul Kennedy, *op. cit.*, pp. 127–139.

18. Margaret Gowing, *Britain and Atomic Energy 1939–45*, London: Macmillan 1964.

19. Andrew J. Pierre, *Nuclear Politics: The British Experience with an Independent Strategic Force, 1939–1970*, London: Oxford University Press 1972, p. 196.

20. Mary Kaldor, 'Defence Costs and the Defence Industry' in Mary Kaldor, Dan Smith and Steve Vines (eds), *Democratic Socialism and the Cost of Defence*, London: Croom Helm 1979, p. 283.

21. D.C. Paige, 'Defence Expenditure', *National Institute Economic Review*, 11, 1960, pp. 28–39.

22. Mary Acland-Hood, 'Statistics on Military Research and Development Expenditure', *SIPRI Yearbook 1984*, London: Taylor and Francis 1984, p. 171.

23. *House of Commons Debates*, Written Answer, 25 April 1983, Hansard col. 267.

24. Lawrence Freedman, *Britain and Nuclear Weapons*, London: Macmillan 1980, pp. 53–4.

2. Opportunity lost: the 1940s

1. Paul Kennedy, *The Realities Behind Diplomacy*, London: Fontana 1981, p. 316. For a wide-ranging study of the economics of the Second World War, see Alan S. Milward, *War, Economy and Society 1939–1945*, London: Allen Lane 1977.

2. Wm. Roger Louis, *Imperialism At Bay: The United States and the Decolonization of the British Empire, 1941–45*, New York: Oxford University Press 1978, p. 8.

3. Richard W. Clarke, *Anglo-American Economic Collaboration: British Economic Policy 1942–49*, London: Oxford University Press 1982, pp. 34–5.

4. See Joyce and Gabriel Kolko, *The Limits of Power: The World and United States Foreign Policy 1945–54*, London: Harper and Row 1972, pp. 300–329.

5. Angus Calder, *The People's War: Britain 1939–45*, London: Granada 1971, contains a fascinating account of the popular mood in those years.

6. *Ibid*, p. 674.

7. C.J. Bartlett, *The Long Retreat: A Short History of British Defence Policy 1945-70*, London: Macmillan 1972, p. 12. Somewhat different figures are given in David Greenwood, 'Defence and National Priorities since 1945', in John Baylis (ed.), *British Defence Policy in a Changing World*, London: Croom Helm 1977, pp. 174-207. It should be noted, however, that not all the workers withdrawn from war production entered paid employment in the civilian sector. A large proportion – particularly of women – withdrew from the labour market altogether.

8. Quoted in Richard W. Clarke, *op. cit.*, p. xvi.

9. J.C.R. Dow, *The Management of the British Economy, 1945-60*, London: Cambridge University Press 1964, p. 14.

10. S. Pollard, *The Wasting of the British Economy*, London: Croom Helm 1982, pp. 31-2.

11. *Statement Relating to Defence: 1947*, Cmd 7042, p. 4.

12. Hugh Dalton, *Memoirs, 1945-60: High Tide and After*, London: Muller 1962, pp. 101, 112, 193-202.

13. *House of Commons Debates*, 16 May 1947, col. 1965.

14. One of the most thorough accounts of the origins of the Cold War in 1945-8 is contained in Daniel Yergin, *Shattered Peace: The Origins of the Cold War and the National Security State*, London: Penguin 1980. For Britain's role in changing United States policy towards the Soviet Union during this period, see Terry H. Anderson, *The United States, Great Britain and the Cold War 1944-1947*, London: University of Missouri Press 1981.

15. C.J. Bartlett, *The Long Retreat*, *op. cit.*, p. 13.

16. *Ibid*, p. 46.

17. R.N. Rosecrance, *The Defense of the Realm: British Strategy in the Nuclear Epoch*, New York: Columbia University Press 1968, pp. 34-51.

18. Andrew Pierre, *Nuclear Politics: The British Experience with an Independent Strategic Force 1939-1970*, London: Oxford University Press 1972, pp. 75-77. Pierre argues that 'if America had not ruptured the special relationship, . . . if British security had been guaranteed then as it came to be in the NATO treaty two years later, the decision of 1947 to start on an independent nuclear weapons capability may have been different.'

19. A fascinating account of this process is included in Teddy Brett, Steve Gilliatt and Andrew Pople, 'Planned Trade, Labour Party Policy and US Intervention: The Success and Failures of Post-War Reconstruction', *History Workshop Journal*, 13, Spring 1982, pp. 130-142.

20. C.J. Bartlett, *A History of Postwar Britain 1945-74*, London: Longman 1977, p. 25.

21. *House of Commons Debates*, 13 December 1945, Hansard pp. 652-3.

22. *Economist*, February 8, 1947.

23. *Economist*, March 27, 1948.

24. Daniel Yergin, *op. cit.*, p. 178. Also see Richard N. Gardner, *Sterling Dollar Diplomacy*, New York: McGraw Hill 1969.

25. Minute, 22 February 1947, quoted in Richard W. Clarke, *op. cit*, p. 152.

26. *Ibid*, p. 70.

27. J.C.R. Dow, *op. cit.*, p. 22.

28. *Ibid*, p. 23.

29. Daniel Yergin, *op. cit.*, p. 280.

30. *Ibid*, p. 281.

31. *Ibid*, p. 307.

32. Joyce and Gabriel Kolko, *op. cit.*, pp. 384–402.

33. John Baylis, *Anglo-American Defence Relations, 1939–1980*, London: Macmillan 1981, p. 44.

34. From Lord Curzon's presidential address to the Birmingham and Midland Institute, 1907. Quoted in Phillip Darby, *British Defence Policy East of Suez 1947–1968*, London: Oxford University Press 1973, p. 1.

35. C.J. Bartlett, *The Long Retreat, op. cit.*, p. 12.

36. *Ibid*, pp. 15–16.

37. J.C.R. Dow, *op. cit*, p. 34.

3. Rearmament and rethink: the early 1950s

1. C.J. Bartlett, *The Long Retreat*, London: Macmillan 1972, p. 52.

2. Daniel Yergin, *Shattered Peace*, London: Penguin 1980, pp. 400–408. On the decision to build the 'super', see also Peter Pringle and James Spigelman, *The Nuclear Barons*, London: Sphere 1983, pp. 95–103; and Gregg Herken, *The Winning Weapons: The Atomic Bomb in the Cold War 1945–50*, New York: Alfred Knopf 1980, pp. 304–329.

3. Daniel Yergin, *op. cit.*, p. 402.

4. Quoted in R.N. Rosecrance, *Defense of the Realm*, New York: Columbia University Press 1968, p. 125.

5. *Ibid*, p. 137.

6. C.J. Bartlett, *The Long Retreat, op. cit.*, pp. 60–1.

7. Joan E. Mitchell, *Crisis in Britain: 1951*, London: Secker and Warburg 1963, pp. 32–3.

8. Minutes of special meeting of Ministers, 8 September 1950, 'Effects of Defence Programme on National Economy', *Public Records Office*.

9. C.J. Bartlett, *A History of Postwar Britain 1945–74*, London: Longman 1977, p. 86.

10. Nitze was speaking at a Pentagon meeting on 3 December 1950. Cited in *Foreign Relations of the United States 1950*, Washington DC: Government Printing Office 1976, p. 1328.

11. *Ibid*, p. 1364.

12. Attlee-Truman meeting in White House, 6 December 1950, in *Foreign*

Relations of the United States 1950, op. cit., Volume III.

13. *Defence Programme: Statement made by the Prime Minister in the House of Commons on Monday, 29 January 1951*, London: HMSO 1951, Cmd 8146; *Economic Survey for 1951*, London: HMSO 1951, pp. 5–6. Andrew Shonfield, *British Economic Policy Since the War*, London: Penguin 1958; pp. 92–3, however, suggests that the full story of this decision has not yet been told.

14. Quoted in Richard Rose, 'The Relations of Socialist Principles to British Labour Foreign Policy, 1945–51', unpublished D.Phil thesis (Nuffield College, Oxford, 1959), p. 334.

15. J.C.R. Dow, *The Management of the British Economy*, London: Cambridge University Press 1964, pp. 39, 74.

16. *Statement made by the Prime Minister, op. cit.*, p. 5.

17. D.C. Paige, 'Defence Expenditure', *National Institute Economic Review*, 11, 1960, pp. 28–39

18. Cited in Raymond Fletcher, *£60 a Second on Defence*, London: MacGibbon and Kee 1963, p. 30.

19. *Statement made by the Prime Minister, op. cit.*, pp. 6–7

20. *Economic Survey for 1951, op. cit.*, p. 19.

21. Joyce and Gabriel Kolko, *The Limits of Power*, New York: Harper and Row 1972, p. 633.

22. *Ibid*, p. 634. See also Denis Healey, 'Britain and NATO', in Klaus Knorr (ed.), *NATO and American Security*, Princeton: Princeton University Press 1959, p. 215; A.C.L. Day 'The Economics of Defence', *Political Quarterly*, 1, 1960, pp. 57–65.

23. Joan E. Mitchell, *Crisis in Britain 1951, op. cit.*, is the most comprehensive account of this period. See also 'Political and Economic Planning', *Growth in the British Economy*, London: Allen and Unwin 1960; S. Pollard, *The Wasting of the British Economy*, London: Croom Helm 1982, pp. 36–8, 138–9; Andrew Shonfield, *British Economic Policy Since the War*, London: Penguin 1959, pp. 56–8.

24. J.C.R. Dow, *op. cit.*, pp. 57–61; S. Pollard, *op. cit.*, pp. 36–8.

25. C.J. Bartlett, *A History of Postwar Britain, op. cit.*, pp. 89–91.

26. Harold Macmillan, *Tides of Fortune*, London: Macmillan 1969, p. 378; C.J. Bartlett, *The Long Retreat, op. cit.*, p. 79.

27. *Statement on Defence 1952*, London: HMSO 1952, Cmd. 8475, p. 9.

28. Estimated from *Economic Survey for 1951, op. cit.*, pp. 5–6.

29. R.N. Rosecrance, *Defense of the Realm, op. cit.*, pp. 159–164.

30. *Ibid*, p. 160.

31. Presentation by Sir John Slessor to United States Joint Chiefs of Staff in July 1952. Quoted in *The History of the Joint Chiefs of Staff*, Volume IV 1950–52, Washington DC: Historical Division, Secretariat, Joint Chiefs of Staff, pp. 307–310.

32. *Statement on Defence: 1955*, London: HMSO 1955, Cmd. 9391, p. 6.

33. Margaret Gowing, *Independence and Deterrence: Britain and Atomic Energy 1945–52*, London: Macmillan 1974, pp. 273–321. Also R.N. Rosecrance, *op. cit.*, pp. 164–8.

34. Andrew Brookes, *V-Force: The History of Britain's Airborne Deterrent*, London: Jane's Publishing Company 1982, p. 100.

35. Margaret Gowing, *op. cit.*, pp. 449–450.

36. Sir John Slessor, *Strategy for the West*, London: Cassell 1954, pp. 105–6.

37. Margaret Gowing, *op. cit.*, p. 407.

38. Alastair Buchan, Director of the Institute for Strategic Studies, quoted in Raymond Fletcher, *op. cit.*, p. 122.

39. Susan Strange, *Sterling and British Policy*, London: Macmillan 1971, pp. 181–2; W.A.P. Manser, *Britain in Balance*, London: Penguin 1971, p. 31; Phillip Darby, *British Defence Policy East of Suez*, London: Oxford University Press 1973, pp. 1–8.

40. 'Britain and the Tide of World Affairs', *Listener*, 52/1314 (11 November 1954), p. 788. Quoted in Phillip Darby, *op. cit.*, p. 22.

41. *Statement on Defence 1954*, London: HMSO 1954, Cmd. 9075, para. 12.

42. C.J. Bartlett, *The Long Retreat, op. cit.*, p. 106.

43. *Ibid.*, p. 113.

44. R.N. Rosecrance, *op. cit.*, pp. 6–7, 194–8.

45. C.J. Bartlett, *The Long Retreat, op. cit.*, p. 82.

46. Phillip Darby, *op. cit.*, p. 36.

47. C.J. Bartlett, *A History of Postwar Britain, op. cit.*, p. 114.

48. Phillip Darby, *op. cit.*, especially pp. 35, 276–282.

49. Anthony Eden, *Full Circle*, London: Cassell 1960, pp. 29–59; F.S. Northedge, *Descent From Power: British Foreign Policy 1945–73*, London: Allen and Unwin 1974, pp. 159–172.

50. Anthony Eden, *op. cit.*, p. 36.

51. C.J. Bartlett, *A History of Postwar Britain, op. cit.*, pp. 105–9.

52. Matthew A. Evangelista, 'Stalin's Postwar Army Reappraised', in *International Security*, Winter 1982/83, pp. 110–138.

53. See David Alan Rosenberg, 'The Origins of Overkill: Nuclear Weapons and American Strategy, 1945–60', *International Security*, Spring 1983; Fred Kaplan, *The Wizards of Armageddon*, New York: Simon and Schuster 1983.

54. Cited in full C.J. Bartlett, *The Long Retreat, op. cit.*, p. 94.

55. Andrew Shonfield, *op. cit.*, pp. 100–8.

56. R.N. Rosecrance, *op. cit.*, pp. 173–5.

57. *The History of the Joint Chiefs of Staff*, Volume IV 1950–52, *op. cit.*, p. 307.

4. Fall from grace: 1957–68

1. J.C.R. Dow, *The Management of the British Economy*, London: Cambridge University Press 1964, p. 91.
2. Harold Macmillan, *Riding the Storm*, London: Macmillan 1971, p. 53.
3. Anthony Eden, *Full Circle*, London: Cassell 1960, p. 371.
4. *Ibid*, pp. 370–372. See also C.J. Bartlett, *The Long Retreat*, London: Macmillan 1972, pp. 105–7.
5. Raymond Dawson and Richard Rosecrance, 'Theory and Reality in the Anglo-American Alliance', *World Politics*, XIX, 1, 1966, pp. 37–41; C.J. Bartlett, *A History of Postwar Britain*, London: Longman 1977, pp. 132–6; and many other works.
6. Phillip Darby, *British Defence Policy East of Suez*, London: Oxford University Press 1973, p. 103.
7. *Defence: Outline of Future Policy*, London: HMSO 1957, Cmnd. 124, p. 10.
8. *Ibid*, pp. 2, 10.
9. *Ibid*, p. 9.
10. Phillip Darby, *op. cit.*, p. 224.
11. *Defence: Outline of Future Policy, op. cit.*
12. *Ibid*, p. 2.
13. Andrew Pierre, *Nuclear Politics*, London: Oxford University Press 1972, pp. 188–191; Phillip Darby, *op. cit.*, pp. 161–2.
14. F.S. Northedge, *Descent from Power*, London: Allen and Unwin 1974, p. 282.
15. Phillip Darby, *op. cit.*, p. 222.
16. *Ibid*, p. 111.
17. *Defence: Outline of Future Policy, op. cit.*, p. 6.
18. Phillip Darby, *op. cit.*, pp. 255–266.
19. Phillip Darby, 'East of Suez Reassessed', in J. Baylis (ed.), *British Defence Policy in a Changing World*, London: Croom Helm 1977, p. 59.
20. *Defence: Outline of Future Policy, op. cit.*, p. 4; Phillip Darby, *British Defence Policy East of Suez, op. cit.*, pp. 120–1.
21. *House of Commons Debates*, 17 April 1957, col. 1958.
22. Phillip Darby, *British Defence Policy East of Suez, op. cit.*, pp. 203–13, pp. 276–282.
23. Susan Strange, *Sterling and British Policy*, London: Oxford University Press, 1971, p. 184.
24. Phillip Darby, *British Defence Policy East of Suez, op. cit.*, pp. 249–50; Mary Kaldor, 'Defence Costs and the Defence Industry', in Mary Kaldor, Dan Smith, and Steve Vines (eds), *Democratic Socialism and the Cost of Defence*, London: Croom Helm 1979, p. 295.
25. Andrew Pierre, *op. cit.*, p. 196.
26. A.J.R. Groom, *British Thinking About Nuclear Weapons*, London:

Frances Pinter 1974, p. 495.

27. *The Times*, 14 November 1958.

28. *Report of the Fifty-Sixth Annual Conference of the Labour Party, 1957*, London: The Labour Party 1957, pp. 181–2.

29. Andrew Pierre, *op. cit.*, pp. 217–262.

30. John Baylis, *Anglo-American Defence Relations 1939–1980*, London: Macmillan 1981, pp. 66–75. Also see Richard E. Neustadt, *Alliance Politics*, New York: Columbia University Press 1970.

31. John Baylis, *op. cit.*, p. 73.

32. F.S. Northedge, *op. cit.*, pp. 291–2. Also see Andrew Pierre, *op. cit.*, pp. 251–72.

33. C.J. Bartlett, *A History of Postwar Britain, op. cit.*, pp. 192–3; F.S. Northedge, *op.cit.*, p. 293.

34. J.C.R. Dow, *op.cit.*, p. 91.

35. Samuel Brittan, *Steering the Economy*, London: Penguin 1971, pp. 238–45.

36. Harold Wilson, *The Labour Government 1964–70*, London: Penguin 1974, p. 43.

37. Table 13 in Chapter 6.

38. Christopher Mayhew, *Britain's Role Tomorrow*, London: Hutchinson 1967, p. 35.

39. *The National Plan*, London: HMSO 1965, Cmnd 2764, Chapter 19.

40. C. Freeman, 'Technical Innovation and British Trade Performance' in Frank Blackaby (ed.), *De-industrialisation*, London: Heinemann 1978, pp. 65–73; C.J. Bartlett, *A History of Postwar Britain, op. cit.*, p. 249.

41. *The National Plan, op. cit.*, chapter 9, para. 36.

42. Samuel Brittan, *op. cit.*, pp. 291–4.

43. *Ibid*, pp. 291–4, 334–9.

44. Bruce Reid and Geoffrey Williams, *Denis Healey and the Politics of Power*, London: Sidgwick and Jackson 1971, p. 175.

45. *House of Commons Debates*, 16 December 1964, col. 423–4.

46. Harold Wilson, *op.cit.*, p. 69; Andrew Pierre, *op. cit.*, pp. 283–5; Bruce Reid and Geoffrey Williams, *op. cit.*, pp. 168–70

47. Phillip Darby, *op. cit.*, pp. 286–8.

48. C.J. Bartlett, *A History of Postwar Britain, op. cit.*, p. 233.

49. Bruce Reid and Geoffrey Williams, *op. cit.*, p. 217.

50. *The National Plan, op. cit.*, p. 182.

51. Christopher Mayhew, *op. cit.*, pp. 131–6.

52. Bruce Reid and Geoffrey Williams, *op. cit.* pp. 177–80

53. C.J. Bartlett, *The Long Retreat, op. cit.*, p. 200.

54. *Statement on the Defence Estimates, 1965*, London: HMSO 1965, Cmnd 2592, paras 9–10; *The National Plan, op.cit.*, p. 182.

55. Bruce Reid and Geoffrey Williams, *op. cit.*, pp. 252–61.

56. Phillip Darby, *op. cit.*, p. 292.

57. *Ibid*.
58. C.J. Bartlett, *The Long Retreat, op. cit.*, pp. 216–17; Phillip Darby, *op. cit.*, pp. 292–3.
59. *Statement on the Defence Estimates, 1966,* London: HMSO 1966, Cmnd 2901, pp. 6–7.
60. Christopher Mayhew, *op. cit.*, p. 25.
61. *Statement on the Defence Estimates, 1966, op. cit.*, pp. 10–11
62. *Ibid*, p. 11.
63. *Ibid*, p. 7.
64. *The Times*, 3 February 1966.
65. C.J. Bartlett, *A History of Postwar Britain, op. cit.*, pp. 227–9.
66. Fred Halliday, *Arabia without Sultans*, London: Penguin 1974, pp. 214–22.
67. 'The Cost of Peacekeeping', *Financial Times*, 23 February 1966.
68. Richard Crossman, *The Diaries of a Cabinet Minister, Volume 2*, London: Jonathan Cape 1976, p. 85.
69. *Ibid*, p. 86.
70. *Ibid*, p. 308.
71. *Supplementary Statement on Defence Policy 1967*, London: HMSO 1967, Cmnd 3357, Chapter III, para. 9.
72. *Ibid*, Chapter VI, para. 1.
73. Phillip Darby, *op. cit*, pp. 322–3.
74. Richard Crossman, *op. cit.*, pp. 619–22, 634–40, 646–53.
75. *Ibid*, p. 622.
76. In 1964–5 cost terms, defence spending in 1969–70 was £1,780 million.
77. *Supplementary Statement on Defence Policy, 1968*, London: HMSO 1968, Cmnd 3701, p. 1.
78. Denis Healey, 'British Defence Policy', *Royal United Services Institute Journal*, December 1969, p. 16.
79. In 1964–5 cost terms, defence spending in 1972–3 was £1,960 million.

5. Yearning for redemption: the 1970s

1. OECD, *Main Economic Indicators*, Paris: OECD various dates.
2. *Economic Trends: 1984 Annual Supplement*, London: HMSO 1983, pp. 4, 80.
3. *Supplementary Statement on Defence Policy 1968*, London: HMSO 1968, Cmnd 3701, pp.7–8
4. *Ibid*, pp. 8–11. See also David Greenwood, *Budgeting for Defence*, London: Royal United Services Institute 1972, pp. 70–1
5. C.J. Bartlett, *The Long Retreat*: London: Macmillan 1972, p. 225; *Supplementary Statement on Defence Policy 1968, op. cit.*, p. 11.
6. *Supplementary Statement on Defence Policy 1967*, London: HMSO 1967, Cmnd 3357, Chapter IV, para. 3.

7. *Supplementary Statement on Defence Policy 1970*, London: HMSO 1970, p. 5.

8. John E. Woods, 'The Royal Navy Since World War II', *Proceedings: US Navy Institute*, March 1982, p. 88.

9. *Ibid*, p. 86.

10. Paul Bracken, *The Command and Control of Nuclear Forces*, London: Yale University Press 1983, pp. 129–78.

11. A.J.R. Groom, 'The British Conservative Government's Defence Policy', London: manuscript December 1971, prepared for Etudes Internationales (Quebec), mars 1972 (in French), pp. 16–18.

12. See Lawrence W. Martin, *British Defence Policy: The Long Recessional*, London: Institute for Strategic Studies 1969, pp. 7–8, 15–16.

13. Duncan Campbell, *The Unsinkable Aircraft Carrier: American Military Power in Britain*, London: Michael Joseph 1984, pp. 316–18.

14. An interesting discussion of the economic policies of the 1970–4 government is contained in Andrew Glyn and John Harrison, *The British Economic Disaster*, London: Pluto 1980, pp. 57–90.

15. Michael Chichester and John Wilkinson, *The Uncertain Ally: British Defence Policy 1960–1990*, London: Gower 1982, p. 41.

16. *The Labour Party Manifesto, February 1974*, London: Labour Party 1974, p. 14.

17. *Statement on the Defence Estimates 1975*, London: HMSO 1975, Cmnd 5976, p. 4.

18. *Ibid*. Also see David Greenwood, 'Sights Lowered: The United Kingdom's Defence Effort 1975–1984', *Royal Air Forces Quarterly*, 15, 3, Autumn 1975, pp. 187–8.

19. Barbara Castle, *The Castle Diaries 1974–76*, London: Weidenfeld and Nicolson 1980, p. 333.

20. *Statement on the Defence Estimates 1975, op. cit.*, p. 24. GNP at factor cost was still used as the denominator at this time. This accounts for most of the disparity between these figures and those in Table 16. For a contemporary critique of the government's White Paper, see Robin Cook, David Holloway, Mary Kaldor, Dan Smith, *Defence Review: An Anti-White Paper*, London: Fabian Society 1975, Fabian research series 323.

21. *Times*, 19 March 1975. See also 'When Is a Cat not a Cat?', *Economist*, 15 March 1975.

22. The report of the Study Group, together with the main discussion papers upon which its work was based, were published in Mary Kaldor, Dan Smith and Steve Vines (eds), *Democratic Socialism and the Cost of Defence*, London: Croom Helm 1979.

23. 'Mulley in Sea of Troubles', *Financial Times*, 13 January 1977; 'Is this the Last of the Defence Cuts?', *Economist*, 15 January 1977.

24. 'Defence as the Treasury's Scapegoat', *Times*, 1 December 1975; 'Defence Chiefs and Cabinet Face Clash on £1300 m. Cuts', *Telegraph*, 3

December 1975; *Financial Times*, 26 November 1975: Barbara Castle, *op.cit.*, pp. 596–7.

25. *Guardian*, 15 December 1975; *Telegraph*, 3 December 1975.

26. *Times*, 1 December 1975; *Times*, 15 January 1976.

27. *Observer*, 23 May 1976.

28. *Statement on the Defence Estimates 1975, op. cit.*, pp. 10–15.

29. Michael Chichester and John Wilkinson, *op.cit.*, pp. 57–62.

30. *Sunday Times*, 19 October 1976. See also Dan Smith, *The Defence of the Realm in the 1980s*, London: Croom Helm 1980, pp. 146–8.

31. *Sunday Times*, 19 October 1976.

32. *Statement on the Defence Estimates 1977*, London: HMSO 1977, Cmnd 6735, pp. 1–2; David Greenwood, 'Defence Programme Options to 1980–81', in Mary Kaldor, Dan Smith and Steve Vines (eds), *op. cit.*, pp. 178–80.

33. *Ministerial Guidance 1977, Final Communique of the NATO Defence Planning Committee*, Brussels: NATO 1977.

34. Richard Crossman, *Diaries of a Cabinet Minister*, London: Hamish Hamilton 1976, p. 647.

35. *Times*, 1 December 1975.

36. Denis Healey, 'British Defence Policy', *Royal United Services Institute Journal*, December 1969, p. 17.

37. R.B. Pengelley, 'The Royal Navy's Invincible-class Cruisers', *International Defense Review*, 8, 1979.

38. Michael Chichester and John Wilkinson, *op. cit.*, p. 41.

39. *Ibid.*

40. Mary Kaldor and Albert Booth, 'Alternative Employment for Naval Shipbuilding Workers: A Case Study of the Resources Devoted to the Production of the ASW Cruiser', in Mary Kaldor, Dan Smith and Steve Vines (eds), *op. cit.*, pp. 397–8.

41. *Statement on the Defence Estimates 1975, op. cit.*, p. 39.

42. James Cable, *Britain's Naval Future*, London: Macmillan 1983, pp. xii–xiii.

43. *House of Commons Debates*, 24 January 1980, col. 681.

44. *Ninth Report from the Committee of Public Accounts*, London: HMSO 1982, HC 269 (1981–82), p. 24.

45. Lawrence Freedman, *Britain and Nuclear Weapons*, London: Macmillan 1980, p. 45.

46. This pledge is repeated in *Statement on the Defence Estimates 1975, op. cit.*, p. 10.

47. *Ninth Report from the Committee of Public Accounts, op. cit.*, pp. 1–3. All these figures are expressed at Autumn 1972 prices.

48. In 1980, it was estimated that Chevaline would cost £1,000 million ('The Development of the Chevaline Improvement to the Polaris Missile System', *Memorandum submitted by the Ministry of Defence*, contained in

Ninth Report from the Committee of Public Accounts, op. cit., p. 1). This has been interpreted wrongly by most commentators to mean £1,000 million *at 1980 prices*. In fact, the £1,000 million estimate was an amalgam of 'actual sunk costs', before 1980 (which are expressed in cash rather than 'real' terms) and 'projected costs' at September 1980 price levels.

The cost of Chevaline in today's prices can, however, be readily deduced. The same MoD memorandum estimates the cost in *Autumn 1972* prices to be £530 million. Allowing for inflation, this is equal to £1,670 million in *Autumn 1980* prices, and £2,200 million in *Autumn 1984* prices.

49. 'Strategic Nuclear Weapons Policy', *Fourth Report from the Defence Committee*, London: HMSO 1981, HC 674 (1979–80), p. 229. Here the Ministry of Defence estimates the capital cost of Polaris at £330 million at *1963* prices: £2,260 million at *Autumn 1984* prices.

50. *Ninth Report from the Committee of Public Accounts, op. cit.*, p. 24.

51. Lawrence Freedman, *op. cit.*, pp. 51–3.

52. *Statement on the Defence Estimates 1976*, London: HMSO 1976, Cmnd 6432, p. 53; *Sunday Times*, 2 March 1976; *Daily Mail*, 16 May 1977; John Simpson, *The Independent Nuclear State: The United States, Britain and the Military Atom*, London: Macmillan 1983, p. 170.

53. *Statement on the Defence Estimates 1980*, London: HMSO 1980, Cmnd 7826–II, p. 21.

54. See Richard Crossman, *op. cit.*, p. 622; Barbara Castle, *op. cit*, p. 228.

55. Quoted in Mary Kaldor, *The Baroque Arsenal*, London: Andre Deutsch 1982, p. 189.

56. The government has estimated the total capital cost at £11,300 million at September 1981 prices (*Statement on the Defence Estimates 1982*, London: HMSO 1982, Cmnd 8529–1, p. 6). At September 1984 prices, this would be £13,400 million, assuming no 'real' cost escalation since 1982.

57. This is an estimate based on the discussion in Dan Smith, 'Tornado: Cancellation, Conversion and Diversification in the Aerospace Industry', in Mary Kaldor, Dan Smith, and Steve Vines (eds), *op. cit*, p. 441.

58. David Greenwood, *Reshaping Britain's Defences*, Aberdeen: Centre for Defence Studies 1981, Aberdeen Studies in Defence Economics No. 19, pp. 33–5; *Statement on the Defence Estimates 1980*, London: HMSO 1980, Cmnd 7826–1, pp. 70–1.

59. The Future European Fighter Aircraft (FEFA). See '£14 bn. Facelift Reshapes RAF', *Flight International*, 18 February 1984; 'European Fighter Project Will Cost Over DM 50 bn.', *Financial Times*, 17 December 1983.

60. *Economist*, January 15 1977.

61. Rae Angus, 'The Tornado Project', in Martin Edmunds (ed.), *International Arms Procurement: New Directions*, New York: Pergamon Press 1981, pp. 164–87.

62. Dan Smith, *Defence of the Realm in the 1980s, op. cit.*, pp. 134–5.

63. This is the lowest estimate available and is quoted in Dudley Saward,

'*Bomber' Harris*, London: Cassell 1984, p. 298.

64. This has led one commentator to suggest that Tornado GRI should be sold in order to pay for an increased Royal Navy presence outside Europe:

> It is worth noting that a substantial part of Britain's continental costs arise from the large proportion of the Tornado strike force intended to support the Central Region. Savings in this area would have little political impact compared with an equivalent troop reduction; and military reaction would be muted, because the prospects of interdicting Red Army reinforcements by conventional air attack are becoming less plausible as the air defences covering Eastern Europe become ever denser. Tornadoes can be sold, as *Invincible* nearly was.

(Captain F.D. Stanley, RN (Retd), 'The Royal Navy and its Future', *Navy International*, July 1984, p. 327.)

Also see David Greenwood, 'Some Economic Constraints on Force Structure', in E.J. Feuchtwanger and R.A. Mason (eds), *Air Power in the Next Generation*, London: Macmillan 1979, pp. 12–38.

65. Wing Commander Alan Parkes, 'Air Interdiction in a European Future War', *Air University Review (US)*, 1976, XXVII, 6, p. 18.

66. General Bernard Rogers, 'Sword and Shield: ACE Attack of Warsaw Pact Follow-On Forces', *NATO's Sixteen Nations*, Feb–March 1983, pp. 16–26.

67. European Security Study, *Strengthening Conventional Deterrence in Europe*, London: Macmillan 1983, especially pp. 222–33.

68. See Malcolm Chalmers, 'Can NATO Afford a Non-suicidal Strategy?' in Gwyn Prins (ed.), *The Choice*, London: Chatto and Windus 1984, pp. 218–33; and Matthew Evangelista, 'Offense or Defense: A Tale of Two Commissions', *World Policy Journal*, Fall 1983, pp. 45–69.

69. *Minutes of Defence and External Affairs Sub-Committee of House of Commons Expenditure Committee*, London: HMSO 1976, HC 236-v (1975–76), pp. 106–7.

70. *Financial Times*, 1 July 1977.

6. Military spending and the British economy

1. Quoted in C.J. Bartlett, *The Long Retreat: A Short History of British Defence Policy, 1945–70*, London: Macmillan 1972, p. 149.

2. *The National Plan*, London: HMSO 1965, Cmnd 2764, p. 182.

3. Robert De Grasse Jr., *The Costs and Consequences of Reagan's Military Build-up*, New York: Council on Economic Priorities 1982, p. 13. Also see: Bruce Russett, *What Price Vigilance?* New Haven: Yale University Press 1970, p. 22; Kurt W. Rothschild, 'Military Expenditure, Exports and Growth', *Kyklos*, 1973, pp. 804–13; Ron Smith, 'Military Expenditure

and Capitalism', *Cambridge Journal of Economics*, March 1977; Ron Smith, 'Military Expenditures and Investment in OECD Countries 1954–73', *Journal of Comparative Economics*, 4, 1, 1980; George Georgiou, 'The Political Economy of Military Expenditure', *Capital and Class*, 19, Spring 1983; Robert De Grasse Jr., *Military Expansion, Economic Decline*, New York: Council on Economic Priorities 1983.

Most recently, a study by United States Congressman Les Aspin, chairman of the House Budget Committee's Task Force on Economic Policy and Growth, contends that 'the current defense buildup threatens to undermine long-term US economic growth by drawing money away from civilian industrial investment and research.' (*Wall Street Journal*, 24 April 1984.)

4. Sidney Pollard, *The Wasting of the British Economy*, London: Croom Helm 1982, p. 27.

5. *Guardian*, 23 February 1984.

6. Andrew Glyn and Bob Sutcliffe, *British Capitalism, Workers and the Profits Squeeze*, London: Penguin 1972.

7. Andrew Glyn and John Harrison, *The British Economic Disaster*, London: Pluto 1980, p. 50.

8. See Robert Bacon and Walter Eltis, *Britain's Economic Problem: Two Few Producers*, London: Macmillan 1976.

9. Ron Smith (1980), *op. cit.*, p. 19.

10. Robert De Grasse Jr., *The Costs and Consequences of Reagan's Military Build-up, op. cit.*, pp. 16, 54.

11. D.C. Paige, 'Defence Expenditure', *National Institute Economic Review*, 11, 1960, p. 32.

12. *Economic Survey for 1951*, London: HMSO 1951, p. 8.

13. Denis Healey, 'Britain and NATO' in Klaus Knorr (ed.), *NATO and American Security*, Princeton: Princeton University Press 1959, p. 215.

14. See Table 17 in Chapter 7.

15. D.C. Paige, *op. cit.*, pp. 23–39; *Economist*, 8 September 1956.

16. C.J. Bartlett, *The Long Retreat, op. cit.*, p. 133.

17. Mary Acland-Hood, 'Statistics on Military Research and Development Expenditure', *SIPRI Yearbook 1984*, London: Taylor and Francis 1984, Table 6.4.

18. *Ibid*, Table 6.3.

19. 'IT Industry in Grave Danger says Neddy', *Guardian*, 21 June 1984.

20. Cited in C.J. Bartlett, *A History of Postwar Britain 1945–74*, London: Longman 1977, p. 250.

21. Sheila Durie and Rob Edwards, *Fuelling the Nuclear Arms Race: The Links between Nuclear Power and Nuclear Weapons*, London: Pluto 1982, pp. 11–30.

22. *Annual Review of Government Funded R & D, 1983*, London: HMSO 1984, Table 9.

23. *Shipbuilding Inquiry Committee 1965–1966 Report*, London: HMSO 1966, Cmnd 2937, p. 129.

24. E. Sciberras, 'The UK Semi-conductor Market', in K. Pavitt (ed.), *Technical Innovation and British Economic Performance*, London: Macmillan 1980, p. 289. See also Sir Ieuan Maddocks, *Commercial Exploitation of Defence Technology*, London: National Economic Development Office 1983.

25. *Los Angeles Times*, 10 July 1983.

26. *Statement on the Defence Estimates 1984*, London: HMSO 1984, Cmnd 9227-I, p. 41.

27. Figure for 1982–3 in *House of Commons Debates*, Written Answer, 25 April 1983, cols. 265–6.

28. *SIPRI Yearbook 1984*, London: Taylor and Francis 1984, p. 199.

29. Frederic S. Pearson, 'The Question of Control in British Defence Sales Policy', *International Affairs*, 59, 2, Spring 1983, p. 232.

30. Lawrence Freedman, *Arms Production in the United Kingdom: Problems and Prospects*, London: Royal Institute of International Affairs 1978, p. 29.

31. Kurt W. Rothschild, 'Military Expenditure, Exports and Growth', *Kyklos*, 1973, p. 813.

32. *Statement on the Defence Estimates 1984, op. cit.*, Volume II, p. 13.

33. *The Government's Expenditure Plans 1984–85 to 1986–87*, London: HMSO 1984, Cmnd. 9143-1, Table 1.3.

34. *Sunday Times*, 21 May 1978 and 28 May 1978.

35. Samuel Brittan, *Steering the Economy: The Role of the Treasury*, London: Penguin 1971, pp. 492–4.

36. Susan Strange, *Sterling and British Policy*, London: Oxford University Press 1971.

37. Harold Macmillan, *Tides of Fortune*, London: Macmillan 1969, p. 380.

38. Eric Hobsbawm, *Industry and Empire*, London: Penguin 1969, pp. 258–9.

39. Susan Strange, *op. cit*, pp. 188–9.

40. C.J. Bartlett, *The Long Retreat, op. cit.*, p. 186.

41. Susan Strange, *op. cit.*, pp. 182–3.

42. Cited in Susan Strange, *op. cit.*, pp. 306–7.

7. The Empire strikes back: the 1980s

1. *The Government's Expenditure Plans 1984–85 to 1986–87*, London: HMSO 1984, Cmnd 9143-1, Tables 1–10, 1–14.

2. *SIPRI Yearbook 1984*, London: Taylor and Francis 1984, Table 3A.

3. *The Government's Expenditure Plans 1979–80 to 1982–83*, London: HMSO 1979, Cmnd 7439, p. 9; *Economic Trends: 1984 Supplement*, London: HMSO 1983, p. 4.

4. *Economist*, 26 February 1983, pp. 53–6.

5. Much of which is being used to finance the United States' massive arms build up. See *Economist*, 11 February 1984.

6. *The Government's Expenditure Plans 1984–85 to 1986–87, op. cit.*, Table 1.11.

7. Spending on child benefits in 1984–5 is estimated to be £3,892 million (in 1982–83 cost terms). (*Ibid.* Volume II, p. 82.)

8. *Economist*, 25 February 1984; *SIPRI Yearbook 1984, op. cit.*, Table 6.4.

9. *House of Commons Debates*, 7 May 1982, col. 143.

10. *The Government's Expenditure Plans 1984–85 to 1986–87, op. cit.*, Table 1.3.

11. *Statement on the Defence Estimates 1984*, London: HMSO 1984, Cmnd 9227-II, Table 2.10.

12. 'Britain Happier than Most Allies with Expanded Role of Alliance', *Washington Star*, 20 May 1980. 'Britain Planning Its Own "Rapid Strike" Force', *New York Times*, 13 November 1983; *Statement on the Defence Estimates 1984, op. cit.*, Volume I, pp. 7, 29–33.

13. The increased emphasis on intervention in the Third World has been paralleled in United States defence policy. See Fred Halliday, *The Making of the Second Cold War*, London: Verso 1983.

14. *The United Kingdom Defence Programme: The Way Forward*, London: HMSO 1981, Cmnd 8288, p. 11.

15. *The Falklands Campaign: The Lessons*, London: HMSO 1982, Cmnd 8758, p. 6.

16. *Statement on the Defence Estimates 1984, op. cit.*, p. 32. The government has also announced that: 'For operations outside the NATO area, we intend to improve the readiness and capability of our "out of area" forces to provide, effectively, a divisional-sized force'.

17. Announced in *The Falklands Campaign: The Lessons, op. cit.*, p. 34.

18. *The United Kingdom Defence Programme: The Way Forward, op. cit.*, p. 11.

19. 'Hormuz Straits Defence "Global Responsibility" ', *Jane's Defence Weekly*, 3 March 1984.

20. Including all three operational carriers, *Invincible, Illustrious*, and *Hermes*. (*Times*, 14 October 1983.)

21. For the naval commitment to the Falklands see Paul Rogers, *A Note on UK Naval Deployments in the Falklands*, Bradford: Peace Studies 1983.

22. *Statement on the Defence Estimates 1984, op. cit.*, Figure 7 shows that in early 1984 one of the two operational carriers was in the Far East and the other was in the Caribbean area.

23. *House of Commons Debates*, 28 November 1983, cols 443–54.

24. Simon Lunn, *Burden-sharing in NATO*, London: Routledge and Kegan Paul 1983, pp. 35–43.

25. John E. Woods, 'The Royal Navy Since World War II', *Proceedings:*

US Naval Institute, March 1982, pp. 88–90.

26. As shown by its two 'Defence Open Government Documents' on the Trident decision.

27. *House of Commons Debates*, 18 June 1984, col. 40.

28. *The United Kingdom Trident Programme*, London: HMSO 1982, Defence Open Government Document 82/1.

29. See Jerry W. Sanders, *Peddlers of Crisis*, London: Pluto 1983, pp. 235–315.

30. Simon Lunn, *op. cit.* p. 41.

31. 'Strategic Nuclear Weapons Policy', *First Special Report from the Defence Committee*, London: HMSO 1983, HC266 (1981–82), pp. 14–15, 24.

32. *Economist*, 3 March 1984, pp. 23–5.

33. *Telegraph*, 3 March 1984.

34. Michael Chichester and John Wilkinson, *The Uncertain Ally*, London: Gower 1982, pp. 60–1.

35. *Times*, 9 August 1980.

36. *The United Kingdom Defence Programme: The Way Forward, op. cit.*, pp. 8–10.

37. *The Falklands Campaign: The Lessons, op. cit.*, pp. 32–5, 'The Future Defence of the Falkland Islands', *Third Report House of Commons Defence Committee,* London: HMSO 1983, HC154 (1982–83).

38. *House of Commons Debates*, 27 June 1983, cols. 345–50.

39. *Guardian*, 3 October 1983.

40. 'Strategic Nuclear Weapons Policy', *First Special Report from the Defence Committee*, London: HMSO 1982, HC266 (1981–82), p. 13.

41. European Security Study, *Strengthening Conventional Deterrence in Europe*, London: Macmillan 1983.

42. *Christian Science Monitor*, 25 November 1983; Raymond L. Garthoff, 'The "Spending Gap" ', *Bulletin of the Atomic Scientists*, May 1984, pp. 5–6.

43. *Statement on the Defence Estimates 1982*, London: HMSO 1982, Cmnd 8529–1, p. 27.

44. International Institute for Strategic Studies, *The Military Balance 1973–74*, London: Chatto & Windus 1974, and *The Military Balance 1982–83*, London: IISS 1983.

45. Memorandum by Ron Smith and Dan Smith, 'Strategic Nuclear Weapons Policy', *Fourth Report from the Defence Committee*, London: HMSO 1981, HC 674 (1979–80), p. 286; Written Answer, *House of Commons Debates*, 10 March 1983, col. 485; Written Answer, *House of Commons Debates*, 15 June 1984, col. 577.

46. *Statement on the Defence Estimates 1984, op. cit.*, pp. 10–18.

47. *The Government's Expenditure Plans 1983–84 to 1986–87, op. cit.*, p. 9.

48. *Guardian*, 14 March 1983, and *Guardian*, 14 December 1983.

49. *New Statesman*, 11 November 1983.

50. *Financial Times*, 18 November 1983; *Times*, 15 May 1984.

51. David Greenwood, *Trident: The Budgetary Impact*, Aberdeen: mimeo 1984, p. 12.

52. *Statement on the Defence Estimates 1983*, London: HMSO 1983, Cmnd 8951-II, p. 11.

53. *Third Report from the Defence Committee, op. cit.*, pp. 184, 225.

54. Anthony Cordesman, 'British Defense: A Time for Hard Choices', *Armed Forces Journal International*, September 1983, pp. 58–68, 114.

55. David Hobbs, *Alternatives to Trident*, Aberdeen: Centre for Defence Studies 1983, p. 65.

56. *Third Report from the Defence Committee, op. cit.*, p. 184.

57. *Ibid.* p. 225.

58. *Ibid.* p. vi.

59. Anthony Barnett, 'Iron Britannia', *New Left Review*, July–August 1982, p. 98.

60. *House of Commons Debates*, 1 July, 1982, cols. 1069–77.

61. Admiral of the Fleet Lord Hill-Norton, 'Return to a National Strategy', in John Baylis (ed.), *Alternative Approaches to British Defence Policy*, London: Macmillan 1983, p. 134.

62. Field Marshall Lord Carver, 'Getting Defence Priorities Right', in *ibid.* pp. 76–91.

63. *Statement on the Defence Estimates 1983, op. cit.*, p. 11.

8. Paying for a real defence

1. Daniel Ellsberg, 'Call to Mutiny', in *END Papers One*, Winter 1981–2, pp. 4–24.

2. For a rather different emphasis, see Michael Randle, 'Constructing Defensive Strategies', *ADIU Report*, 5, 2, March/April 1983, p. 3.

3. A point reinforced by the possibility of a 'nuclear winter'. See R.P. Turco, O.B. Toon, T.B. Ackerman, J.B. Pollack, Carl Sagan, 'Nuclear Winter: Global Consequences of Multiple Nuclear Explosions', *Science*, 23 December 1983, pp. 1283–1300.

4. Jeff McMahan, *British Nuclear Weapons: For and Against:* London: Junction Books 1981; Malcolm Chalmers, *Trident: Britain's Independent Arms Race*, London: CND 1984.

5. *Statement on the Defence Estimates 1984*, London: HMSO 1984, Cmnd 9227-II, p. 9.

6. David Greenwood, 'Setting Defence Priorities', *ADIU Report*, 3, 3, p. 5.

7. Malcolm Chalmers, *The Cost of Britain's Defence*, Bradford: School of Peace Studies 1983, p. 65.

8. Gwyn Prins (ed.), *Defended to Death*, London: Penguin 1983, pp. 271–8.

9. Table II, *NATO Review*, 6, 1983, p. 31.

10. Union of Concerned Scientists, *No First Use*, Cambridge, Mass.: UCS

1983; John D. Steinbruner and Leon V. Segal (eds), *Alliance Security: NATO and the No-First-Use Question*, Washington DC: Brookings Institution 1983.

11. Malcolm Chalmers, 'Steps to a Bomb-free Britain', *New Socialist*, July/August 1983, pp. 13–15.

12. The best survey of such proposals for Britain is the Report of the Alternative Defence Commission, *Defence Without the Bomb*, London: Taylor and Francis 1983.

13. Samuel P. Huntingdon, 'Conventional Deterrence and Conventional Retaliation in Europe', *International Security*, Winter 1983/4, Vol. 8, No. 3, p. 46.

14. See Per Berg and Gunilla Herolt, ' "Deep Strike": New Technologies for Conventional Interdiction', *SIPRI Yearbook 1984*, London: Taylor and Francis 1984, p. 309.

15. Ian Bellany, 'Defence Procurement – A Heretical View?', *Royal United Services Institute Journal*, March 1972, pp. 37–9; M. Asteris, 'British Arms Procurement: Protection versus Free Trade', *Royal United Services Journal*, March 1984, pp. 30–6.

16. There is, however, a strong case on both moral and security grounds for a rapid reduction in the export of arms to the Third World, particularly to areas of tension.

17. Keith Hartley, *NATO Arms Co-operation: A Study in Economics and Politics*, London: Allen and Unwin 1983, Chapter 3.

18. *Annual Review of Government funded R & D 1983*, London: HMSO 1984. These figures may understate the distortion in R&D allocation. A further 14.0 per cent of government-funded R & D is the 'imputed' R & D element in Universities Grants Commission (UGC) funding – an improbably high proportion (around 40 per cent) of total university spending.

19. *Financial Times*, 17 December 1983.

20. Mary Kaldor, Dan Smith, Steve Vines (eds), *Democratic Socialism and the Cost of Defence*, London: Croom Helm 1979, pp. 360–505.

21. Dan Smith and Ron Smith, *The Economics of Militarism*, London: Pluto 1983, p. 107.

22. Sir Ieuan Maddocks, *Commercial Exploitation of Defence Technology*, London: National Economic Development Council 1983.

23. Robert de Grasse and others, *The Costs and Consequences of Reagan's Military Build-up*, New York: Council on Economic Priorities 1982, pp. 24–7.

24. J.P. Dunne and R.P.Smith, *The Economic Consequences of Reduced UK Military Expenditure*, London: Birkbeck College 1983.

25. *Statement on the Defence Estimates*, London: HMSO various years; Chris Pite, 'Employment and Defence', *Statistical News*, November 1980, pp. 15–19; *Annual Abstract of Statistics*, London: HMSO various years.

26. *Statement on the Defence Estimates 1984*, London: HMSO 1984, Cmnd 9227-II, Tables 4.2 and 5.1.

27. *House of Commons Debates*, Written Answer, 3 May 1983, col. 37.

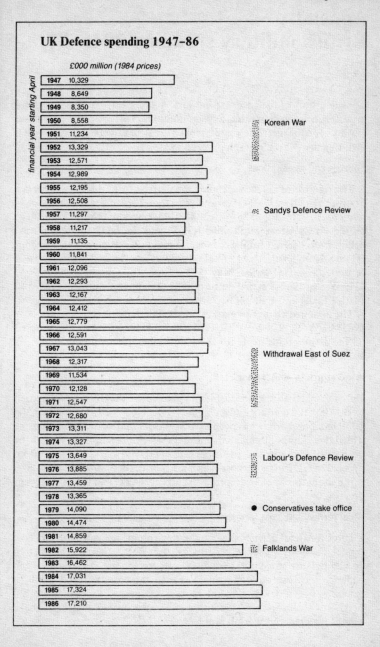

UK Defence spending 1947–86

financial year starting April

£000 million (1984 prices)

Year	Amount	Note
1947	10,329	
1948	8,649	
1949	8,350	
1950	8,558	Korean War
1951	11,234	
1952	13,329	
1953	12,571	
1954	12,989	
1955	12,195	
1956	12,508	
1957	11,297	Sandys Defence Review
1958	11,217	
1959	11,135	
1960	11,841	
1961	12,096	
1962	12,293	
1963	12,167	
1964	12,412	
1965	12,779	
1966	12,591	
1967	13,043	Withdrawal East of Suez
1968	12,317	
1969	11,534	
1970	12,128	
1971	12,547	
1972	12,680	
1973	13,311	
1974	13,327	
1975	13,649	Labour's Defence Review
1976	13,885	
1977	13,459	
1978	13,365	
1979	14,090	Conservatives take office
1980	14,474	
1981	14,859	
1982	15,922	Falklands War
1983	16,462	
1984	17,031	
1985	17,324	
1986	17,210	

Appendix
British military spending 1945–87

Consideration of defence expenditure data is often complicated by inconsistencies in definitions and assumptions. This appendix provides a few notes on the methodology employed in calculating the statistics in the text, together with the graph on page 193.

Sources and assumptions

1. The figures for defence spending are derived from *Annual Abstract of Statistics*, London: HMSO (various years) and *The Government's Expenditure Plans 1984/85 to 1986/87*, Cmnd 9143, London: HMSO 1984. Data on the Gross Domestic Product (GDP) and the GDP (market prices) deflator are derived from *Economic Trends: 1984 Supplement*, London: HMSO 1984. Projections of GDP growth are derived from *National Institute Economic Review*, May 1984.
2. 1945–6 to 1982–3 actual outturn. 1983–4 estimated outturn. 1984–5 to 1986–7 Plans in Cmnd 9143.
3. The assumed change in market price GDP deflator is:
1983–4 +5½%, 1984–5 +4¾%, 1985–6 +4¼%, 1986–7 +4%. This is based on the assumptions made for the 1984 Budget (see *House of Commons Debates* (Written Answer) 13 March 1984, Hansard, cols. 77–8).

'Market prices' and 'factor cost'

Until the mid-1970s, it was customary to calculate the UK military burden by dividing the military budget by the GDP *at factor cost*. Since then, the GDP *at market prices* has been used as the denominator. The difference which this change has made is considerable. For example, in 1980–1 the military burden constituted 4.8 per cent of GDP at market prices, but 5.6 per cent of GDP at factor cost. The market prices definition has been used throughout this book in accord with current NATO and UK government practice.

'Real terms' and 'cost terms'

Figures for 'real' defence spending in this volume are calculated in 'cost terms', i.e. using a general price index (the GDP deflator). The use of a special defence price index has been avoided for two reasons. First, in order to measure the opportunity cost to the economy as a whole, a general price index is thought more appropriate. Second, there are persistent problems in the definition of defence 'output' which can make figures for defence inflation problematic.

Guide to further reading

1. Britain's decline

For a masterly account of Britain's economic history since 1750, see Eric Hobsbawm, *Industry and Empire*, London: Penguin 1969. Andrew Gamble, *Britain in Decline*, London: Macmillan 1981, examines the collapse of British power and its relation to current political debate. For the post-war period, C.J. Bartlett, *A History of Postwar Britain, 1945–74*, London: Longman 1977, is a comprehensive account of Britain's changing role. The political economy of decline also forms the subject of Stephen Blank, 'Britain: The Politics of Foreign Economic Policy, the Domestic Economy, and the Problem of Pluralistic Stagnation', *International Organisation*, 31, 4, 1977.

Sidney Pollard, *The Wasting of the British Economy*, London: Croom Helm 1982, Andrew Glyn and John Harrison, *The British Economic Disaster*, London: Pluto 1981, and Robert Bacon and Walter Eltis, *Britain's Economic Problem: Too Few Producers*, London: Macmillan 1976, provide three very different economic perspectives on post-war decline. See also Keith Smith, *The British Economic Crisis*, London: Pelican 1984.

Susan Strange, *Sterling and British Policy*, London: Oxford University Press 1971, is a fascinating account of the role of sterling in Britain's economic policies; Samuel Brittan, *Steering the Economy*, London: Penguin 1971, exposes the failures of the Treasury in British economic management since the Second World War; and Anthony Sampson, *The Changing Anatomy of Britain*, London: Coronet 1983, provides a perceptive picture of the British ruling class with many useful insights into its continuing power.

2. British defence policy

Several general narratives exist on the evolution of defence policy since the Second World War, including C.J. Bartlett, *The Long Retreat: A Short History of British Defence Policy 1945–70*, London: Macmillan 1972, and F.S. Northedge, *Descent from Power: British Foreign Policy 1945–73*,

London: Allen and Unwin 1974. A Conservative perspective is provided in Michael Chichester and John Wilkinson, *The Uncertain Ally: British Defence Policy 1960–1990*, London: Gower 1982. For a powerful radical critique see Dan Smith, *The Defence of the Realm in the 1980s*, London: Croom Helm 1980.

A longer view of Britain's foreign and defence policy is taken in Paul Kennedy's excellent *The Realities Behind Diplomacy*, London: Fontana 1981. Also see *The Rise and Fall of British Naval Mastery*, London: Allen Lane 1976, by the same author.

The most thorough discussion of non-nuclear defence policy is the Report of the Alternative Defence Commission, *Defence Without the Bomb*, London: Taylor and Francis 1983. Also see chapter ten of Gwyn Prins (ed.), *Defended to Death*, London: Penguin 1983. For a useful collection of essays on the current debate on defence policy, see John Baylis (ed.), *Alternative Approaches to British Defence Policy*, London: Macmillan 1983.

3. Britain's nuclear force

Andrew Pierre, *Nuclear Politics: The British Experience with an Independent Strategic Force, 1939–70*, London: Oxford University Press 1972, is excellent. For the early years Margaret Gowing, *Britain and Atomic Energy 1939–45*, London: Macmillan 1964; *Britain and Atomic Energy 1945–52*, London: Macmillan 1974, in two volumes, is the authoritative work. Lawrence Freedman, *Britain and Nuclear Weapons*, London: Macmillan 1980, concentrates on the more recent period. The reports of the House of Commons Defence Committee into Britain's strategic nuclear force also provide a wealth of detailed information.

4. The imperial commitment

The most thorough history is Phillip Darby, *British Defence Policy East of Suez 1947–1968*, London: Oxford University Press 1973. Also see Phillip Darby, 'East of Suez Reassessed', in John Baylis (ed.), *British Defence Policy in a Changing World*, London: Croom Helm 1977. Christopher Mayhew, *Britain's Role Tomorrow*, London: Hutchinson 1967, contains useful material.

On the persistent strength of imperial attitudes, see Anthony Barnett, 'The Dangerous Dream', *New Statesman*, 17 June 1983. The links between these attitudes and the Labour Party's debate on the EEC is the subject of Tom Nairn's provocative *The Left Against Europe?*, London: Penguin 1973.

5. NATO, Britain and the nuclear arms race

Daniel Yergin, *Shattered Peace*, London: Penguin 1980, is a balanced and authoritative account of the origins of the Cold War in the 1940s. On more recent events, see Fred Halliday, *The Making of the Second Cold War*, London: Verso 1983.

Gwyn Prins (ed.), *Defended to Death*, London: Penguin 1983, is one of the most informative analyses of the nuclear arms race. It includes a thorough dissection of the British government's case for nuclear weapons. On Britain's role as a forward base for US nuclear weapons, see Duncan Campbell, *The Unsinkable Aircraft Carrier*, London: Michael Joseph 1984. Campbell's book, together with Malcolm Spaven's *Fortress Scotland*, London: Pluto 1983, are invaluable guides to the military presence in the UK.

On the relations between military technology, the arms industry and the economy, see Mary Kaldor's *The Baroque Arsenal*, London: Andre Deutsch 1982.

A growing literature exists on alternatives to current NATO defence policies. Two recent books are particularly useful: John D. Steinbruner and Leon V. Sigal (eds), *Alliance Security: NATO and the No-First-Use Question*, Washington: Brookings Institution 1983; Gwyn Prins (ed.), *The Choice: Nuclear Weapons Versus Security*, London: Chatto and Windus 1984.

Index